PRAISE FOR FOOD FIRST

"It is a pleasure to congratulate Food First on four decades of valuable work educating the public and thus laying the basis for constructive efforts to address growing crises that we cannot evade. The significance and urgency of this work is even greater today than before, as the very serious threat of environmental catastrophe becomes more evident and imminent. This is no time to relax our efforts. Rather, to redouble them."

— Noam Chomsky, Professor Emeritus, Massachusetts Institute of Technology

"For 40 years, Food First has been at the forefront of deep thinking about the consequences of agricultural and food consumption practices and injustices, and what needs to be done to achieve food systems that are healthier for people and the planet. It is an invaluable resource for students, scholars, and advocates. May it flourish for another 40 years at least!"

— Marion Nestle, Professor of Nutrition, Food Studies, and Public Health, New York University, and author of *Food Politics: How the Food Industry Influences Nutrition and Health*

"Food First is a champion of farmworkers' rights in the US! Lifting the voices of farmworkers in the national dialogue on food sovereignty. ¡Que viva pa siempre!"

— Rosalinda Guillen, Executive Director, Community to Community Development, Bellingham, WA

"Want to know what the world will be discussing tomorrow about the food system? Look to Food First today. Where else to find astute politics, accountable research, and cutting edge thinking on how we eat today, and how we'll eat tomorrow? Happy birthday, and thank you, Food First!"

— Raj Patel, author, *Stuffed and Starved: The Hidden Battle for the World Food System*

"Thanks to 40 years of pioneering and progressive work by Food First, we have a clearer and more critical understanding of the roots of hunger, the injustices of the world's food system, corporate control, and the ecological footprint of industrial agriculture. Thanks to this revolutionary work we also have deeper insights into the agroecological alternatives and the path that food system transformation must take. I am proud to have been associated with such a unique think tank for more than 20 years."

— Miguel Altieri, Professor of Agroecology, University of California Berkeley

"Food First is the best independent think tank on global food politics. It is my political compass on food issues. I wish you more power as we celebrate your 40th anniversary!"

— Jun Borras, Professor of Agrarian Studies, Institute of Social Studies (ISS), The Hague

FOOD FIRST

SELECTED WRITINGS FROM 40 YEARS
OF MOVEMENT BUILDING

Edited by Tanya M. Kerssen and Teresa K. Miller

Oakland, CA

Food First Books
Institute for Food and Development Policy
398 60th Street, Oakland, CA 94618 USA
Tel (510) 654-4400
foodfirst@foodfirst.org
www.foodfirst.org

Cover and text design by Design Action Collective
Copy editor: William Wroblewski
Cover artwork by Federico "Boy" Dominguez
Interior illustrations by Leonor Hurtado

Library of Congress Cataloging-in-Publication Data

Food first : selected writings from 40 years of movement building / edited by Tanya M. Kerssen and Teresa K. Miller.
    pages cm
Includes bibliographical references.
ISBN 978-0-935028-46-1 (pbk.) — ISBN 978-0-935028-47-8 (e-book)
1. Food relief. 2. Food supply. 3. Food security. 4. Hunger—Prevention. I. Kerssen, Tanya M., 1981- editor. II. Miller, Teresa K., author. III. Food first.
HV696.F6F6426 2015
363.8—dc23
                    2015033174

ACKNOWLEDGMENTS

This book is dedicated to the women, men, and youth from the frontline communities who are changing the world by transforming the food system. Their struggle for dignity, justice, and liberation are taking us to new, uncharted ground ripe with possibility. We are here today because of those who came before—who gave the best they had so that others would benefit. We honor them. Our gratitude and appreciation also go out to all of the colleagues, interns, volunteers, members, friends, and allies who have made Food First the organization it is today. And special thanks to our loyal supporters for funding this special 40th anniversary book, in particular: Sudha Balakrishnan, Robert Berman, Robin Broad & John Cavanagh, Harvey Chang, Douglas Constance, Dean Cycon, Jonathan Fox, Katrina & Jonathan Frey, Steve Hayden, Gordon James, Henry Kahn, Aleksey Kovalyov, Marjorie Kuipers, Peter Laursen, Dennis Macdonald, Abby Mohaupt, Fei Mok, Loretta Pirozzi, Debbie Ruben, Joel Siegal, Joey Smith, Dale Sorensen, Lisu Thachet, Gail Thomas, Estelle Voeller, Masahiro Watarida, Charles Whitney, and David Zebker.

TABLE OF CONTENTS

NO ONE SAID POLITICS WOULD BE EASY

Benedita da Silva, 1997[i]

Politics is a man's game
I heard that all my life
You have to be well-educated
have tons of experience
a degree in philosophy
better yet, economics
or else you're not competent.

You have to have lots of money
come from a traditional family
listen carefully to what I say
if you're a worker
not an intellectual
you're out of the running
this is for professionals.

Power is never shared
nor given away
power is taken
it's not easy
I always say.

Política é coisa pra macho
ouvi isso a vida inteira
tem que ter sabedoria
experiência voraz
formado em filosofia
melhor mesmo economia
ou você não é capaz.

Tem que ter muito dinheiro
ser de família tradicional
ouça bem o que te digo
se você é operário
não é intelectual
cai fora desse pedaço
isso é pra profissional.

O poder não se divide
não se dá
mas se conquista
não e fácil
sempre disse.

---

i   From *Benedita da Silva: An Afro-Brazilian Woman's Story of Politics and Love*, as told to Medea Benjamin and Maisa Mendoça (Oakland. CA: Food First Books, 1997), 52.

FOREWORD

Frances Moore Lappé

I am elated that Food First is thriving in its 40th year. In honor of its four decades, let me share some powerful memories of the sparks that triggered the birth of this extraordinary organization.

What was alive in our culture 40 years ago?

A few years before Food First's founding, Paul Ehrlich's book *The Population Bomb* had frightened humanity with a warning that famine was inevitable. And the early seventies seemed to bear his warnings out: in 1974, famine in Bangladesh, and then in the African Sahel. Television brought images of skeletal babies.

In response, the United Nations called the first World Food Conference in Rome. Some of you may recall its takeaway: Kissinger's line, "In ten years' time, no child shall go to bed hungry."

Joseph Collins—co-founder of Food First, then with the Institute for Policy Studies—and I were both at this historic 1974 gathering, though we didn't meet.

Mainly, I remember the shock. Wait, my naïve-self thought, hadn't *Diet for a Small Planet* proven that scarcity was not the cause of hunger? Yet corporate leaders were still touting their diagnosis—scarcity—and their solution—more production—of course requiring *their products*, and government leaders were falling in line.

At the same time, the frame of scarcity was being unwittingly reinforced by sincere, dedicated people in religious communities who seized on hunger as a central concern. I worried that their message—"We have so much while they have so little"—could reinforce the scarcity message. From that frame, what's the answer? Ship our great bounty over there!

It was in this moment, early 1975, that Joe and I met at a hunger conference at the University of Michigan, where Rodale Institute leader Jerry Goldstein introduced us. Joe told me he was beginning to work on a book to explode this false diagnosis. "Oh wait," it dawned on me, "that's the book I want to write!"

Within weeks, Joe had moved to my town, Hastings-on-Hudson, New York, and we were typing away in tiny offices above the A&P grocery.

Soon, it became obvious: we weren't just creating a book—one whose name, *Food First*, was the brainchild of my clever brother Gil. One book was hardly enough to break the grip of this false frame. The world needed an ongoing center transforming the mindset generating the unjust, anti-democratic power relationships at the root of hunger.

We wanted to be that organization. But what to call it? It had to sound serious, so no one would ever guess we were just "kids" barely past our 30th birthdays! The Institute for Food and Development Policy. Now *that* sounds serious.

By early 1977, *Food First: Beyond the Myth of Scarcity* was published, and we'd moved our fledgling institute to the Mission District of San Francisco. Thus was Food First's birth 40 years ago.

During the Reagan eighties, among Food First's proudest moments was its work in support of progressive movements in Central America, including the publication of *What Difference Could a Revolution Make?*

Jumping to 2015, Joe and I have completed a new book that is a descendent of Food First's founding book. First released in booklet form in 1977, the new *World Hunger: 10 Myths* addresses 21st-century realities. It begins with an impassioned call for a redefinition of hunger itself.

The Food and Agriculture Organization's (FAO) long-used definition, measured by calorie availability, produces a total estimate of 800 million hungry people worldwide. The FAO acknowledges that it misses a significant number of hungry people—for instance, those who experience seasonal hunger between harvests.

When Food First began, we could not have imagined the strength of peasant-led efforts now operating in solidarity through the global food sovereignty movement La Vía Campesina, nor that more than two dozen nations would include the right to food in their constitutions.

But the definition is terribly inadequate for another reason. Food doesn't necessarily mean nutrition anymore. As monocultures and monopoly capital spread nutritionless food, calories and nutrition become disconnected.

In *World Hunger: 10 Myths*, we argue that the world needs a measure of hunger based on nutrition. We don't have it yet. But we do know that an estimated two billion of us are deficient in at least one essential nutrient and that one of four young children are stunted, commonly bringing life-long harms. Bottom line? At least one in four of us suffer what we call "nutritional deprivation." By this we mean being actively prevented from access to nutritious food by an unjust—and ultimately deadly—concentration of economic and political power.

Forty years ago, I could never have imagined the dimensions of what is unfolding now. I could never have guessed that 40 years after Food First's founding, the science and practice of agroecology would have advanced so far, and its productive potential would be solidly documented. Back then, I didn't even know the word "agroecology'!

I could not have imagined it would be displacing the failed model of industrial agriculture even in India—the testing ground for industrial agriculture in the Global South. That country's first "Green Revolution" state, the Punjab, has now publicly admitted its disastrous consequences.

Two million farmers on 15 percent of the arable land in two southern Indian states are now using agroecology. And another, the state of Kerala, is aiming to be 100 percent organic in just a few years. They're telling pesticide sellers: stay away from our villages!

When Food First began, we could not have imagined the strength of peasant-led efforts now operating in solidarity through the global food sovereignty movement La Vía Campesina, nor that more than two dozen nations would include the right to food in their constitutions.

And so much more.

As you read this book, I feel confident that many of you will share my "ah-ha!"—that it's just not possible to know what's possible.

In closing, let me share a light-hearted moment from Food First's early years. At a Food First party in the late seventies, we had invited a friend who was a stand-up comic. "Well," he tells the group, "I did once consider going into Frances Moore Lappé's line of work myself—trying to change the world—but you know, trouble is, you can go for *weeks* and not see any change at all!"

I thought that was pretty funny. So I used it one night in a talk in Steven's Point, Wisconsin. But opening the local paper the next morning, I read, "Last night Frances Moore Lappé told a packed auditorium that it can take up to two weeks to change the world!"

For real.

Yes, it *can* take more than two weeks! But here we are at 40 years, and we do see that real change—change necessary for life to survive—is underway. Now at 71, I get it: *life loves life*, and, as we are joined together in struggle, what could be better than to know we have life on our side?

The accomplishments of Food First and all you'll find in this book are big reasons why I can say any of this. So, thank you, Food First, for leading—with courage and persistence—in this slow but endlessly rewarding work on behalf of life itself.

Frances Moore Lappé is the author or co-author of 19 books, including the bestselling *Diet for a Small Planet*. She was named by Gourmet Magazine as one of 25 people—including Thomas Jefferson, Upton Sinclair, and Julia Child—whose work has changed the way America eats. Her most recent work, co-authored with Joseph Collins, is *World Hunger: 10 Myths* (Grove Press and Food First Books, 2015). She is the co-founder of three organizations including Food First and the Small Planet Institute.

INTRODUCTION

For four decades, Food First has been generating progressive analyses of development issues at home and abroad, and amplifying the voices of local and global movements for peace, social justice, human rights, and the right to food. When we look back, we are amazed at the breadth of topics Food First has taken on over the years, speaking to the timeliest challenges facing humanity while always highlighting the struggles of ordinary people.

We are humbled by this remarkable history because it reminds us that we stand on the shoulders of visionary analysts and activists like Frances ("Frankie") Moore Lappé, Joseph Collins, Walden Bello, Peter Rosset, Medea Benjamin, Christine Ahn, Raj Patel, and countless others—who pushed the envelope and gave us new ways of seeing the world. As part of Food First and beyond, they exploded the myths that, as Raj says, "do a lot of thinking for us." Food First's goal, then as now, is to give people the tools to take back the power—to think for themselves; to understand how our food (and economic) system works; and to engage in deeply informed activism.

The 1977 book *Food First Beyond the myth of scarcity* is Food First's hallmark (and namesake) publication. Frankie and Joe's pioneering book argued that the root causes of hunger were not to be found in underproductive agriculture, the whims of nature, or insufficient food aid—but rather in an unjust distribution of wealth, resources, and political power. The implications of this analysis are far-reaching: only through a radical reorganization of society will we achieve genuine solutions to poverty and hunger.

The 1970s and '80s saw a number of struggles around the world fighting for precisely this kind of radical change—including revolutionary movements in Central America. Through its solidarity activism and publications, Food First provided a window onto these movements and the US-supported campaigns to crush them. Foreign aid, Food First pointed out, often worsened hunger and dependency, fanning the flames of conflict rather than promoting peace and development. And in the 1980s and 90s, when the aid agenda turned into a "free trade" agenda with the creation of the World Trade Organization (WTO) and the North American Free Trade Agreement (NAFTA), Food First continued to inform the public about the devastating consequences for countries of the Global South as well as for workers and farmers in the United States.

In numerous publications, Food First outlined the disaster of neoliberal globalization, including *Chile's Free Market Miracle* by Joe Collins, *A Siamese Tragedy* by Walden Bello, and *Shafted: Free trade and America's working poor* by Christine Ahn. From the wreckage of neoliberal globalization, which pushed people—especially communities of color, women, peasants, and indigenous people—to the edge of survival, new movements emerged such as the Zapatistas in southern Mexico; the international peasant movement La Vía Campesina with its cry for "food sovereignty"; Brazil's Landless Workers Movement (MST); and the US community food security movement.

Food First participated in many of these movements—organizing, protesting, debating, giving congressional testimony, teaching courses, leading delegations, and facilitating workshops. In recent years, we have witnessed and celebrated the unprecedented advance of people power around the world. In the US, Occupy Wall Street, the climate justice movement, food and farm worker organizing, and anti-racism protests have contributed to a richer definition of "food justice" and broader alliances for transformation. Informed by global peasant movements, the UN now touts agroecology and peasants' rights as the way forward.

This book brings together selected writings from Food First's rich 40-year history, organized around some of the critical themes and questions that have guided our work and activism over the last four decades. They demonstrate both the evolution of Food First thinking and the continued relevance of early writings by Food First thinkers. We also know that the issues we address going forward will shift and evolve in lock step with global struggles for justice, and their ever-expanding power, creativity, and visions of a better world.

As we look around us in 2015, we are energized, inspired, and eager to face the future arm-in-arm with the vast family of supporters, allies, and friends who have shaped 40 years of Food First. We hope you enjoy this book, which is a chronicle of our shared journey.

I. BEYOND THE SCARCITY SCARE

TOO LITTLE FOOD, TOO MANY PEOPLE?

Frances Moore Lappé and Joseph Collins, 2015[i]

MYTH: Food-producing resources are already stretched to their limits, and in many places there's just not enough to go around. More people inevitably mean less for each of us. So continuing population growth, which could lead to several billion more people by mid-century, is a major crisis. To end hunger today and to have any hope of preventing ever-greater hunger in the future, we must stop population growth.

OUR RESPONSE: "Too many people pressing on too few resources" is perhaps the most common and intuitive explanation for continuing hunger. But sometimes our intuitions just don't line up with the evidence. The world produces more than enough food today. And, given the striking decline in population growth in recent decades, there's every reason to believe it is possible to halt population growth before we overshoot the Earth's capacity.

Let's begin by probing more deeply the extent of hunger that many assume to be evidence of too little food for too many mouths. How we measure hunger turns out to be trickier than we'd long assumed.

The UN Food and Agriculture Organization (FAO) defines hunger only in terms of calorie deficiency, and reports about 800 million hungry people.[1] In this widely used measure, the FAO explained to us, those who lack calories for many months at a stretch—say, between harvests or jobs—do not register if their calorie supply averaged over a year is minimally sufficient. Yet, medical authorities tell us that even short-term calorie deficiency can have devastating effects, especially on children and anyone weakened by disease.

Appreciating the inadequacy of this single measure, in 2013 the FAO began to emphasize a "suite of food security indicators" that includes not only the adequacy of available protein and calorie supplies but also stunting and factors such as grain-import dependency and access to safe water and sanitation that signal vulnerability to hunger. The FAO also added an assessment tool called Voices of the Hungry drawing on self-reported experiences of food insecurity.[2] We applaud these efforts to gain a truer understanding of the depth of hunger.

Still, only *one* hunger measure—that of calorie deficiency—reaches the broad public, even as this measure increasingly fails to capture nutritional well-being.

Why do we say "increasingly"?

We say this because the quality of food in many parts of the world is degrading, so more of us can be suffering from lack of nutrients even when our calories are more than sufficient. Take

i   Adapted from Frances Moore Lappé and Joseph Collins, *World Hunger: 10 Myths* (New York: Grove Press and Oakland, CA: Food First Books, 2015). See original for full references.

India, for example, where one in seven people is "hungry" by the current calorie measure, yet at the same time four in five infants and toddlers and half of all women suffer from iron deficiency, with potentially deadly consequences.[3]

From 1990 to 2010, unhealthy eating patterns outpaced dietary improvements in most parts of the world, including the poorer regions, reports a 2015 *Lancet* study. As a consequence, "most of the key causes" of non-communicable diseases are diet related and predicted by 2020 to constitute nearly 75 percent of all deaths worldwide, the study emphasizes.[4] By 2008 nearly four-fifths of deaths from cancer, heart disease, and other non-communicable diseases were not in the Global North, long associated with these largely diet-related ailments, but rather in "low- and lower middle-income countries," according to the World Health Organization (WHO).[5]

In these alarming trends, the *Lancet* study implicates "transnational marketing and investment."

This widening disconnect between calories and nutrients has another devastating outcome: worldwide, roughly one in eight people is now obese, a risk factor for heart disease and diabetes among other ailments.[6] Almost two-thirds of obese people live in the Global South.[7]

These realities hit us when a doctor working in a rural Indian clinic serving 2,000 impoverished farmers each month described a major change in his practice over the last few decades: "My patients get enough calories, but now 60 percent suffer diabetes and heart conditions."[8]

Clearly, the world urgently needs a more meaningful primary indicator of the nutritional crisis than one based on calories alone—a measure of what we call "nutritional deprivation" that captures both calorie and nutrient deficiencies. Since we don't yet have one, let's review the indicators we do have and then see where we stand.

In addition to the calorie-deficiency measure, arriving at 800 million people worldwide in 2014, another is "stunting," estimated by the WHO in collaboration with UNICEF and the World Bank. In children under five, stunting is diagnosed when a child's height is significantly below the median compared with the "reference population."[9] To most ears, "stunting" merely suggests being unusually short; but it actually defines a set of medical problems including a depressed immune system and impeded cognitive development.

One-quarter of the world's children are stunted, report these agencies, with many factors conspiring to cause the problem, including too little food and nutritionally poor food for pregnant women and children, along with other deprivations.[10] New research underscores that poor sanitation also contributes to poor nutrition, and thus perhaps to as much as one-half or more of stunting, even when a child is well fed, because repeated bacterial infection associated with unsafe water interferes with nutrient absorption.[11]

Stunting remains "disturbingly high," notes the FAO. Without China, the global decline in stunting since 1990 would be significantly less than the decline in calorie deficiency—to us more evidence of a widening gap between calorie and nutritional sufficiency.[12]

Evidence grows that the consequences of stunting commonly last a lifetime, including cognitive impairment and a weakened immune system, as noted—and, for females, reproductive problems. All show up in reduced educational and economic achievement. Thus, we believe, because stunting brings life-long harm, individuals designated as stunted during childhood should be counted throughout their lives among those suffering the consequences of nutritional deprivation.

By this reasoning, stunting affects not just one-quarter of our children but one-quarter of our whole population, or 1.8 billion people. We know this approach breaks with conventional wisdom, but we ask you to weigh it seriously.

One might counter by observing that surely not every stunted child experiences its significant harms as adults, so isn't applying the same percentage to a whole population bound to overstate the problem? Unfortunately, no. Because stunting afflicted prior generations as well, this measure actually undercounts many adults born when stunting was even more common. Those in their 30s today, for example, were themselves under five years old at a time when stunting was much more widespread than it is today.

Beyond calorie deficiency and stunting, are there any additional indicators that might help us to grasp the magnitude of the nutritional crisis?

A third is WHO's estimate that *two billion* of us are deficient in at least one nutrient essential for health—a deficit often causing great harm. Vitamin A deficiency, for example, means blindness for as many as half a million children each year, and iron deficiency is linked to one in five maternal deaths.

So taking into consideration these three indicators, with considerable overlap—calorie deficiency at about 800 million, stunting at 1.8 billion, and nutrient deficiency at two billion—arguably at least one-quarter of the Earth's 7.3 billion people suffer from nutritional deprivation. That's roughly twice as many as are "hungry" measured by calorie deficiency.

We've chosen "nutritional deprivation" to define the crisis, mindful that it isn't a common term. With this background, we can now clarify its meaning. Nutritional deprivation means being so deprived of healthy food—and the safe water needed to absorb its nutrients—that one's health suffers. It thus captures both calorie and nutrient deficiency. "Being deprived" in this definition refers to the result of inequities in power relationships that block people's access to food and sanitary conditions. It therefore conveys a social malady—not simply being in a state of deficiency but the widespread harm caused by being actively deprived.

The implication of all of this?

We'll say it again: *in a world of abundant food resources, at least one in four of us suffers from nutritional deprivation*, yet humanity still lacks a comprehensive measure of this crisis.

Because the word "hunger" carries such powerful emotion, we will continue to use it. We hope that you do, too. Only, we want to be clear that for us hunger means not only calorie deficiency but the much broader, and often more devastating, dimensions captured in "nutritional deprivation." In this sense, "hunger" is no longer understood primarily as an uncomfortable, even painful experience but as a condition creating great and often lasting harms that we can all be part of ending.

Now let's tackle head-on the premise that scarcity explains the widespread misery of not being able to secure a healthy diet. Does a scarcity explanation hold up in light of the facts?

Behind the scarcity scare

Global population more than doubled between 1961 and 2013, but world food production grew even faster. So today there's about 50 percent more food produced for each of us.[13] In fact, the world produces enough food to provide every human being with nearly 2,900 calories a day.[14] That's enough to make many people chubby!

Plus, those 2,900 calories are just from the "leftovers"—what's left after we've diverted about half of the world's grain and most soy protein into feed for livestock and nonfood uses. World-wide, 9 percent of major crops are now used to produce ethanol—what we call "agrofuel" to remind us of its agricultural roots—and for other industrial purposes.[15]

Nor do the 2,900-and-climbing calories for each of us include much of the breathtakingly large amount of food we waste each year, about one-third of all edible parts of food, amounting to 1.3 billion tons in 2009.[16] As a result, we lose one out of every four calories produced.[17] Consumers in industrialized countries waste almost as much as the net food production of sub-Saharan Africa.

Beyond the vast abundance represented by these numbers are the uncounted but sizeable quantities of food that 1.6 billion people living in or near forests secure for themselves from herbs, animals, fruits, nuts, and berries. A sense of the richness that's not counted in the world's food supply is suggested in a finding of the National Academy of Sciences that "most of Africa's edible native fruits are wild—rarely cultivated or maintained or improved."[18]

While we hear from longtime food analyst Lester Brown that scarcity is the "new norm," the UN agency responsible for forecasting our future food supply, the FAO—even after taking into account expected population growth—forecasts global calories available per person in 2050 to be even slightly higher than the generous supply we have today.[19]

Abundance, not scarcity, best describes the world's food supply.

But don't price spikes prove scarcity?

On average, global food prices in 2014 were 45 percent higher than a decade ago, after adjusting for inflation, a huge increase in a short time.[20] And they are predicted to rise further as climate change affects agriculture.

But are shortages really the cause?

From time to time, the world experiences price spikes in grains and other agricultural commodities—accompanied by experts blaming food "shortages." The most recent and deadly price spikes occurred in 2008 and 2011. But such spikes often do not reflect a real shortage of food: over the decade that included this food-price crisis, global per capita agricultural production continued, with one tiny dip, its steady growth of the previous decade. Rather, these spikes are "bubbles" generated in large measure by commodity speculators whose gambles transform small declines in forecasted supply into *much* higher prices.

Unfortunately, for impoverished people increasingly dependent on imports, international price swings bring harsh consequences.

Lessons from home

In reflecting on the relationship between hunger and scarcity, we should also never overlook the experience of the United States. In 2006, the US government chose to abandon the word "hunger" and replace it with "food insecurity" in the official count of the food-deprived. The US Department of Agriculture defines food security as access "at all times to enough food for an active, healthy life." Thus, "food insecurity" is the lack of such access, affecting one of every six Americans. But would anyone argue that there is not enough food in the United States? Surely not.

The United States is the world's leading agricultural exporter. For US farmers, "overproduction"—which knocks down prices—is a persistent worry. Plus, over a third of this country's enormous corn harvest, used for fuel, feeds no one. In the United States, just as in the Global South, hunger is an outrage precisely because it is profoundly needless.

Behind the headlines, the media images, and the superficial clichés, we can learn to see that hunger is real; scarcity is not. Scarcity is a human creation.

With this clarifying evidence of food sufficiency along with vast, wasted potential, let's now turn to the other side of the equation: the number of people who need to eat. After virtually every public talk on hunger we've given over more than 40 years, there's been one question we've had to be ready to answer: "What about population growth—isn't it the *real* problem?"

Clearly, many people who appreciate that there is more than enough food today still worry that, if population continues to grow, very soon there will not be. So let's ask:

What *is* the population problem?

As we examine the relationship between population and hunger, let's first register the obvious but often-overlooked absence of any link between population density and the extent of hunger.

Scanning the globe, we see population density in the European Union at about twice the world average; but the region has the least hunger. Now consider two regions that are home to most of the world's hungry people: India and sub-Saharan Africa. India's population per square kilometer of 416 is many times the world average of 54, while sub-Saharan Africa's density of 39 per square kilometer is considerably below the average.[21] Now imagine this comparison: Bangladesh's density is equivalent to half the entire US population living in an area the size of Alabama, yet the total calories in its food supply could meet the needs of every citizen.[22]

Of course, in localities where people have been pushed off their land and forced to settle on fewer acres of less fertile land, the number of people per unit of land is likely to contribute to hunger. But in no way does such local injustice explain global hunger.

Yet, we all must take seriously the continuing growth of the human population. For who would look forward to our species so dominating the planet that other forms of life were squeezed out, and all wilderness subdued, and the mere struggle to feed and warm ourselves would keep us from more satisfying pursuits? Plus, of course, the size of the human population is one of the key variables in dealing with climate change.

The population question is so vital that we can't afford to be the least bit fuzzy in our thinking. So here we will focus on the most critical questions: is human population growth "out of control"? And what are we learning about the link between halting population growth and ending hunger?

In the early 1950s, the global total fertility rate was five. That's the average number of children a woman would bear if she were to live out her childbearing years and have children in line with the current age-specific fertility rates. This total fertility rate of five was well more than double the "replacement rate"—the point at which a population begins to level off and stops growing over time.

Then, the 1968 bestseller *The Population Bomb* by Paul Ehrlich delivered this frightening verdict: "The battle to feed all of humanity is over. In the 1970s the world will undergo famines—hundreds of millions of people are going to starve to death."[23] A few years later, ecologist Garrett Hardin called for a "lifeboat ethic," in which we must let some starve if the majority is to survive.[24]

People got really worried. And so what has happened?

Food per person, as we've seen, kept climbing while at the same time, by the mid-1990s, the global fertility rate had dropped from five to three. By 2010, globally, it reached 2.5. (The replacement rate is now 2.1.) More specifically:

- In the "more developed" regions as a whole, fertility rates—with major exceptions, including the United States—had dropped to 1.7 by 2010, well below the replacement rate.

- In Asia and Latin America, fertility has fallen steadily from around five in the mid-1970s to about 2.3 in 2010.[25]

- In Africa, the rate of fertility decline has been considerably slower, falling from more than 6.7 in the mid-1970s to 4.7 in 2012.[26] That's about where South Asia and Latin America stood 40 years earlier, just as their accelerated fertility declines began.[27]

Toward a sustainable "demographic transition"

All of this lines up neatly with the concept of "demographic transition," first observed in what are today's industrial countries over the two centuries preceding 1950. It works like this: as public health and living standards improve, mortality falls and population grows fast. But over time, fertility rates drop and overall population growth slows, then stops.

Demographers have observed a similar pattern in countries in the Global South as well. The two most populous countries on the planet, China and India, have experienced dramatic declines in their fertility rates. From the 1950s to 2010, China dropped from 6.1 to 1.7, and India from 5.9 to 2.5.[28]

Thus, the population transition in the Global South as a whole, again with exceptions, has occurred much faster than it did in the Global North. But what about the future? Can we get to replacement-level fertility, while healing the Earth from our current damaging practices, without overwhelming food-growing resources?

Here's what the United Nations lays out: according to its "medium" projection, global population will grow to 9.6 billion people by 2050, or about a third more of us than in 2015. At that point the world fertility rate is predicted to be 2.2. But even at that level, our population would add another billion-plus people by 2100. By then, while estimates vary, the medium projection suggests we'd have reached an average fertility rate of roughly replacement level—2.0 births per woman.

This big picture is vitally important to absorb, but when we think only in terms of "world population" we miss a lot. For example: already almost half the world's people live in countries where fertility rates are below replacement levels.

Even more dramatic: if the UN projections pan out, just *eight* countries, six of them in sub-Saharan Africa, will account for more than half of all population growth worldwide to 2100. Those eight are Nigeria, India, Tanzania, the Democratic Republic of Congo, Niger, Uganda, Ethiopia, and the United States. (The US population increase is expected largely to reflect immigration.) And, within India, the population growth is not occurring throughout the country, but primarily in nine states that are home to only about half the country's population. Already, 11 Indian states are at or below replacement level.

Thus, we see that more than half of the increase in world population is actually occurring in just seven countries, plus nine states in India—together representing just a fifth of the world's population. Beyond this group, the picture among low-income countries is extremely mixed, but overall encouraging. Among 156 countries categorized as "less developed" and with at least 90,000 people,

- 32 have reached below-replacement-level fertility;

- only 31 still have high fertility rates—five or above—but these fast-growing countries constitute only 9 percent of the world's population;[29]

- of the remaining 93 countries among those "less developed," only 11 show increasing fertility, while 88 percent—82 countries—show declining fertility rates.[30]

Taking all this in, we suddenly see not a "world" population crisis but, rather, a challenge in specific areas of our world—areas with high fertility rates where people are experiencing poverty, hunger, the oppression of girls and women, and other human rights violations. Think of the implications.

Roughly four in ten pregnancies worldwide in 2012 were unintended and almost a quarter of all births were unplanned. Three-quarters of these births occurred in Africa and Asia. Thus, working toward a world where all families have access to contraception and the knowledge and power to avoid these births can move us toward a stable world population that our Earth can support.

When pressure to lower birthrates puts women at risk

First, China. Its "one-child" policy, most stringently enforced from 1979 to the late '80s, continues in some form to this day. At its height, women were forced to abort second pregnancies, and those who gave birth to females, who were less favored, were sometimes scorned by their families. Because female fetuses were disproportionately aborted, today China faces a highly uneven sex ratio at birth of 118 boys for every 100 girls.[31]

Then, consider India. Although home to 17 percent of the world's people, more than a third of female sterilizations worldwide occur there. In fact, female sterilization accounts for two-thirds of the country's contraceptive use.[32]

Sterilization can be a good choice—when it is a *choice*.

In India, however, "choice" gets murky when at least some government health workers must meet sterilization quotas or risk having their salaries cut, and when very poor women are paid or offered gifts if they agree to sterilization.[33] In 2014, at least 13 women died and many others were sickened in India's "sterilization camps." At one, the doctor performed 83 operations in six hours. Each woman was paid 1,400 rupees, roughly $22, to undergo the procedure.

Interestingly, in the 1970s it was a public outcry over forced male sterilization that led to a spotlight being put on female sterilizations. So, while studies report that male sterilization via vasectomies is both less risky and less costly, in India today only 1 percent of men are sterilized, compared with 37 percent of women.

On all sides of the population question, there is a lot to learn. But one clear pattern stands out: neither population density nor population growth is the cause of hunger. Rather, the two often occur together because they have similar roots in extreme power inequalities.

Conclusion

The biggest lesson we take from these points is this: precisely because population growth is such a critical problem, we cannot waste time with approaches that do not work. To be serious about bringing human population into balance with the natural world and with our food-producing resources, we must address the unfair structures of economic and political power—from the local to the global level—that lie at the root of the crisis. To attack high birthrates without attacking the causes of poverty, hunger, and the disproportionate powerlessness of women is fruitless. It is a tragic diversion our small planet can ill afford.

NOTES

1 FAO, IFAD, and WFP, "The State of Food Insecurity in the World 2014: Strengthening the enabling environment for food security and nutrition," 2014, 1, 40.

2 FAO, "Voices of the Hungry," 2014, accessed March 24, 2014, http://www.fao.org/3/a-ml872e.pdf.

3 UNICEF, "Guidelines for Control of Iron Deficiency Anemia," 2013, http://www.unicef.org/india/10._National_Iron_Plus_Initiative_Guidelines_for_Control_of_IDA.pdf.

4 Fumiaki Imamura et al., "Dietary quality among men and women in 187 countries in 1990 and 2010: a systemic assessment," *The Lancet* 3 (March 2015): 132-142, http://www.thelancet.com/pdfs/journals/langlo/PIIS2214-109X%2814%2970381-X.pdf.

5 World Health Organization (WHO), "Global burden of noncommunicable diseases," accessed October 23, 2014, http://www.searo.who.int/entity/noncommunicable_diseases/advocacy/global_burden_ncd_advocacy_docket.pdf.

6 WHO, "Obesity and Overweight," Fact Sheet No. 311, updated January 2015, accessed February 24, 2015, http://www.who.int/mediacentre/factsheets/fs311/en/.

7 Marie Ng et al., "Global, regional, and national prevalence of overweight and obesity in children and adults during 1980–2013: A systematic analysis for the Global Burden of Disease Study 2013," *Lancet* 384 (May 2014): 766–781.

8 Dr. Kartik Kalyanram, Rishi Valley Rural Health Centre, personal communication with author, October 16, 2013.

9 FAO, "The State of Food Insecurity in the World: The multiple dimensions of food security," 2013, 16–17, 21, accessed July 29, 2014, http://www.fao.org/docrep/018/i3434e/i3434e.pdf; UNICEF, "Improving child nutrition: The achievable imperative for global progress," April 2013, 8, accessed February 17, 2015, http://www.unicef.org/gambia/Improving_Child_Nutrition_-_the_achievable_imperative_for_global_progress.pdf.

10 WHO, "Childhood Stunting: Context, causes, consequences, WHO conceptual framework," September 2013, accessed February 17, 2015, http://www.who.int/nutrition/events/2013_ChildhoodStunting_colloquium_14Oct_ConceptualFramework_colour.pdf.

11 Gardiner Harris, "Poor Sanitation in India May Afflict Well-Fed Children With Malnutrition," *New York Times*, July 13, 2014, accessed January 12, 2015, http://www.nytimes.com/2014/07/15/world/asia/poor-sanitation-in-india-may-afflict-well-fed-children-with-malnutrition.html; Annette Prüss-Üstün et al., "Safer Water, Better Health: Costs, benefits and sustainability of interventions to protect and promote health," WHO, 2008, 7, accessed July 25, 2014, http://whqlibdoc.who.int/publications/2008/9789241596435_eng.pdf.

12 FAO, "State Food Insecurity in the World 2014," *op. cit.*, 16; China statement calculated from UNICEF, "Improving Child Nutrition: The achievable imperative," 2013, 9, http://www.unicef.org/gambia/Improving_Child_Nutrition_-_the_achievable_imperative_for_global_progress.pdf.

13 Calculated from FAOSTAT, [Production, Production Indices, Country: World + (Total), Item: Food (PIN) + (Total), Year: 1961–2011, Element: Net Per Capita Production Index Number (2004-2006=100)], http://faostat.fao.org/site/612/DesktopDefault.aspx?PageID=612#ancor.; United Nations, Department of Economic and Social Affairs (UNDESA), Population Division, Population Estimates and Projections Section, (World, Population (thousands), medium variant, 1960-2010), accessed October 23, 2014, http://esa.un.org/unpd/wpp/unpp/p2k0data.asp.

14 FAOSTAT [Food Balance Sheets, Country: World + (Total), Year: 2011, Food supply (kcal/capita/day)], accessed March 1, 2015, http://faostat.fao.org/site/368/DesktopDefault.aspx?PageID=368#ancor.

15 Emily S. Cassidy et al., "Redefining Agricultural Yields: From tons to people nourished by hectare," *Environmental Research Letters* 8(3) (2013): 3, accessed July 18, 2014.

16 Robert Van Otterdijk and Alexandre Meybeck, "Global Food Losses and Food Waste: Extent, Causes and Prevention," FAO,, 2011, 4, accessed July 18, 2014, http://www.fao.org/docrep/014/mb060e/mb060e.pdf.

17 Brian Lipinski et al., "Reducing Food Loss and Waste," World Resources Institute Working Paper, installment 2 of Creat ng a Sustainable Food Future (Washington, DC: June 2013), 1, accessed July 18, 2014, http://www.wri.org/sites/default/files/reducing_food_loss_and_waste.pdf.

18 *Lost Crops of Africa*, Volume III, Fruits, National Academy of Sciences, 2008, accessed January 2, 2015, http://sites.nationalacademies.org/PGA/cs/groups/pgasite/documents/webpage/pga_054647.pdf.

19 Lester R. Brown, "The New Geopolitics of Food," *Foreign Policy*, May/June 2011, http://www.foreignpolicy.com/articles/2011/04/25/the_new_geopolitics_of_food?page=0,0.; FAO Agricultural Development Economics Division, "World Agriculture: Towards 2030/2050, The 2012 Revision," Summary, Figure 1, http://www.fao.org/fileadmin/user_upload/esag/docs/AT2050_revision_summary.pdf.

20 "FAO Food Price Index in nominal and real terms," Excel data download from "World Food Situation: FAO Food Price Index," FAO, last modified February 5, 2015, accessed March 2, 2015, http://www.fao.org/worldfoodsituation/foodpricesindex/en/.

21 World Bank, (Data, By Country: European Union, Sub-Saharan Africa, India, World), Indicator: Population Density (people per sq. km. of land area), accessed May 22, 2014, http://data.worldbank.org/country.

22 World Bank, (Data, Incicator, Population density (people per sq. km of land area, Bangladesh), accessed January 14, 2015, http://data.worldbank.org/indicator/EN.POP.DNST; FAOSTAT, (Browse Data, Food Balance, Bangladesh, 2011, Average), accessed October 24, 2014, http://faostat3.fao.org/browse/FB/*/E.

23 Paul Ehrlich, *The Population Bomb* (New York: Sierra Club-Ballantine, 1968).

24 Garrett Hardin, "Lifeboat Ethics: The case against helping the poor," *Pyschology Today*, September 1974, accessed May 21, 2014, http://www.garretthardinsociety.org/articles/art_lifeboat_ethics_case_against_helping_poor.html.

25 United Nations Department of Economic and Social Affairs, Population Division, "World Population Prospects: The 2012 Revision, Highlights and Advance Tables," Working Paper No. ESA/P/WP.228, 2013, Table II.1, 12, accessed December 9, 2014, http://esa.un.org/unpd/wpp/Documentation/pdf/WPP2012_HIGHLIGHTS.pdf.

26 Population Reference Bureau, "2012 World Population Data Sheet," 2012, 10, accessed December 9, 2014, http://www.prb.org/pdf12/2012-population-data-sheet_eng.pdf.

27 UNDESA, Population Division, "World Population Prospects," *op. cit.*, 12.

28 Merrick, "Population Cynamics in Developing Countries," 82; UNdata, (Total fertility rate, Country: India and China, Years: 1950–95 and 2010–15); accessed December 8, 2014, https://data.un.org/Data.aspx?d=PopDiv&=variableID%3A54.

29   UNDESA, Population Division, "World Population Prospects," *op. cit.*, xix.

30   UNDESA, Population Division, "Definition of Regions."; Calculated from United Nations, Department of Economic and Social Affairs, Population Division, Population Estimates and Projections Section, "World Population Prospects: The 2012 Revision—Excel Tables—Fertility Data," Data File, Total Fertility (TFR), accessed December 17, 2014, http://esa.un.org/wpp/Excel-Data/fertility.htm.

31   Monica das Gupta, "Explaining Asia's Missing Women: A New Look at the Data," *Population and Development Review*, no. 3 (2005): 529–535, accessed October 24, 2014.

32   Calculated from United Nations, Department of Economic and Social Affairs, Population Division, "World Contraceptive Use 2011," last modified December 2010, accessed May 21, 2014, http://www.un.org/esa/population/publications/contraceptive2011/wallchart_front.pdf.

33   Ellen Barry and Suhasini Raj, "Web of Incentives in Fatal Indian Sterilizations," *New York Times*, November 12, 2014, accessed November 13, 2014, http://www.nytimes.com/2014/11/13/world/asia/web-of-incentives-in-fatal-indian-sterilizations.html?module=Search&mabReward=relbias%3Ar%2C%7B%222%22%3A%22RI%3A16%22%7D&_r=0; The Editorial Board, "India's Lethal Approach to Birth Control," *New York Times*, November 20, 2014, accessed November 21, 2014, http://www.nytimes.com/2014/11/21/opinion/indias-lethal-birth-control.html?_r=0.

THE PARADOX OF HUNGER IN A FERTILE LAND

Betsy Hartmann and James Boyce, 1979[i]

In US news media, Bangladesh is usually portrayed as an "international basket case," a bleak, desolate scene of hunger and despair. But when we arrived in Bangladesh in August 1974, we found a lush, green, fertile land. From the windows of buses on the decks of ferryboats, we looked over a landscape of natural abundance, everywhere shaped by the hands of men. Rice paddies carpeted the earth, and gigantic squash vines climbed over the roofs of the bamboo village houses. The rich soil, plentiful water, and hot, humid climate made us feel as if we had entered a natural greenhouse.

As the autumn days grew clear and cool and the rice ripened in the fields, we saw why the Bengalis in song and verse called their land "golden Bengal." But that autumn we also came face-to-face with the extreme poverty for which Bangladesh has become so famous. When the price of rice soared in the ean season before the harvest, we witnessed the terrible spectacle of people dying in the streets of Dacca, the capital. Famine claimed thousands of lives throughout the country. The victims were Bangladesh's poorest people who could not afford to buy rice and had nothing left to sell.

As we tried to comprehend the contrast between the lush beauty of the land and the destitution of so many people, we sensed that we had entered a strange battleground. All around us silent struggles were being waged, struggles in which the losers met slow, bloodless deaths. In 1975, we spent nine months in the village of Katni, collecting material for a book on life in the Third World. There we learned more about the quiet violence which rages in Bangladesh.

Katni is a typical village. The majority of its 350 people are poor: most families own less than two acres of land, and a quarter of the households are completely landless. The poorest often work for landlords in neighboring villages who own over 40 acres apiece. Four-fifths of the villagers are Muslims, and one-fifth are Hindus. Except for two rickshaw pullers, all make a living from agriculture.

The villagers taught us what it means to be hungry in a fertile land.

Golden Bengal

Bangladesh lies in the delta of three great rivers—the Brahmaputra, the Ganges, and the Meghna—that flow through it to empty into the Bay of Bengal. The rivers and their countless tributaries meander over the flat land, constantly changing course, since most of the country lies less than 100 feet above sea level. The waters not only wash the land, they create it; their sediments have built the delta over the centuries. The alluvial soil deposited by the rivers is among the most fertile in the world.

---

i Adapted from Betsy Hartmann and James Boyce, *Needless Hunger: Voices from a Bangladesh Village* (San Francisco: Food First Books, 1979).

Abundant rainfall and warm temperatures give Bangladesh an ideal climate for agriculture. Crops can be grown 12 months a year. The surface waters and vast underground aquifers give the country a tremendous potential for irrigation in the dry winter season. The rivers, ponds, and rice paddies are alive with fish; according to a report of the United Nations Food and Agriculture Organization (FAO), "Bangladesh is possibly the richest country in the world as far as inland fishery resources are concerned."[1]

The country's dense human population bears testament the land's fertility; historically the thick human settlement of the delta, like that along the Nile River, was made possible by agricultural abundance. Today, with more than 80 million people, Bangladesh is the world's eighth most populous nation. Its population density is the highest of any country in the world except for Singapore and Hong Kong,[2] a fact which is all the more remarkable in light of the country's low level of urbanization. Nine out of ten Bangladeshis live in villages, where most make their living from the land.

Bangladesh's soil may be rich, but its people are poor. The average annual income is less than $100 per person, the life expectancy only 47 years—and like all averages, these overstate the wellbeing of the poorest.[3] Twenty-five percent of Bangladesh's children die before reaching the age of five.[4] Malnutrition claims the lives of many. Over half of Bangladesh's families consume less than the minimal calorie requirement, and 60 percent suffer from protein deficiencies.[5] Healthcare is poorly developed and concentrated in urban areas. Less than a quarter of the population is literate.[6]

Why is a country with some of the world's most fertile land also the home of some of the world's hungriest people? A look at the history of Bangladesh sheds some light on this paradox. The first Europeans who visited eastern Bengal, the region that is now Bangladesh, found a thriving industry and a prosperous agriculture. It was, in the optimistic words of one Englishman, "a wonderful land, whose richness and abundance neither war, pestilence nor oppression could destroy."[7] But by 1947, when the sun finally set on the British Empire in India, eastern Bengal had been reduced to an impoverished agricultural hinterland.

The making of hunger: who owns the land?

The pattern of landownership in Bangladesh profoundly affects both the production and distribution of food. Although Bangladesh is often called a "land of small farmers," the reality in the villages is more complex. On the one hand, many villagers own no land at all and depend upon wage labor for their livelihoods. On the other hand, landlords' holdings, though modest by American standards, are large enough to free them from the necessity of working in the fields.

According to a 1977 study by the United States Agency for International Development (USAID), less than ten percent of Bangladesh's rural households own over half the country's cultivable land, while 60 percent of rural families own less than ten percent of the land. One-third of rural households own no cultivable land at all, and by including those who own less than half an acre, the study concludes that 48 percent of the families of rural Bangladesh are "functionally landless." Pointing to the difficulties of collecting reliable data, the authors of the study note that these figures probably *underestimate* the actual extent of landlessness and the true level of concentration of landownership.[8]

A villager in Katni told us, "Without land, there is no security." Indeed, without land there is often no food. An International Labour Organization (ILO) study reports that landless laborers consume only 78 percent as much grain as those who own over 7.5 acres of land, despite the fact that the landless need 40 percent more calories because they work harder.[9] Landownership not only determines who will have enough to eat, but also affects how much food is actually produced.

Not surprisingly, the small minority of rural families who own over half of the country's farmland are, in the words of the USAID study, "at the apex of the structure of power in rural Bangladesh; the political economy of the countryside is controlled by them."[10] Land is the key to their power, power that in turn brings them control over other food-producing resources such as irrigation facilities and fertilizer. Since these agricultural inputs are often highly subsidized by the government, they are all the more desirable to the rural elite.

Similarly, the large landowner is better able to receive low-interest loans from government banks. His land serves as collateral, and he knows how to deal with the bank officials: how to fill out the necessary forms and when to propose a snack at the nearest tea stall. The large landowners also usually dominate village cooperatives, which have access to government credit.

The rural poor, meanwhile, must turn to the village moneylender when they need cash, often paying interest rates of more than 100 percent a year. Not coincidentally, the moneylender and the large landowner are often one and the same person. Since Islam, Bangladesh's main religion, condemns the taking of interest, moneylenders ease their consciences through such simple expedients as buying a peasant's crop before the harvest—at half the market rate. To get credit, small farmers frequently mortgage their land, forfeiting the right cultivate it until they repay the loan.

Farmers in Bangladesh (Photo by Balaram Mahalder)

The large landowners' control of food-producing resources—land, inputs, and credit—allows them to appropriate much of the wealth produced in the countryside. As a result, they are able to buy out hard-pressed smaller farmers, driving them into the ever-growing ranks of the landless. One study found that peasants who own less than an acre of land sell half the remaining land every year.[11] Land, the ultimate source of wealth and power in rural Bangladesh, is becoming concentrated in fewer and fewer hands.

Who works, who eats?

Surplus is siphoned from poor peasants and landless laborers by the twin mechanisms of sharecropping and wage labor, production relationships that determine who works the land and who eats its fruits.

In Katni's vicinity, landlords and rich peasants generally cultivate about three-fourths of their land by means of sharecroppers and the remaining one-fourth with hired labor. The landowner and sharecropper normally split the crop equally, although in some districts the landowner often takes two-thirds.[12] The sharecropper usually must bear the costs of seed and fertilizer, so that in practice his share is really less than half the crop.

Although the rewards from sharecropping may seem meager, those of wage labor are even less. In Katni, the standard wage for male laborers is about 33 cents US per day, paid in a combination of rice, cash, and a morning meal that ensures the laborer has enough strength to work all day in the fields. Women from poor families who work processing crops in well-to-do households earn even less—about 20 cents for a day's hard labor.

The number of landless laborers in Bangladesh is rising rapidly due to population growth and the displacement of small farmers. The dramatic rise in landlessness has not been matched by a rise in employment opportunities. As a result, in 1974 real wages for agricultural laborers had fallen to less than two-thirds of their 1963 level.[13] As Dalim, a landless laborer, told us: "I earn two pounds of rice, one *taka* (about seven cents) and a meal for a day's work. With that taka I used to be able to buy two more pounds of rice, with a little left over for oil, chilies, and salt. But today one taka won't even buy one pound of rice. Employers used to let their workers take a few free vegetables when they went home in the evening, but nowadays they aren't so generous. Times are getting harder for men like me."

With wages declining, it is becoming more profitable for the landowner to cultivate with hired labor than to give lands to sharecroppers. The largest landowners in Katni's vicinity calculate that wage labor only costs them one-fourth to one-third of the crop. They are slowly shifting more and more land to hired labor.

Poor peasants and landless laborers are caught on an economic treadmill. No matter how hard they run, they keep slipping backwards. The siphoning of the surplus makes it almost impossible to save enough money to buy land of their own. Instead, illness and unemployment often force them to sell their remaining tiny plots of land and their meager household possessions. Though they devote their lives to growing and processing food, they face perpetual hunger.

What happens to the surplus once it passes into the landowners' hands? If it were used productively, the suffering of the poor might not be entirely in vain. After all, any society must generate a surplus for investment if the economy is to grow. But in Bangladesh very little of the surplus finds its way into productive investment. Luxury consumption absorbs much of the income of the rural elite. Nafis, a big landlord, bought himself a new Japanese motorcycle while we were in Katni. It cost him as much as a laborer working on his land would earn in 20 years.[14]

Large landowners are reluctant to invest in agriculture, for farming is a difficult and risky business. They may buy more land, but this is simply a transfer of resources (usually from small farmers), which adds nothing to the nation's productive base. Even less of the surplus is mobilized for investment elsewhere in the economy through taxes or savings because the government does not want to tax the large landowners for fear of losing their political support, and the interest paid on savings deposits cannot compare with other more profitable uses to which the landowner can put his money. Trade and moneylending—both of which siphon surplus from the peasants while leaving the production process untouched—offer by far the most lucrative and easy avenues for investment.

Conclusion

Just as Bangladesh is often called a land of small farmers, so the country's agriculture is sometimes described as "subsistence farming." The implication is that the peasants grow barely enough to feed themselves, with little left over for anyone else. Once again, reality is more complex. Large landowners, moneylenders, and merchants siphon much of the wealth that the peasants produce in the fields. The hunger of Bangladesh's poor majority is intimately related to the ways this wealth is extracted and used.

NOTES

1   Food and Agriculture Organization (FAO), "Bangladesh Country Development Brief, 1973," cited in Frances Moore Lappé and Joseph Collins, *Food First: Beyond the Myth of Scarcity* (New York: Ballentine Books, 1979).

2   World Bank, *Bangladesh: Development in a Rural Economy, Vol. 1: The Main Report*, September 15, 1974, 1.

3   According to the World Bank, *Bangladesh: Current Trends and Development Issues*, December 15, 1978, iv, per capita income is $91. Life expectancy from US Agency for International Development (USAID) FY 1978, Submission to Congress: Asia Programs, February 1977, 16.

4   World Bank, *Bangladesh: Development in a Rural Economy*, 2.

5   Institute of Nutrition and Food Science, *Nutrition Survey of Rural Bangladesh, 1975-1976* (Dacca, Bangladesh: University of Dacca, 1977).

6   World Bank, *Bangladesh: Current Trends and Development Issues, op. cit.*.

7   Rice yields for 1928-32 can be found in Nafis Ahmad, *An Economic Geography of East Pakistan* (London, UK: Oxford University Press, 1968), 129.

8   F. Tomasson Jannuzi and James T. Peach, *Report on the Hierarchy of Interests in Land in Bangladesh* (Washington, DC: Agency for International Development, 1977), xxi, 30.

9   Azizur Rahman Khan, "Poverty and Inequality in Rural Bangladesh," in *Poverty and Landlessness in Rural Asia* (Geneva, Switzerland: International Labor Organization, 1977), 142.

10   Jannuzi and Peach, *Report on the Hierarchy of Interests in Land in Bangladesh, op. cit.,* 70.

11   Khan, "Poverty and Inequality in Rural Bangladesh," *op. cit.,* 159.

12   Jannuzi and Peach, *Report on the Hierarchy of Interests in Land in Bangladesh, op. cit.,* 42-43.

13   Edward J. Clay, "Institutional Change and Agricultural Wages in Bangladesh," (paper presented at Agricultural Development Council Seminar on Technology and Factor Markets, Singapore, August 9–10, 1976).

2. QUESTIONING US FOOD AND MILITARY AID

HELP OR HINDRANCE:
US AID IN CENTRAL AMERICA IN THE 1980s

Medea Benjamin, Kevin Danaher, and Phillip Berryman, 1987[i]

US economic and military aid to Central America, which in 1980 stood at $150 million, reached a peak of $1.16 billion in 1985. From 1980 to 1987 US bilateral aid to Central America totaled more than $5.2 billion. Yet during the very years when aid was increasing rapidly, the economic crisis in the region deepened.

The crisis has numerous manifestations: economic growth rates are stagnant; regional trade has plummeted; capital flight is draining the region of investment funds; foreign debt payments absorb a large share of the region's export earnings; and unemployment and underemployment have soared throughout the region, approaching 50 percent in El Salvador, Honduras, and Guatemala. A natural response to this situation of human need is to send yet more economic aid. The very term *aid* conjures up images of hungry people receiving food, children being vaccinated, homes and schools being built, and wells being dug.

Yet if US aid to the region during the 1980s has already totaled more than $5.2 billion, what assurance is there that further aid will improve the lot of the Central American people? Recent developments such as the Iran-Contra arms scandal, the disarray among the contras themselves, and renewed peace efforts by Latin American governments suggest the need for a broader reexamination of US policy in Central America.

Central America's worst economic crisis in decades

Economic growth in Central America, measured on a per capita basis, declined in 1986 for the fifth year in a row.[ii] Real per capita income, with the exception of Costa Rica, has deteriorated, lowering real wages and salaries to levels of 15 years ago.[1] Unemployment—even accepting understated official data—remains dangerously high. Escalating conflict in the region has exacerbated the problem of capital flight. The mass exodus of investment capital, combined with consistent balance of trade deficits, has driven Central American countries deep into debt. Honduras, El Salvador, Costa Rica, Guatemala, and Nicaragua had accumulated $11.5 billion in foreign debt by 1986.[2] Total debt and debt service as a percentage of export earnings have grown to unmanageable proportions. This drain of resources is making economic development in the region impossible.

---

i   Adapted from Medea Benjamin, Kevin Danaher, and Phillip Berryman, "Help or Hindrance: United States Economic Aid in Central America," Food First Development Report, No. 1, September 1987.

ii Most of this chapter is based on data from the UN Economic Commission on Latin America and the Caribbean (ECLAC). See "Economic Decline Continues in 1986," Central America Report, (Guatemala City: Infopress Centroamericana, 13 February 1987).

Military presence in rural Honduras (Photo by Roger Harris)

Government austerity programs designed to satisfy international lenders are requiring cuts in social services such as education, housing, and healthcare. These austerity measures, combined with unemployment, inflation, and declining real wages, are depressing the living standards of the majority and touching off strikes, protests by peasant organizations, and routine government repression.

Most US aid to Central America is designed to support governments and their armies

Between 1980 and 1987, annual US foreign assistance to the four countries surrounding Nicaragua (El Salvador, Honduras, Guatemala, and Costa Rica) increased nearly sixfold, from $150 million in 1980 to $895 million in 1986.[iii] During the period from 1980 through 1987, we have sent more than $5.2 billion of economic and military aid to these four countries. In addition, the Reagan administration has spent billions of dollars on military maneuvers, CIA programs, reconnaissance flights, and counterrevolutionary guerrillas (contras)—all aimed at overthrowing the government of Nicaragua.

Administration officials have claimed that the bulk of our aid is economic. This assertion is based on defining Economic Support Funds (ESF)—the single largest category of aid to the region—as economic. But ESF, while not military aid, is best understood as security assistance: cash transfers which free up funds for governments considered strategically important. Thus,

---

iii These figures are for direct bilateral funds and do not include regional money such as Central America Regional funds and the Regional Office for Central America and Panama (ROCAP). All years for aid figures are fiscal years.

of the total US aid to Central America during the Reagan administration, more than two-thirds has been security assistance.

The emphasis on security in the 1980s marked a radical break with the past. During the Carter administration, security assistance (military assistance and ESF) accounted for just 15 percent of total aid packages. In 1981, security assistance rose to 40 percent of total aid to Honduras, El Salvador, Costa Rica, and Guatemala. By 1983, the security assistance portion had risen to two-thirds of the totals.

Economic Support Funds

ESF is officially designated as part of the Security Assistance Program under the human rights section of the Foreign Assistance Act of 1974. Aid to Central America in the form of ESF has burgeoned from $9.1 million in 1980 to $407 million in 1986—more than a 44-fold increase. ESF money serves several purposes.[iv] It can be tied to development projects, fund Commodity Import Programs, or—as is the dominant method in Central America—take the form of cash transfers to governments with chronic balance-of-payments deficits.[v] The money freed up is then available for the governments' own programs, payroll, and in the cases of El Salvador and Guatemala, for fighting wars.

Section 531(e) of the Foreign Assistance Act prohibits the diversion of ESF money to military uses. Yet a 1987 investigation by the US General Accounting Office (GAO) concludes that there is potential for such diversions:

> Many cash transfers have been commingled with other recipient government revenues, which has made a specific accounting for some of these resources impossible. Providing dollar assistance frees up other resources to be used as the recipient chooses. AID operates in an environment that makes the funds it administers vulnerable to misuse without detection. It must rely on recordkeeping by recipient country institutions.[3]

In exchange for ESF transfers, recipient governments are often required to allocate equivalent amounts of local currency for development projects. But as the GAO reports:

> AID officials told us that they do not attempt to closely control or monitor local currencies. They receive data on local currency uses but do not always visit the activity sites to determine how the funds are actually used.[4]

Another problem with ESF cash transfers is that there are few safeguards to keep the money from lining the pockets of powerful people in government and the private sector. In a survey of El Salvador, Honduras, and Costa Rica, the GAO found that controls to limit capital flight were

---

iv For more details see Larry Q. Nowels, "An Overview of the Economic Support Fund," Report No. 85-93 F, Congressional Research Service, the Library of Congress, April 24, 1985.

v For example, in 1986 the following percentages of total ESF were cash transfers: Costa Rica, 100 percent; El Salvador, 83 percent; Guatemala, 99 percent; Honduras, 100 percent. U.S. General Accounting Office, *Foreign Aid: Potential for Diversion of Economic Support Funds to Unauthorized Use*, GAO/NSIAD-87-70, January 14, 1987, 27.

either weak or nonexistent.[5] Our own research confirms that large amounts of US aid money are being siphoned off into private accounts outside the recipient countries.[vi]

Figure 1: Types of aid as percentage of total aid to Central America, 1979 and 1987

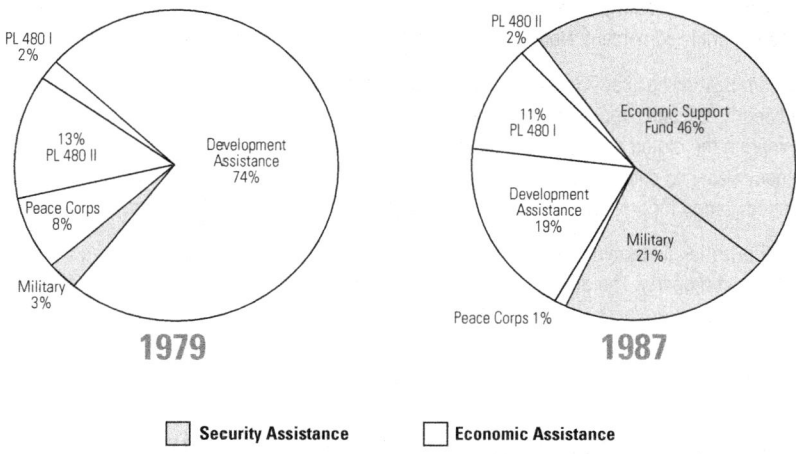

☐ **Security Assistance**   ☐ **Economic Assistance**

Food aid

Many Americans might be surprised to learn that most food aid to Central America does not go to hungry people but serves a function similar to that of ESF. Most US food aid comes under two programs, Public Law (PL) 480 Title I and Title II. Title II consists of direct distribution of food, mainly via private voluntary organizations.

But 84 percent of US food aid to Central America during the Reagan administration has been Title I, and is designed to help financially strapped governments, not hungry people. Under Title I, governments get low interest loans to import US agricultural commodities to sell on the open market. This generates local currency for the recipient government, but because the food is sold, the poor do not get access. Thus, even most "food aid" is really little more than a budgetary transfer to recipient governments and serves a function similar to ESF—it frees up government resources for other things.

Given that most US "economic" aid to Central America consists of non-project cash transfers with little control over end use, the Reagan administration's claim that only a fourth of US aid is security assistance is highly misleading.

---

vi The New York Times cited US government audits revealing "the illegal diversion of funds for private gain, fraudulent accounting procedures and spending that never reached the people it was intended to help." (Philip Taubman, "Abuses Disclosed in Aid Programs in Latin America," New York Times, February 20, 1984, 1.)

Militarization undermines economic development

The Reagan administration's emphasis on security assistance has exacerbated the economic crisis by fostering a shift in regional priorities away from economic development to military might. The size and cost of the region's armies has increased 400 percent since 1977.[6] Individual nations have expanded their air forces and upgraded the size and quality of their ground troops. Governments devote large shares of their national budgets to the military (Nicaragua and El Salvador roughly 50 percent, Honduras and Guatemala more than 25 percent).

This militarization has caused widespread suffering. Since the late 1970s, regional warfare has killed nearly 250,000 people and forced another 2 million to flee their homes and communities.[7] Considering the region has a population of just 24 million, these casualty levels are staggering. For many years to come, the region will spend millions of dollars recuperating thousands of wounded, caring for orphans, and rebuilding bridges, homes, and factories destroyed by war.

But militarization undermines development in many ways beyond the outright destruction of human life and property. The arms buildup is taking investment capital away from social services and development projects, workers in their most productive years are drawn off into military service, investors are scared away by the increasing militarization of social conflicts, and intra-regional trade has plummeted to levels of the early 1970s.[8]

US-promoted development deepens the crisis

Of the 32 percent of US aid to Central America designated for economic development (1981-1987), much aims to encourage export-led growth initiated by the private sector.[9] Aid officials argue that most Central Americans are too poor to constitute a market for locally produced goods. Therefore, each country must orient its production for export markets, the closest and largest being the United States. In theory, the foreign exchange earned from exports will pay for needed imports of equipment and consumer goods, and the entire society will benefit.

The record of the last three decades shows that export-led growth in Central America greatly exacerbated the conflicts currently wracking the region because it intensified inequalities.[10] Based on exports of sugar, bananas, cotton, coffee, and cattle, Central American economies showed remarkable growth, averaging between 5 and 6 percent from the 1950s until the late 1970s. This expansion was led by the private sector. Yet even as overall economic indicators climbed, inequality worsened. In 1960 the poorest 40 percent of the population received 8.7 percent of national income. By 1975 their share of national income had declined to 7.7 percent.

To expand production of export crops, the large landowners took control of the best farmland. Thousands of peasants were thrown off their small farms as land and other productive resources became concentrated into fewer and fewer hands. By the mid-1970s, 73 percent of Central America's land was owned by 4 percent of the population, while the poorest 77 percent of the population owned just 7 percent of the land.[11] The relatively capital-intensive industries that grew in the cities could not absorb the growing labor supply.

The roots of today's crisis can be traced not to a lack of development, but to a particular model of agro-export development that impoverishes the many while rewarding the few. It is this tendency to concentrate wealth and power in a few hands—not exports per se—that is the central flaw of this economic model.

Central American governments were able to keep the lid on this explosive inequality until the global recession beginning in the late 1970s sharply reduced the earnings of their export-dependent economies. The end of economic growth, added to decades of grinding poverty and political repression, touched off a wave of political organizing among workers and peasants.

The response of governments to this popular discontent varied. In Costa Rica and Honduras, the governments' response to mass pressure was less repressive than in Guatemala, El Salvador, and Nicaragua. In the latter countries, widespread brutality by government forces led to further mass mobilization: the overthrow of the Somoza dictatorship in Nicaragua, and deeply rooted insurgencies in Guatemala and El Salvador.

As for US development aid, there is no reason to believe that the revival of an export strategy—even the current emphasis on "nontraditional" exports such as flowers, spices, fruits, and vegetables—will have any different impact from that of earlier decades. The export-oriented model has proven that it will not get money into the hands of the majority to create the demand needed to support a local market.

In addition to fostering dependence on exports, US policy has failed to support the kind of agrarian reform that could redress severe inequalities in landownership. This official US hostility to agrarian reform has sometimes been blatant: for example, the 1954 CIA backed overthrow of the reform-minded Arbenz government in Guatemala. In other cases, lack of US commitment to agrarian reform has been subtler: in El Salvador, a US-designed reform (which ignores the needs of most landless people) has been stalled by a government that is totally dependent on US aid.[12]

Development assistance programs make up only a small percentage of total US aid to the region. Programs for agriculture, rural development, and nutrition in 1984 through 1986, for example, constitute just 7.6 percent of total aid to Central America.[13] As numerous examples from individual countries illustrate, US aid strategy is seeking to stabilize and reinforce the kind of development that has led to the crisis, rather than allowing a transition to a social order meeting the basic needs of the majority.

NOTES

1   Infopress Centroamericana, "Economic Decline Continues in 1986."

2   Richard E. Feinberg, vice president, Overseas Development Council, "Economic Assistance to Central America," Statement before the Senate Subcommittee on Western Hemisphere Affairs, 19 March 1987, 10.

3   General Accounting Office (GAO), *Foreign Aid: Potential for Diversion of Economic Support Funds to Unauthorized Use*, GAO/NSIAD-87-70, January 14, 1987, 27, 2-3.

4   GAO, *US Economic Assistance to Central America,* GAO/NSIAD-84-71, March 8, 1984, 5.

5   GAO, *US Economic Assistance to Central America,* 4.

6   "Fueling the Fires," *Central America Report,* October 3, 1986. Figure includes Nicaragua.

7   "Fueling the Fires," *op. cit.*

8   *Central America Report,* February 13, 1987, 43.

9   GAO, *US Economic Assistance to Central America, op. cit.,* 5.

10   Billie R. DeWalt, "The Agrarian Bases of Conflict in Central America" in *The Central American Crisis: Sources of Conflict and the Failure of US Policy,* eds. Kenneth Coleman and George Herring (Wilmington: Scholarly Resources, Inc., 1985); Robert G. Williams, *Export Agriculture and the Crisis in Central America* (Chapel Hill: University of North Carolina Press, 1986); Richard S. Newfarmer, "The Economics of Strife" in *Confronting Revolution: Security Through Diplomacy in Central America,* eds. Morris J. Blachman et al. (New York: Pantheon Books, 1986); Walter LaFeber, *Inevitable Revolutions: The United States in Central America* (New York: W.W. Norton and Co., 1984).

11   Inter-American Development Bank (IADB), *Report on Demographic Trends and Projections for Central America* (Washington, DC: Inter-American Development Bank, 1977).

12   Martin Diskin, *Land Reform in El Salvador* (San Francisco: Food First Books, 1984).

13   Martin Diskin, *Land Reform in El Salvador, op. cit.*

US SPONSORED LOW-INTENSITY CONFLICT IN THE PHILIPPINES

Walden Bello, 1987[i]

Recent dramatic events in the Philippines have underlined the volatile, revolutionary process that is underway in the country. The US response has been to mount a major effort to stabilize the government of President Corazon Aquino and intensify its campaign to contain the escalating insurgency of the New People's Army (NPA). The US establishment sees itself as having vital stakes in the Philippines, the most important of which are two of the largest US overseas bases, Subic Naval Base and Clark Air Base. But beyond this, the US elite has long considered its relationship with the Philippines, a former colony, as a "special relationship" that justifies a more pervasive intervention in that country's internal affairs than in most other Third World countries. In short, Washington still regards the Philippines as a part of US territory that can never be allowed to "go red."

This report examines the strategies of low-intensity conflict (LIC) or counterinsurgency that the United States has employed in the Philippines since the turn of the century. US LIC strategy in the Philippines has developed through four major confrontations: the US colonization of the Philippines, 1899-1903; the campaign to defeat the Huk insurgency from 1950 to 1953; the struggle to contain the New People's Army (NPA) during the Marcos period from 1966 to 1986; and the current counterinsurgency effort fronted by the Aquino government and the Armed Forces of the Philippines (AFP).

While the US counterinsurgency strategy during the colonization campaign was to rely on massive military repression, later efforts to contain rising insurgencies emphasized political initiatives aimed at defusing discontent. A counterinsurgency strategy using political and ideological initiatives was developed during the campaign against the Huk guerrillas in the early 1950s. Instrumental in this process was Edward Lansdale, an influential CIA operative. We call his approach the "strategy of the Third Force" because its main feature was the creation of a populist, reformist alternative—Ramon Magsaysay—to both the right and left.

Other elements of the strategy were fair elections, the promise of land reform, and military "civic action." While political reforms were emphasized, the "streamlining" of the armed forces as an effective repressive force was nevertheless not neglected. The Huks were eventually crushed, but the striking feature of their defeat was that they were first beaten politically, and then destroyed militarily.

During the rule of Ferdinand Marcos, from 1966–86, emphasis on containing insurgency shifted

i   Adapted from Walden Bello, "US Sponsored Low-Intensity Conflict in the Philippines," Food First Development Report No. 2, December 1987.

back to the military solution. The United States had no substantial direct hand in containing the rise of the New People's Army (NPA), and it largely limited its support to providing military aid to a military establishment that quadrupled in size in less than a decade. To counter the NPA, counterinsurgency tactics borrowed from Vietnam, like strategic hamleting, were employed. But with the political legitimacy and credibility of the Marcos regime severely eroded, military repression simply created more and more alienation among the populace.

As the NPA threat to US interests became magnified and the Marcos regime was increasingly isolated, influential sectors of the US national security bureaucracy were able to successfully transform US policy from supporting Marcos to cutting him loose. This reorientation was part of a larger reorientation of counterinsurgency strategy from one based principally on escalating force to one that put the priority on political initiatives. Tactics employed during the Lansdale-Magsaysay period reappeared: for example, pushing the corrupt regime to loosen its grip on political power; free elections; reform in the military; and, finally, supporting a "centrist" alternative to both the right and the left—Corazon Aquino.

Since the ouster of Marcos, the thrust of US policy has been to assist in the consolidation of the Aquino government and the institutionalization of formal democratic institutions. The Third Force strategy is, however, threatened by several factors, including the military's lack of any desire to reform, the rise of death squads, and the Aquino government's inability to deliver basic economic reforms. Very damaging is the continuing failure of the civilian government and the military to achieve consensus on a counterinsurgency approach.

In a very real sense, the current battle is merely "round four" of the confrontation between the US imperial power and Philippine nationalism that began in 1898. Threading through the continuing conflict has been the insurgents' goal of liberating the country from domination by the United States. When the nationalist element is joined to the lower classes' struggle for land and equality, as it has been in the Philippines, then the revolutionary enterprise has turned out to be both explosive and enduring. And the costs of mounting a counterinsurgency campaign are getting progressively higher.

US intervention in the Philippines also has a broader significance in Third World affairs. Given its status as a quasi-colony, the Philippines has, in the past, enjoyed the dubious distinction of serving as America's principal proving ground for developing and testing strategies and tactics for LIC. America's first major overseas LIC engagement, the Philippine-American War, allowed the US Army free rein to develop and test a variety of counterinsurgency tactics that are still emulated today. Fifty years later, in the early 1950s, there was an effort to transfer to Vietnam some of the "lessons" that the United States had gained in the struggle against the Huk guerrillas in the Philippines.

Today's generation of insurgents have proven to be far more sophisticated practitioners of guerrilla warfare than the Huks. They have patiently rooted themselves in peasant and urban working-class populations, carefully expanded their influence throughout the country, and relied mainly on political organizing and ideological influence. Now a political force in almost all of the Philippines' provinces, the insurgents continue to have an infrastructure of support that will be very difficult to destroy. The left may be on the defensive, and its work in the cities and with the middle classes may be in some disarray, but its rural bases remain intact for the most part. These areas will undoubtedly serve as springboards for future political initiatives.

Today, the Philippines, together with Central America, serves as a laboratory for experimenting with LIC, which have been revitalized and revised after the debacle in Vietnam. These tactics may register temporary successes in containing the revolutionary left, but how lasting these will be is in doubt. Provided it can keep its head above water, the progressive movement is likely to find time on its side.

THE PROFITS OF FAMINE: SOUTHERN AFRICA'S LONG DECADE OF HUNGER

Raj Patel with Alexa Delwiche, 2002[i]

At the end of September 2002, US Secretary of State Colin Powell requested an altogether earthly intercession from Archbishop Jean-Louis Tauran, the Vatican foreign minister. Powell wanted the Vatican to persuade the Zambian government to accept US-supplied genetically modified (GM) food aid. With a population under 10 million and with the vast majority of people earning under $1,000 a year,[1] Zambia is a mouse that has roared. In refusing to accept US GM corn, and by dealing with its famine by sourcing grain from within the region, the Zambian government has sent a clear signal that it understands both why famines happen and that US aid is part of the problem, not the solution.

By the end of 2002, a little under 15 million people will have faced starvation in Southern Africa.[2] Lesotho, Malawi, Mozambique, Swaziland, Zambia, and Zimbabwe are among the most severely affected. Thus, while the US State Department blames the Zimbabwean government for the famine there, that explanation is clearly inadequate to account for a famine that has affected the entire region. For a meaningful explanation, we need to understand what famine means, and put it into the context of a phenomenon that has affected the entire region—structural adjustment.

How to define a famine

Definitions of famine run a gamut. The World Health Organization (WHO), for example, declares a famine when "the severity of critical malnutrition levels exceed 15 percent of children aged six to 59.9 months."[3] The Food and Agriculture Organization of the United Nations (FAO) defines famine as "an extreme collapse in local availability [of] and access to food that causes [a] widespread rise in mortality from outright starvation or hunger-related illnesses."[4]

These definitions focus on the threshold a situation crosses in order for chronic hunger to be officially declared acute. But this threshold is essentially arbitrary. For example, because rates of acute malnutrition have remained stable in most Southern African countries, the WHO has not yet declared a state of famine in every country.

Mike Davis, who has written on famine in recent history, points us away from this sort of threshold thinking: "We must acknowledge that famine is part of a continuum with the silent violence of malnutrition that precedes and conditions it, and with the mortality of the shadow of debilitation and disease that follows it."[5] Famine does not arise spontaneously with the failure

---

i   Raj Patel with Alexa Delwiche, "The Profits of Famine: Southern Africa's Long Decade of Hunger," Food First Backgrounder, Vol. 8, No. 4, Fall 2002.

of the harvest season; rather it is the outcome of the system that places greater importance upon the market than upon those going hungry.

The silent violence of malnutrition

It's no wonder the people of Southern Africa are starving in 2002—they have been starving for over a decade. The Southern African Development Community reports that in Zambia in 1991, the chronic malnutrition (stunting) rate of children between the ages of six and 59 months was 39 percent.[6] Since then it has increased to (and leveled off at) about 55 percent. At the same time, acute malnutrition (wasting) rates have thus far remained stable at 4.4 percent in Zambia. In Malawi, the rate of chronic malnutrition has remained at 49 percent since 1990.[7] It is only acute malnutrition that has slightly increased over the same period, by one percent, for a total rate of six percent. The United Nations Development Programme (UNDP) estimated in 2000 that 35 percent of the people in the famine region were undernourished, with 54 percent of Mozambique's population undernourished.[8] Among those most vulnerable to chronic hunger are women, children, and the elderly. The UNDP reported in 2000 that 20 percent of children in the region under the age of five were underweight.[9]

In 2002, rampant hunger in Southern Africa was tipped over the official "famine" threshold by two years of bad harvests. That is one reason we are now hearing news of it. Another likely reason is that some Southern African countries aren't behaving as the US would want them to, and the word "famine," with the desperate urgency it conveys, helps put pressure on those governments. That sense of emergency also masks the question we must ask: why, even before the current food crisis, have so many people suffered for so long from chronic malnutrition?

The ingredients for hunger

Manmade famine isn't new in world history. For example, in 1878 a study published in the prestigious *Journal of the Statistical Society* found 31 serious famines in 120 years of British rule in India and only 17 recorded famines in the entire previous two millennia.[10] The reason for the change? According to Mike Davis's recent commentary, it happened because the British integrated the Indian food system into the world economy while simultaneously removing the traditional supports that had existed to feed the hungry in times of crisis—supports that were rejected as the trappings of a hopelessly backward and indolent society. And so, by the end of the 1800s, "Millions died, not outside the 'modern world system,' but in the very process of being dynamically conscripted into its economic and political structures. They died in the golden age of Liberal Capitalism."[11]

This lesson was not lost on the first generation of African governments. At the beginning of the 1980s, African states had a very clear idea of what their economies and societies needed in order to flourish. In the Lagos Plan of Action,[12] heads of state called for a type of economic growth disconnected from the vicissitudes of the world market, relying on import-substitution policies, food sovereignty and trade within Africa, and, critically, a reduction in the level of external indebtedness that was systematically siphoning value out of Africa.

The World Bank disagreed, insisting in its Berg Report[13] that state interference in the smooth functioning of the market was precisely the cause of low levels of growth.[14] As most African governments were buried in debt, their futures mortgaged on declining commodity prices, the Bank's plan prevailed.[15] Under the Bank's regime, African nations are forced to produce foreign exchange—earning (i.e., cash) crops to pay off increasing debt, and find themselves importing more and more food. In a perfect, stable market, this ought not pose a problem: the farmer will grow an export crop in which she or he has a comparative advantage, and will use the cash to buy imported food, goods, and services. But in the real world, this model increases farming communities' vulnerability to a number of risks:

1. **Commodity price fluctuations and decline:** Primary commodity prices have been falling consistently for 30 years, and have been exceptionally variable within this timeframe. In part, the World Bank is to blame; its structural adjustment programs enforced the export of the few key commodities in high demand in the North, putting Southern countries on the receiving end of volatile and decreasing prices for their exports.[16]

2. **Currency fluctuations:** Southern countries have also suffered fluctuations in the currency market. Even the most efficient farmers are unable to buy food on the world market if their currency is undervalued. Yet this is what every economic model suggests will happen when countries follow World Bank recommendations to liberalize exchange markets: the currency will depreciate and require stabilization, which these countries, because of their debt burden and structural adjustment obligations, cannot provide.[17]

3. **Loss of food sovereignty:** The World Bank and the international aid community tend to use the term "food security" to talk about the availability of food and people's access to it.[18] Since the 1996 World Food Summit, La Vía Campesina, the international farmers' movement, has pushed for an alternative concept: food sovereignty, which it defines as "the right of countries and peoples to define their own agricultural and food policies which are ecologically, socially, economically, and culturally appropriate for them."[19] The difference between these approaches lies in the issue of who controls access to food, seed, land, and the market. Movement toward a free-trade economy takes control away from the majority of rural people. This is a fundamental issue of justice, dignity, and democracy.

Debt: the tie that binds

Vast debt was instrumental in forcing Third World governments to accept World Bank control. The level of debt is staggering. The bank itself suggests that debt is "unsustainable" if it is above five percent of the total gross national product of a country.[20] Meanwhile, Zambia, for example, is paying three times as much in debt service as on healthcare.[21]

But the debt level isn't the whole story. Debt is also a discipline wielded over Southern economies. High levels of external debt mean foreign creditors call the shots. And when countries with limited foreign cash decide which creditor gets paid and which has to wait, they always put

the World Bank first. This special position gives the Bank considerable power. On behalf of itself and other creditors—and in return for an increased line of credit—it imposes conditions on the governments that owe it money. These conditions, though clothed in the language of impartial economics, are nevertheless political decisions. Ideas about interest rates, exchange rates, and the "appropriate" level of unemployment are always politically motivated,[22] and are always justified by talking about untouchable, mysterious phenomena like "investor confidence."[23] Governments transform their economies to make them "credible" places for investors to come, and to pull back capital that has flown the country in the wake of structural adjustment policies. [ii] Investors who want to be "confident" about Southern economies essentially control those economies, overseeing outflows of resources and wealth that invariably make the lives of the people in those countries less democratic and less secure.

Trade: the gift that keeps on taking

Within Southern Africa—where, for example, tobacco production has expanded by 50 percent per year over the past three years in communal, small-scale, and resettlement areas[24]—the most desirable land is continually used for export agriculture, and food production is sacrificed to boost agricultural production. After each year's harvest, the soil is often left unprotected, accelerating erosion.[25] And small farmers are pushed ever farther into marginal land. This marginalization is not trivial: it affects the African majority, who remain wage laborers and small-scale farmers without savings or capital to devote to expansion.

Exports and foreign exchange-oriented trade has consigned most African farmers to shrinking returns. The declining real price of all primary commodities forces many farmers to sell what land they have to pay the debts their crop income can no longer sustain. Still, even until the

---

ii Capital flight, the phenomenon of money leaving one country in search of higher returns in another, prevents at least 25 African countries from being net creditors, instead of net debtors. This is an example of the sort of disciplining that financial markets can dole out to poorer countries.

1990s in Southern Africa, government-run marketing boards protected farmers by assuring a fixed price for their crops, published in advance. Structural adjustment decreed the effective elimination of marketing boards in favor of private buyers. Now, in addition to enduring direct exposure to international market fluctuations, farmers are often unsure when private buyers will appear next, and are thus forced to sell cheap to the first trader. Finally, many remote areas remain unserviced by private traders, who prefer to buy from a few large farmers near better roads.

The World Bank's policies of increased trade, lower government spending on health and education, and increased debt have made poverty blossom. As Giovanni Arrighi, a scholar of the world economy, has noted: "In 1975, the regional GNP per capita of sub-Saharan Africa stood at 17.6 percent of 'world' per capita GNP; by 1999 it had dropped to 10.5 percent."[26] And in these countries, the removal of social supports to redistribute what little there is has rendered the poorest destitute.

Between 1996 and 2001, the population living below the poverty line in Zambia rose from 69 percent to 86 percent. Twenty-eight million people, or 51 percent of those living in Lesotho, Malawi, Mozambique, Swaziland, Zambia, and Zimbabwe, lived below the national poverty lines.[27] And we know that the face of the poorest ten percent is likely to be black and female:[28] since women are responsible for 70 percent of food production in Africa, the shift away from food production toward export production has been extremely detrimental to them.[29] Men's leaving the farm for wage labor makes women responsible for all domestic responsibilities as well.

A shortage of food?

Famine is not caused by a lack of food, but by poverty.[30] According to the World Food Programme (WFP), there are no shortages of food products in the markets in Lesotho. However, two-thirds of the population lives below the poverty line, and half is classified as destitute. Purchased cereals comprise 75 percent of annual food needs for Lesotho's poor,[31] and over 70 percent of the households classified as "very poor" in Lesotho have no cereal in reserve.[32] Rapidly escalating prices and vanishing incomes are a lethal combination. The people of Lesotho cannot afford to buy the food that is available.[33]

The situation is similar in Malawi where, in 2001, the IMF told the government to slash its strategic grain reserve from 165,000 metric tons (MT) to between 30,000 and 60,000 MT. The IMF advocated this on cost grounds, and because erroneous data persuaded them that the coming year's harvest would increase stocks. A year later, when people were already beginning to die of starvation, the IMF denied disbursement of the $47 million tranche of loans to the Malawian government amid accusations of impropriety in the government's efforts to mitigate the famine.[34] The government accused the IMF of causing the famine, while the IMF blamed the government for corruption before admitting that it had, perhaps, behaved insensitively. Horst Koehler, managing director of the IMF, said at a British parliamentary hearing:

In the past we (the IMF) have not given enough attention to poverty and social safety nets when proposing structural changes. But structural changes are always accompanied by dislocation. We must live with permanent change in order to achieve economic growth in developing countries...[developing countries] should be able to produce food for themselves—and we should help them strengthen capacity to produce food.[35]

Meanwhile, thousands were starving, and grain was being stockpiled by speculators betting that the famine would drive up maize prices—behaving, in short, precisely as they ought in a free market with high demand and a tight supply.

Who benefits from famine?

It is a continuing tragedy that still today, when we know what causes famine, we continue to witness it. Why does it persist? To answer this, we need to ask a still more painful question: who benefits from famine?

Consumers in the US and EU do well by having food and agricultural products that are cheap compared to the true cost of production. But the greatest beneficiaries are the transnational food corporations that market the food and control our food systems. Altria, the Philip Morris group of companies, which includes Kraft and Miller, made over $8 billion in profits last year.[36] In the past six months, Switzerland-based Nestlé SA posted profits of a little under $4 billion on sales of $29 billion.[37] To put this in perspective, the entire gross domestic product for all six countries in the African famine region was a little over $20 billion in 2001.[38]

These corporations depend on cheap inputs, such as the agricultural products grown in the Third World, to make their food processing profitable. In fact, with the decline of every currency in Southern Africa against the US dollar and the oversupply (and hence falling prices) of primary commodities, food industry inputs have never been cheaper. And profits have never been higher.

The role of US policy

Such profits would never be possible without the constant mentorship of the US government. It has a 20-year history of first generating hunger through macroeconomic policy that, while selling itself as "austere," systematically enriches large corporations and impoverishes working families. Then the government hen-feeds the hungry with the surplus food this policy produces.[39] This two-step trick was perfected within the US. In 1981, Congress told the USDA to reduce the storage costs associated with its dairy support program. Simultaneous cuts in welfare provisions for the poor and the incipient recession provided a ready market for the surplus.[40] Now this discipline is being applied in Southern Africa as a way to force open markets for US-produced genetically modified (GM) grain.

The US GM grain stockpile, created through the vast, ongoing subsidy of US agriculture,[41] needs a home. This grain cannot be sold to the EU or Japan because of their embargoes on genetically modified food for human consumption. The figures for US farm exports tell the story: US corn exports to the European Union shrank from $426 million in 1995 to $1 million in 1999.[42]

Particularly while EU and US negotiators are bickering over US farm supports in the run-up to

---

iii Of course, this doesn't stop the OECD countries' subsidizing their agriculture to the tune of just under $1 billion a day. It just means that they're doing it more discreetly. See www.oecd.org/pdf/M00030000/M00030609.pdf.

the World Trade Organization ministerial in Cancun, Mexico, in 2003, explicit subsidies for agri-business aren't in vogue.[iii] But food aid serves as the de facto means of product support and has an unimpeachable veneer of humanitarianism, as the United States Agency for International Development (USAID) spends over $1 billion a year buying American crops from agricultural corporations and shipping them to the starving. By insisting that this food aid be purchased from US companies, Congress is able to support US industry while appearing to help the Third World.[43] United Nations agencies (the WHO, the WFP, and the UNDP) have all lauded the safety of GM food. However, no independent scientific human trials of GM food have yet taken place. And scientists in Africa remain concerned about their inability to limit the sort of genetic pollution that resulted from GM contamination of corn in Mexico. [44]

In recent months, many countries in the region have protested a food aid arrangement that they see as a cynical ploy by the US to dump its GM corn on a captive and starving market. However, discreet threats to slash nonfood aid budgets and suspend funding for other projects soon brought these countries into line. Except Zambia.

Glimmers of an alternative in Zambia

The Zambian government has recognized that the problem is the lack of food available within the means of the poor. Their short-term solution is to reject the output of US agribusinesses (which are subsidized at a rate of $1 million in taxpayer dollars per hour). Instead, they have purchased grain from domestic and regional suppliers and made it available to the hungry. This approach directly threatens US business interests. But it has begun to feed the hungry in Africa. Of course it needs to be supplemented by more enduring social change for the poor—investment in education and health, serious measures to tackle HIV/AIDS, and land reform are key issues, and ones that cannot be resolved with the vast debt that currently shackles the region. Yet bypassing the US aid industry is a heaven-sent idea, as it gives governments of poor countries some control over their economies and their farming systems.

NOTES

1   World Bank, *World Development Indicators 1999* (CD-ROM), Washington, DC: World Bank, 2002, www.worldbank.org/data/wdi2002.

2   United Nations, "14.4 Million Face Starvation," *United Nations News Centre*, September 19, 2002.

3   World Health Organization (WHO), "First Needs Assessment Situation Report," WHO, July 2002, www.who.int/disasters.sitrep/ref-val.htm.

4   Food and Agriculture Organization (FAO), "FEWS Net Glossary," FEWS Net, www.fews.net.

5   Mike Davis, *Late Victorian Holocausts: El Niño Famines and the Making of the Third World* (London: Verso, 2000).

6   SADC-FANR Vulnerability Assessment Committee, "Zambia Emergency Food Security Assessment Report," August 2002, sadc-fanr.org.zw/vac/Zambi%20Emergency%20Assessment%20Report.pdf.

7   SADC-FANR Vulnerability Assessment Committee, "Malawi Emergency Food Security Assessment Report," August 2002, sadc-fanr.org.zw/vac/Zambi%20Emergency%20Assessment%20Report.pdf.

8   United Nations Development Programme (UNDP), "Human Development Report 2002," UNDP, 2002.

9   UNDP, "Human Development Report 2002."

10   Mike Davis, *Late Victorian Holocausts, op. cit.*

11   *Ibid.*

12   Organisation of African Unity, "The Lagos Plan of Action for the Economic Development of Africa 1980-2000," Geneva: Organisation of African Unity, 1981.

13   World Bank, "Accelerated Development in Sub-Saharan Africa: An Agenda for Action," Washington, D.C.: World Bank 1981.

14   Giovanni Arrighi, "The African Crisis: World Systemic and Regional Aspects," *New Left Review* 15, May-June 2002: 5-35.

15   Kevin Danaher and Abikok Riak, "Myths of African Hunger," Food First Backgrounder, Spring 1995.

16   Bill Peters, "The Third World Debt Crisis—Why a Radical Approach is Essential," *Round Table* 354, April 2000: 195-204.

17   See Romilly Greenhill and Ann Pettifor, "The United States as a HIPC—How the Poor Are Financing the Rich," Jubilee Research at the New Economics Foundation, London, April 2002, www.jubilee2000uk.org/analysis/reports/usa190402.htm.

18   For a compendium of definitions, see the USAID policy determination of food security PD-19, April 13, 1992, at www.usaid.gov/pubs/ads/200/pd19.pdf.

19   See www.voiceoftheturtle.org/library/viacampesina.php.

20   Giovanni Arrighi, "The African Crisis," *op. cit.*

21   UNDP, "Human Development Report 2002."

22   World Bank, *World Bank Developments Indicators 1999.*

23   Ilene Grabel, "Creating 'Credible' Economic Policy in Developing and Transitional Economics," *Review of Radical Political Economics* 29 (3), 1997: 70-78.

24   UNDP, "Human Development Report 2002."

25   SADC-FANR Vulnerability Assessment Committee, Zimbabwe Emergency Food Security Assessment Report," SADC, August 2002, www.sadc-fanr.orgzw/vac/Zimbabwe%20Emergency%20Assessment%20Report.pdf.

26   Giovanni Arrighi, "The African Crisis," *op. cit.*

27   UNDP, "Human Development Report 2002."

28   World Bank, *World Development Indicators 1999.*

29   World Bank, *World Development Indicators 1999.*

30   Kevin Danaher and Abikok Riak, "Myths of African Hunger," *op. cit.*

31   SADC-FANR Vulnerability Assessment Committee, "Lesotho Emergency Food Security Assessment Report," SADC, August 2002, www.sadc-fanr.orgzw/vac/Lesotho%20Emergency%20 Assessment%20Report.pdf.

32   *Ibid.*

33   World Food Programme (WFP), "Food Shortages in Lesotho: The Facts," WFP, September 2002, www.wfp.org/newsroom/in_depth/Africa/sa_lesotho020705.htm.

34   Stephen Devereux, "State of Disaster: Causes, consequences and policy lessons from Malawi," Actionaid, www.actionaid.org/resources/pdfs/malawifamine.pdf.

35   *Ibid.*

36   *Fortune Magazine Online,* www.fortune.com/lists/F500/snap_1047.html?ref=articles.

37   Nestlé S. A., "2002 Half Yearly Report," www.ir.nestle.com/4_publications/4_1-frameset. asp?txt=4_1_1-txt.asp&left=4_1-left.asp?bold=2002.

38   World Bank, *World Development Indicators 1999.*

39   Frances Moore Lappé, Rachel Schurman, and Kevin Danaher, *Betraying the National Interest* (New York: Grove, 1987).

40   Michael Lipsky and Marc Thibodeau, "Feeding the Hungry with Surplus Commodities," *Political Science Quarterly* 108 (2), 1988: 223-244.

41   Anuradha Mittal, "Giving Away the Farm: The U.S. Farm Bill," Food First Backgrounder, Summer 2002.

42   USDA economic research service. See especially www.ers.usda.gov/Briefing/Corn/.

43   Food First, "Food Aid in the New Millennium—Genetically Engineered Food and Foreign Assistance," fact sheet, December 2000, and "New Food Aid: Same as the old food aid?," Food First Backgrounder, Winter 1995.

44   ETC Group, "Genetic Pollution in Mexico's Center of Maize Diversity," Food First Backgrounder, Spring 2002.

DON'T BE AFRAID, GRINGO

Elvia Alvarado, 1987[i]

When I hear that all this military buildup in Honduras is just trying to maintain peace in our country, I ask myself what peace they're talking about. Maybe it's peaceful for the politicians. The congressmen make $3,000 a month; their bellies are full of food and drink; they've got a wad of bills in their pockets. So for them, there is peace.

But not for the campesinos. Do you think a mother who can't send her children to school because she doesn't have any clothes to put on their backs feels at peace? Do you think a mother who watches her child die because she doesn't have a penny to take her to the doctor feels at peace?

To protect this great peace we have, the politicians have sold our country off to the United States. They've made us a colony of the United States. They're only doing it, they say, to protect our national security. What national security? They're protecting the fat checks that come pouring in from the United States.

We've lived for years with only our beans and tortillas, and we'll go on living with our beans and tortillas. If the US stopped sending money, it would be the rich who'd be hurt, not us. They're the ones who live off the dollars. All that money does for the campesinos is divide us. The US Agency for International Development (USAID) dangles some bills in front of the campesino groups to try to buy them off, to corrupt the leaders.

But the worst thing the US money does is strengthen the Honduran military. For us campesinos, this just means more repression, more human rights abuses, more disappeared. We see the US policy as very dangerous.

The reason we haven't had a civil war here in Honduras is that we campesinos have had an alternative—our campesino movement. Any gains we've made have been thanks to our organizations, thanks to the fact that we work together. But if the United States is determined to break up the campesino movement, we'll be left with no alternative but to take up arms just like our neighbors have done.

I must admit that sometimes I get so overwhelmed by the odds against us that I break down and cry. I see our children dying of hunger, and the ones that live have no jobs, no education, no future. I see the military getting more and more repressive. I see us being persecuted, jailed, tortured. I get exhausted by all the internal problems between the campesino organizations. And I see all of Central America going up in flames. I start to wonder if it's worth it. I start to think maybe I should just stay home making tortillas.

But whenever I have these doubts, whenever I start to cry, I put my hands into fists and say

---

i   Adapted from Elvia Alvarado, *Don't be Afraid, Gringo: A Honduran Woman Speaks from the Heart*, edited and translated by Medea Benjamin (San Francisco: Food First Books, 1987).

to myself, "Make your tears turn into anger, make your tears turn into strength." As soon as I stop crying, I feel a sense of power go through my body. And I get back to work with even more enthusiasm, with more conviction than ever.

One thing that gives us a great boost is when we hear that there are other people in other countries who are on our side. Not long ago I was in a meeting with a group of Hondurans working for peace in Central America. Two gringos were visiting and joined the meeting. They weren't gringos from the United States. They were gringos from other countries I'd never heard of, some countries in Europe, they said. And they were here to show support for our struggle.

They asked me to write a message to the people in their country. I picked up the pen and I don't know how I did it—because I really don't write very well—but I wrote something and they understood it. I wrote that I was just a poor Honduran, but that we were fighting for justice in our country. I told them how happy I was that there were people from other countries who were working for peace in Central America. I said I might not know what they look like, what language they speak, or even the names of the countries they come from, but that we were all brothers and sisters.

I later learned that there are also gringos in the United States who don't agree with their government's policies in Central America. You can't imagine how much courage and hope it gives me to know that we have friends in the United States. It's hard to think of change taking place in Central America without there first being changes in the United States. As we say in Honduras, "*Sin el perro, no hay rabia*" ("Without the dog, there wouldn't be rabies").

So you Americans who really want to help the poor have to change your own government first. You Americans who want to see an end to hunger and poverty have to take a stand. You have to fight just like we're fighting—even harder. You have to be ready to be jailed, to be abused, to be repressed. And you have to have the character, the courage, the morale, and the spirit to confront whatever comes your way.

We campesinos are used to planting seeds and waiting to see if the seeds bear fruit. We're used to working on harsh soil. And when our crops don't grow, we're used to planting again and again until they take hold. Like us, you must learn to persist.

You also have to be clear about your objectives, about why you're struggling. You can't struggle just because someone else tells you it's a good idea. No, you've got to feel the struggle. You've got to be completely convinced that what you're struggling for is just. And then you have to have a plan. What are you trying to achieve? What methods will you use? How many people do you have? Who can you count on for help? How much money do you have? How long will it take you to reach a certain number of people? What will you ask them to do?

You have to begin educating people, telling them the truth about what's happening in the world. Because if the press in the United States is anything like it is in Honduras, the people aren't well informed. You have to teach them what's really happening in the United States, what your government is really doing. And once you've educated people, get them organized.

Start out forming small groups, first in your own house, then with your neighbors. You might have to start out with just a handful of people. It doesn't matter if you start out small. Things that start out small get bigger and bigger. One group becomes two groups, two groups become four; and before you know it, you have a lot of well-organized people.

Then you start dividing up the tasks, and you make up your committees—the education committee, the women's committee, the youth committee. And soon you branch out to other neighborhoods and other villages and cities.

The other thing you have to do is make allies. I used to think you had to be poor to be part of this struggle. But there are people in Honduras who aren't poor, yet they're on our side. They're well-educated people—doctors, lawyers, teachers, engineers—who identify with the poor. I suppose it's the same in the United States.

I hate to offend you, but we won't get anywhere by just writing and reading books. I know that books are important, and I hope this book will be important for the people who read it. But we can't just read it and say, "Those poor campesinos. What a miserable life they have."

The important thing is for you to do something. We're not asking for food or clothing or money. We want you with us in the struggle. We want you to educate your people. We want you to organize your people. We want you to denounce what your government is doing in Central America.

From those of you who feel the pain of the poor, who feel the pain of the murdered, the disappeared, the tortured, we need more than sympathy. We need you to join the struggle. Don't be afraid, gringos. Keep your spirits high. And remember, we're right there with you!

3. FREE TRADE VS. PEOPLE'S MOVEMENTS

FREE TRADE AND AMERICA'S WORKING POOR

Christine Ahn, 2003[i]

On June 12, 2003, a delegation of America's working poor gathered for a congressional briefing in Washington, DC. Convened by the Congressional Progressive Caucus and Food First, the briefing was a rare chance for working poor people to speak collectively to members of Congress and the American public about the impact of free trade on their lives. *Shafted: Free Trade and America's Working Poor* is based on that briefing.

When Food First began the task of identifying a delegation to testify, we weren't looking for mere victims of free trade; we wanted to bring forward communities who resisted and fought back. The people whose stories you will read are the conscience among us, the ones who spoke up and started organizing when they and their fellow workers were fired as factories shut down and moved overseas. They are the ones who refused to believe that trade policies forcing family farms into foreclosure were progress, or that they were inevitable.

The theory of free trade, which says that these punishing economic policies are part of a natural, fair, and self-correcting mechanism over which we have no control, is collapsing under the weight of real-world experience. Yet the US is pushing for more trade liberalization through the Free Trade Area of the Americas (FTAA) and the World Trade Organization (WTO). This push is occurring without a national review of how the North American Free Trade Agreement (NAFTA) and other existing trade polices have affected the domestic economy.

The global justice movement is making the connection most of our policymakers won't: if free trade hasn't worked for America's poor—and it hasn't—it certainly won't work for the poor in developing countries.[ii]

Ten years of NAFTA: the emperor has no clothes

by Dena Hoff, National Family Farm Coalition

I am a family farmer from eastern Montana and a member of the National Family Farm Coalition, which was founded to bring together farmers and others to strengthen family farms and rural communities.

Free trade is no longer about an exchange of commodities between countries—wheat for coffee or bananas. What free trade is really about is procuring the unregulated movement of unlimited amounts of capital anywhere in the world. To this end, farm families have become pawns in a dangerous game played by powerful people who trade away the futures of the next generations of farm families, who in turn neither understand nor consent to the rules of the game.

---

i Adapted from Christine Ahn, ed., *Shafted: Free trade and America's working poor* (Oakland, CA: Food First Books, 2003).

ii Introductory section is an excerpt from Christine Ahn's preface to *Shafted.*

When Congress gives up the right to debate and amend trade agreements, they stop any meaningful participation by the American people in decisions that will affect every facet of their lives as well as the lives of every person on this planet. Free trade is no longer an economic issue. It is a moral issue.

Will US trade policy mean that farm prices will be above the cost of production for all farmers worldwide? Will countries have the right to determine domestic food and farm policies to benefit their own citizens? Will there be family farms for my own children and other farm children who want to farm? Will countries have the right to protect the public health and welfare of their citizens if their regulations deny a profit to a corporation?

Unless you can answer an unequivocal yes to each question, something is morally wrong with our current trade policy. In the nearly ten years since NAFTA, the facts show that the impacts to family farmers and ranchers in the US, Canada, and Mexico have been disastrous. Yet we stand ready to export this disaster to the rest of the Western Hemisphere.

A trade policy that is secret and undemocratic and that ignores the impacts on family farms, workers, and the environment is a slap in the face to every American who believes he or she lives in a country that proclaims liberty and justice for all. Our future depends on your commitment to making all trade fair trade.

Black farmers: the canary in the mineshaft of US agriculture

by Gary Grant, Black Farmers and Agriculturalists Association

I am a former small family farmer from North Carolina, and president of the Black Farmers and Agriculturalists Association (BFAA). On our farm, we planted row crops such as cotton, tobacco, corn, soybeans, and wheat. Black family farmers and the Black rural community have suffered under US agriculture policies that promote corporate concentration and exports through free trade agreements.

We are the canary in the mineshaft of American agriculture, and what has happened to Black family farmers in this country is what is now happening to the small family farmer in America.

In 1910, Black farmers owned between 16 and 19 million acres, and by 1997, we collectively owned just 1.5 million acres. Twenty years ago, there were 50,000 Black-operated family farms in the US; today there are just over 10,000. My family's struggle to stay on the farm is the same as my parents'. Like many farm families, they left the city with their five young children to realize their dreams of independence and their love for the land.

In the 1950s, we lived in the New Deal resettlement community of Tillery, North Carolina, with 300 other Black farming families. Today, none of those farmers are farming. Large White farmers are now tending 98 percent of that farmland.

My parents worked 16 hours a day, seven days a week as small farmers, and my dad worked weekends as a barber. Even though they worked hard, institutional racism prevented them from staying on the land, and in 1976 the farm went into foreclosure. The destruction of our farm led to high levels of stress and the deterioration of my parents' health, and eventually to their early deaths. Our family is just one example of what has happened to the rest of the Black farmers.

In a 1997 civil rights action report, the USDA admitted it had systematically discriminated against Black farmers. The following year, the *Pigford v. Glickman* case, in which Black farmers sought monetary compensation and debt relief for the discrimination and racism they endured from 1981 through 1996, was declared a class action lawsuit. Although over 100,000 Black farmers have sought to become a part of the lawsuit, only 21,591 have been accepted, and as of December 2002, only 12,972 have actually received any compensation.

Discrimination destroyed the ability of Black farmers to survive. The funding for loans that were denied to Black farmers did not sit idly by. It was used. For every dollar that did not find its way into a Black farmer's operation, a dollar did find its way into a White farmer's operation. In a world of limited financial resources, denial of access and support for one group usually means heightened access and support for another. With resources getting tighter and the destruction of Black farmers so thorough and complete, small White farmers were next.

US agricultural policy believes that Archer Daniels Midland (ADM) can feed a hungry world, and that they can do it better than a robust mixture of vibrant family farmers. In effect, the government subsidizes large corporate giants like ADM, Monsanto, and Tyson, which doesn't reduce hunger in the world, but increases the inequitable distribution of wealth, with wealth trickling upward and away from small family farmers.

The US has implemented trade agreements that are supposed to establish a "fair playing field" and open international markets. Without a doubt, small farmers view these trade agreements as more elaborate mechanisms to cheat ordinary farmers and the people out of their fair share.

The free trade strategies of the US government have destroyed and eradicated small farmers and rural development and employment. We do know that replacing small farmers with the large agricultural complex, with the goal of exporting crops, does nothing to increase America's rural employment or broaden the distribution of income and strategies of nonfarm rural enterprises. It breaks the human spirit of America's family farmers, and is the root and fundamental cause of poverty, disease, ignorance, and injustice in rural America, and in rural Black America in particular.

There is no single formula for saving small farmers and their generations of knowledge, and for achieving rural development. However, we do know that with the right government help and investment, small farmers don't have to perish and be deprived of what they enjoy most—being stewards of the land.

NAFTA and the border crisis

by Guillermo Glenn, Association of Border Workers

I am a member of the Association of Border Workers in El Paso, Texas, which represents over 2,800 workers on the border in efforts to secure labor rights and help displaced workers fight for retraining and job replacement under NAFTA.

In 1995, one year after NAFTA took effect, several electronic and health products manufacturing workers got together to figure out how we could save our jobs, as factories were closing down and moving at a rapid pace.

Communities across the country have been hit hard by loss of jobs due to free trade, but no other city has seen the effects as clearly as we have in El Paso. Since NAFTA, over 29,000 jobs have left El Paso, creating the largest number of NAFTA-displaced workers in the country. The city of El Paso estimates that each lost job costs $50,000/year in lost wages and sales revenue, totaling $1 billion lost by NAFTA-displaced workers alone.

And this trend continues. As of this March, 450 workers were laid off by Jones Apparel, 950 from Vanity Fair Jeans Corporation, 150 from International Garment Processor, and hundreds more from smaller factories. These were good-paying jobs that paid $12 or more per hour. It is no wonder that unemployment in El Paso is two to three times the state and national rates.

Before NAFTA was signed and implemented, a study was released by several research organizations that explained how the garment industry was going to leave El Paso due to NAFTA. The state, however, did nothing to prepare. They did not consider the workers and the diverse resources they would need to help displaced workers secure jobs. They should have implemented a bilingual job corps, eliminated discriminatory treatment toward Spanish speakers, and made resources available for economic development programs. But none of the above happened.

As part of NAFTA's Trade Adjustment Assistance Program, the Department of Labor gave a large grant to El Paso to provide job training to displaced workers. Eighty percent of the displaced workers in El Paso are Spanish speakers. However, no bilingual infrastructure was built to help displaced workers who were Spanish speaking. Without a GED and with limited English skills, the majority of these workers had very few options available to them. As a last resort, we filed a lawsuit in March 2002 against the Department of Labor and the Texas Workforce Development Board for denial of language and relevant job skills to workers in El Paso.

Those hardest hit by the restructuring are older Spanish-speaking factory workers, people defined by the marketplace as not worth training for new jobs, even if they are US citizens. Spanish-speaking displaced workers have become the marginalized targets of harassment and discrimination in virtually all aspects of their lives.

Since NAFTA, El Paso has experienced economic growth, but not everyone has shared the prosperity. Even the mayor of Juarez, just across the Mexican border from El Paso, recently remarked that NAFTA has been very beneficial for international corporations, but as the city creates more and more wealth, Juarez becomes poorer and poorer.

The border is in crisis. Texas state senators have declared it an emergency. One out of three persons live in poverty. Forty percent of schoolchildren live in poverty. The border has one of the nation's highest unemployment rates, at 11.4 percent. We have seen record numbers of deaths caused by diabetes and hepatitis and other liver diseases.

With this kind of displacement and economic loss, neighborhoods and communities must be rebuilt. But how do we create jobs for American workers on the US side of the border when corporations can now pay just one or two dollars an hour for labor right across the border?

It is imperative that displaced workers not be discarded as the inevitable losers in the destructive globalization process facilitated by so-called "free" trade agreements. Massive job loss is equivalent to a natural disaster; it has ramifications beyond the workers' lives, including damage to the community's social and economic fabric. Companies and corporations that displace workers should provide resources toward their reintegration into the workforce and the rebuilding of the community's economy and socioeconomic fabric.

Trade adjustment resources are vital to ensuring that whole communities are not left behind in the new economy, but only if they are used in effective ways that genuinely help displaced workers and communities to rebuild their futures, rather than simply receiving a token handout.

Displaced farmers and unemployed farmworkers

by Dolores Huerta, United Farm Workers of America

The United Farm Workers of America, AFL-CIO, represents 43,000 farmworkers across the US. We have seen the devastating impact free trade has had on farmworkers, and we adamantly oppose any expansion of these agreements.

Free trade, as exemplified by NAFTA, has hurt hundreds of thousands of farmworkers here in the US. Since NAFTA, we have seen new waves of workers emigrating from the coffee growing regions of Veracruz, Mexico, where they were once small family coffee farmers. The free trade of coffee on the world market has destroyed the price coffee buyers once paid small family farmers.

As a result, they are no longer able to support themselves and their families off the revenue generated from the coffee they grow, forcing them to leave their farms, risk their lives crossing the border to the US, and seek employment on farms in this country. Between 1995 and 2001, over 2,200 Mexicans died crossing the US border. Those who survive find a situation not much different than what they left in Mexico.

This displacement is not only limited to coffee growers. It is estimated that 1.75 million Mexican nationals have been displaced due to free trade. Throughout Mexico, thousands of small family farmers grow corn for their own consumption and for sale within Mexico. These farmers, however, cannot compete with the corn from the US. In 2001, US corn exporters dumped over 5 million tons of corn on the Mexican market at 25 percent below market cost. The Mexican government has reduced subsidies for corn production by 61 percent since NAFTA went into effect. Meanwhile in the US, commodity payments continue to favor large multinationals that both grow and purchase corn and other grains from US growers.

In the US, we have witnessed a dramatic decrease in the acreage of crops such as apples, asparagus, broccoli, cauliflower, mushrooms, grapes, and strawberries. In the last five years in the Willamette Valley of Oregon, three major food processors have closed their doors due to the availability of cheaper crops from other countries. In eastern Washington, the largest asparagus processor in the US threatens to close, due in large part to the continued importation of tariff-free asparagus from Peru, which is far cheaper than asparagus grown locally.

The loss of acres of crops and the increasing number of food processors and packers who are closing up shop are wreaking havoc on rural communities throughout the US. Faced with the loss of buyers, growers are increasingly facing the real threat of bankruptcy and the loss of their family farms. Farmworkers, many of whom depended on jobs provided on the farms and in the processors and packing sheds, are now unemployed. In rural communities throughout the US, there is a scarcity of alternate jobs available to the increasing number of unemployed farmworkers and displaced US farmers.

The net impact of these changes caused by free trade is that we in this country, just like our counterparts in Mexico, are importing more and more of the food we consume. We are ultimately placing the security of our food at risk and tearing apart the social fabric of our rural communities.

The continued expansion of unrestricted trade is not a given, nor is it inevitable. US and Mexican agricultural policy can ensure the continued economic viability of family farmers by ensuring a fair playing field in the marketplace for all. But we must first work to remedy the damage that has been done by these free trade agreements and help family farmers from the US and Mexico get back on their feet and earn a fair and just living from their dignified labor. The real human, social, and economic costs of free trade clearly indicate that US trade negotiators should cease to sign any additional free trade agreements.

BASTA! THE ZAPATISTA REBELLION IN CHIAPAS, MEXICO

George A. Collier with Elizabeth Lowery Quaratiello, 1999[i]

On January 1, 1994, the EZLN (*Ejercito Zapatista de Liberación Nacional* or Zapatista Army of National Liberation)—equipped with rubber boots, homemade army uniforms, bandanas, ski masks, and weapons ranging from handmade wooden rifles to Uzi machine guns—seized towns in eastern and central Chiapas, proclaiming a revolution on the inaugural day of the North American Free Trade Agreement (NAFTA).

Taking advantage of the New Year holiday to catch security forces off-guard, the Zapatistas—a force of young, disciplined, and mostly indigenous men and women soldiers—ransacked the town halls of Altamirano, Chanal, Huistan, Las Margaritas, Oxchuc, Ocosingo, and San Cristobal de las Casas—once the colonial seat of government of Chiapas and today an important commercial and tourist center. Some burned district attorney, judicial, and police records (but spared archives in San Cristobal that a local scholar told them had historic value). Others fanned out into the mountains to seek recruits from among the indigenous and other peasants of the region. Treating startled tourists and civilians with courtesy, the EZLN pronounced itself in rebellion against the government, the army, and the police. In printed circulars and broadcasts from captured Ocosingo radio station XOECH, the Zapatistas declared:

> *!Hoy decimos basta!* Today we say enough is enough! To the people of Mexico, Mexican brothers and sisters: we are a product of 500 years of struggle. First against slavery, then during the War of Independence against Spain led by insurgents, then to promulgate our Constitution and expel the French empire from our soil, and later (when) the dictatorship of Porfirio Díaz denied us the just application of the reform laws and the people rebelled and leaders like Villa and Zapata emerged, for men just like us. We have been denied the most elemental education so that others can use us as cannon fodder and pillage the wealth of our country. They don't care that we have nothing, absolutely nothing, not even a roof over our heads, no land, no work, no healthcare, no food, and no education. Nor are we able freely and democratically to elect our political representatives, nor is there independence from foreigners, nor is there peace nor justice for ourselves and our children.[ii]

Invoking Article 39 of Mexico's Constitution of 1917, which invests national sovereignty and

---

i   Adapted from George A. Collier with Elizabeth Lowery Quaratiello, *Basta! Land and the Zapatista Rebellion in Chiapas* (Oakland, CA: Food First Books, 1999).

ii   From the "Declaración de la Selva Lacandona" emitted by the Comandancia General del EZLN from the Selva Lacandona, Chiapas, Mexico, on December 31, 1993.

the right to modify government in the people of Mexico, they called on other Mexicans to help them depose the "illegal dictatorship" of President Carlos Salinas de Gortari's government and party. They declared war on the Mexican armed forces and called on international organizations and the Red Cross to monitor under the Geneva Conventions of 1949. They appealed to other Mexicans to join their insurgency.

Within 24 hours, the EZLN launched an attack on the Rancho Nuevo army base about six miles southeast of San Cristobal and freed 179 prisoners from a nearby penitentiary. They kidnapped Absalón Castellanos Domínguez, governor of Chiapas from 1982 to 1988, announcing he would be tried summarily and shot for crimes of repression. Instead, he was "sentenced" to a life term of hard peasant labor.

The Mexican government quickly moved 12,000 troops and equipment into the region. Within days, and after two pitched battles, the Zapatistas retreated east and southward out of the central highlands and into rugged and inaccessible strongholds in the tropical forests of the eastern lowlands. Backed by airstrikes, federal troops pursued the EZLN in armored vehicles to where roads give way to wilderness.

By that time, journalists from around the world had arrived on the scene to chronicle the Zapatistas' exploits and explore their motives, which struck chords of sympathy with the Mexican public. Reporters portrayed the rebels as Maya Indians upset over years of poverty and discrimination as they began to write poignant articles describing the abuses heaped upon the Indians of Mexico's southernmost state. Human rights organizations that had for some time been trying to alert the world to the plight of the region's poor suddenly found an avid audience as they began to document federal army abuses against Zapatista prisoners and civilians caught up in the warfare.

Subcomandante Marcos in Chiapas

The rebels, disguised with bandanas and ski masks, became instant icons, their images replicated on everything from cloth dolls sold in Mexico's outdoor marketplaces to cartoons in Mexico City's daily newspapers. Zapatista images even appeared on condom wrappers. Guessing the identity of "Subcomandante Marcos," the shadowy, green-eyed ideologue and military director of the uprising, suddenly became a popular obsession.

In the weeks that followed, tensions rose. Citizens seized dozens of town halls in Chiapas and neighboring states to protest that incumbent mayors, most of whom were pawns of the governing party, had stolen office through fraudulent elections. In eastern Chiapas, peasants invaded private ranches. Some landowners fled; others counterattacked with hired gunmen. A broad coalition of peasant and indigenous organizations denounced the government for past neglect and abuse and proclaimed themselves in favor of Zapatista demands for reforms.

The region behind the headlines is a complicated one. Chiapas is sometimes described as a picturesque backwater—a quaint stop on the tourist circuit where time has stood still and Maya Indians can be observed performing their age-old crafts and rituals. But beneath the surface seen by the casual visitor, Chiapas is filled with paradoxes that defy easy categorization. In addition to peasants who weave and wear the traditional *huipul* (tunics) and carry loads on *tumplines*, there are peasants who dress in jeans and drive trucks. Within even the tiniest Indian hamlets there are wealthy entrepreneurs who own such modern luxury items as televisions and videocassette recorders; poor, marginalized farmworkers; and opportunistic political bosses. The state has plenty of wealthy *ladinos* (non-indigenous Mexicans of the region) who sympathize with the Zapatistas, as well as poor peasants who do not. There are disaffected intellectuals, grassroots organizers, elite colonial families, and ranchers, each with their own political agenda. And in this place where Catholics and Protestants have clashed bitterly, where women are praised for passivity rather than activism, a nonsectarian rebellion has arisen, and mothers, wives, and daughters are among those who make up the ranks of the Zapatista army.

What is it that unites those who took up arms with the Zapatistas? In contrast to some analysts, I posit that it is primarily a peasant rebellion, not an exclusively Indian rebellion, because although the Zapatistas are demanding rights for indigenous peoples, they are first and foremost calling attention to the plight of Mexico's rural poor and peasants, both indigenous and nonindigenous. By *peasants* I mean rural people who produce their own food or who are closely connected to others who produce for subsistence, as contrasted with those who farm commercial crops primarily for sale and profit. In southern Mexico, many peasants, but not all, are *indigenous* people, descendants of those who were conquered and subordinated by the Spanish during the period of colonial rule.[iii]

Some may wonder why the rebellion was instigated by peasants and not by the urban poor or those who toil in the *maquiladoras*, people who have certainly suffered greatly in recent years. Although there is no clear answer to this question, one possible explanation is that on top of

---

iii Indigenous people generally speak one of the Native American languages as their first tongue, though many also learn some Spanish. Many indigenous people identify themselves as members of ethnic communities that were classified as "Indian" rather than "Spanish" or *mestizo* (mixed race) under the period of colonial rule. There are also indigenous people who lack such links to specific communities because they have been diasporic throughout history. Indigenous people often experience discrimination at the hands of nonindigenous Mexicans.

the severe hardships peasants have had to endure during the past decade of economic restructuring, they were also disappointed by a number of broken promises from the government: land reform that never occurred; price supports guaranteed, then taken away; and credits extended, then withdrawn. When, in 1992, the government of President Salinas de Gortari brought land reform—the issue on which his party had originally risen to power—to a halt, he signaled an abrupt end to a traditional government covenant with the peasantry and deprived many peasants not just of the possibility of improving their livelihoods, but of their power as a constituency. The Zapatistas are trying to reclaim that constituency.

The Zapatista rebellion bears some resemblance to the revolutionary movements of Central America, in that those movements also involved peasants who had no safety net to help cope with marginalization. Mexico's government, however, has been much more stable than any of Central America's regimes, and has steadfastly—and successfully—fought off involvement in the geopolitics of the Cold War.[iv] Until the 1982 debt crisis, Mexico also catered to peasants as a distinct constituency—something most Central American governments never even pretended to do. One of the paradoxes of the rebellion is that the Zapatistas have responded to the adversity of eastern Chiapas more as Mexican nationals than as doctrinaire revolutionaries. While they are demanding changes for their region and for the rural poor in other areas, they're also holding Mexico's ruling party responsible for undemocratic politics and for betraying historic commitments to social welfare when it opened Mexico up to free trade and foreign investment.

As economic and political forces have transformed peasant farming, peasant communities have become less egalitarian, demarcated by class and by national political affiliation. My observations are drawn from research I performed as an anthropologist during three decades spent studying agrarian change in highland Chiapas, including ways in which Mexico's oil boom of the 1970s and the resulting debt crisis of the 1980s redefined the lives and roles of the region's peasants. Among the indigenous peasants I know, I saw a gap grow ever wider between the wealthy, who were able to infuse their farming with cash derived from wage work near the oil fields, on dam projects, and in urban construction projects, and the poor, who are finding it increasingly impossible to afford to farm even their own land.

Some peasants in Chiapas have been able to weather the changes wrought by Mexico's economic restructuring by diversifying their farming activities, becoming produce and flower merchants, or starting up transport businesses. But many have not. Their successes and failures have often resulted from and contributed to politics, as can be seen by tracing the rise of local political bosses who have used their ties with the Institutional Revolutionary Party (PRI) to establish monopolies on small businesses and quell opposition in their towns. Economic restructuring brought particular suffering to the inhabitants of the eastern part of Chiapas, from which the rebels draw the majority of their members, and where cultural isolation, political exclusion, and economic depression have combined to leave people in what is commonly called Mexico's "last frontier" without hope and without even the most basic necessities of life.

---

iv For more on Central American radical movements as responding to peasants' displacement into marginal lands by developing commercial agriculture and ranching oriented to exports, see: Robert G. Williams, *Export Agriculture and the Crisis in Central America* (Chapel Hill: University of North Carolina Press, 1986).

Because the situation of peasants in Mexico's countryside seems so bleak, the Zapatista rebellion inspired enormous sympathy from people throughout the world who read about the uprising in their newspapers and watched reports about it on television. Journalists tended to paint an image of the poor, honest peasants on one side and the greedy ranchers and corrupt politicians on the other.

This idealization of peasants is inaccurate, however, because some of the inequalities in the countryside are the result of stratification within peasant communities, not merely the result of injustices heaped upon them from outside. Understanding indigenous politics in this way necessarily complicates the sympathies one might hold toward peasants, but I view this as salutary. I think we misrepresent peasants if we allow ourselves to view them in simplistic terms—as either the passive victims of the state or as "noble savages" who can reinvigorate modern society with egalitarian and collective values. By acknowledging tensions and differences in peasant communities, we face up to both the virtue and the vice inherent in peasants' exercise of power over one another, and we integrate individual agency into our understanding of peasant communities. We also arrive at an appreciation of why not all peasants and indigenous groups welcomed the Zapatistas. In some highland communities, some people referred to the Zapatistas in native Tzotzil as "troublemakers" or as "thieves"—a reference to marauders who roamed the countryside in the 1910–1920 decade of the Mexican Revolution. Others told me that when the Zapatistas fanned into the mountains to look for recruits, a giant snake and a whirlwind—ancestor deities—rose in their paths to block off the entrances to Zinacantán and Chamula, communities whose leaders are loyal to the PRI.

The Zapatista uprising has forced a public debate about Mexico's priorities and has galvanized many impoverished Mexicans to demand better lives, even as it has to some extent polarized relations among indigenous peoples' organizations in Chiapas.

THE TRANS-PACIFIC PARTNERSHIP: A THREAT TO DEMOCRACY AND FOOD SOVEREIGNTY

Anders Riel Muller, Ayumi Kinezuka, and Tanya Kerssen, 2013[i]

The Trans-Pacific Partnership (TPP), which began as a small regional free trade agreement, has become one of the primary tools in the United States' geopolitical pivot towards the Asia-Pacific region. The agreement—negotiated in secrecy—will dramatically expand the rights of corporations over those of food producers, consumers, workers, and the environment.

What is the Trans-Pacific Partnership?

The TPP began as a trade agreement signed in 2005 between Brunei, New Zealand, Chile, and Singapore. Since then, several more countries have come on board, including Australia, Canada, Malaysia, Mexico, Peru, Vietnam, the United States, and Japan. Current TPP countries account for nearly 40 percent of global economic output and about a third of world trade. The TPP's "docking mechanism" would also enable other countries to join the agreement in the future.

Considered the most ambitious Free Trade Agreement (FTA) in the world, partners hope the TPP will set the agenda for future World Trade Organization (WTO) negotiations. For the United States, the agreement represents an expansion and deepening of its 19 existing bilateral and regional FTAs and a strengthening of US influence in the Asia-Pacific region. Over 60 percent of US trade is with Asia-Pacific Economic Cooperation (APEC) member nations, and 34 percent is with TPP partners. The US is particularly interested in accessing markets in TPP countries for its agricultural products and financial services, including banking and insurance; streamlining and enforcing intellectual property rights; and placing limits on state-owned enterprises. As the most powerful US ally in East Asia, Japan's participation further strengthens US interest in the TPP. While there is no existing US-Japan FTA, trade with Japan already accounts for 6 percent of total US goods trade and 7 percent of total US services trade as of 2011.

The Asian pivot: TPP, China, and US military strategy

One of the hallmarks of President Obama's foreign policy platform has been the so-called Asian Pivot, a strategic shift of economic, military, and diplomatic resources away from the Middle East (mainly Iraq and Afghanistan) and towards Asia. This geopolitical repositioning comes at

i   Adapted from Anders Riel Muller, Ayumi Kinezuka, and Tanya Kerssen, "The Trans-Pacific Partnership: A Threat to Democracy and Food Sovereignty," Food First Backgrounder, Vol. 19, No. 2, Summer 2013.

a time of increasing tensions with North Korea and China's growing political, economic, and military power, including claims on resource-rich contested territories in the South China Sea.[ii] In 2012, the Pentagon announced plans to move 60 percent of US naval assets to the Pacific by 2020, a massive peacetime deployment.[1]

In April 2013, the USS Freedom—a new class of warship designed for combat in coastal areas—sailed into Singapore's Changi Naval Base.[2] While US officials deny that the move was meant to intimidate China, some, like retired Army general and senior advisor to the Center for a New American Century David Barno, do not mince words: "China should and will take note… the United States is and will remain a Pacific power, even more so in this century than in the last."[3]

Though China has indicated it is evaluating the possibility of joining the TPP, the agreement's restrictions on state-owned enterprises—the cornerstone of China's economic model—make it highly unlikely. By assembling US allies in Asia and institutionalizing them as partners in the world's most far-reaching trade agreement, the TPP is part of a broader US geopolitical strategy to offset China's growing influence in the world, and in the Asia-Pacific region in particular.

Secret negotiations to expand corporate power

Civil society groups have voiced great discontent about the lack of transparency in TPP negotiations, which are conducted in secret under a confidentiality agreement. Trade policy proposals are only shared among a few TPP partner government officials and the "trade advisory groups" dominated by large corporations. The US advisory committees related to agriculture[4] are composed almost entirely of large agro-food corporations and industry associations such as Pepsi-Co, Tyson Foods, ADM, Cargill, Coca Cola, and Kraft Foods, as well as the American Soybean Association and the American Meat Institute.[5]

Covered by the TPP confidentiality agreement, corporate interests are able to influence negotiations through the advisory committees without any scrutiny from civil society. Under the guise of protecting sensitive trade talks, negotiating parties have brazenly cast aside democratic principles, virtually banning the general public from knowing—and debating—the content of negotiations. Furthermore, the White House is pushing negotiations through a rarely used "fast track" procedure that transfers congressional trade authority to the executive branch.[6] A recent letter signed by 36 freshman democratic congressman expressed concern that "the administration has yet to release draft texts after more than three years of negotiations, and the few TPP texts that have leaked reveal serious problems."[7]

The TPP seeks to phase out trade tariffs on more than 11,000 commodity categories and expand WTO rules on intellectual property rights (known as TRIPS), expanding the scope and scale of what is patentable.[iii] Furthermore, TPP seeks to extend patent terms beyond the 20-year TRIPS minimum.[8] By extending patents, large corporations can keep smaller producers out of national

---

ii For example, the Senkaku Islands administered by Japan (known as the Diaoyu Islands in China) include rich marine resources, are located near important shipping lanes, and purportedly contain large oil deposits.

iii The Agreement on Trade Related Aspects of Intellectual Property Rights or TRIPS, administered by the WTO, is the international agreement that sets minimum standards for the regulation of intellectual property.

and local markets to an extent never before seen in FTAs. Many groups have voiced concern that extended patents will benefit Big Pharma, for instance, while limiting access to affordable, life-saving generic medicines. Additional provisions limiting state-owned enterprises and public procurement policies would severely limit governments' ability to manage their own economies or support local producers.

Moreover, a chapter leaked from the draft document in 2012 revealed the TPP would create a special tribunal allowing corporations to sue governments for loss of profits if, for example, labor or environmental regulations restrict their activities—a legal tool already available under some current FTAs.[9] For instance, after the Canadian province of Québec placed a moratorium on hydraulic fracturing, or "fracking," for natural gas in response to widespread civil society protest, the US company Lone Pine Resources sued the Canadian government for $250 million under provisions of the North American Free Trade Agreement (NAFTA).[10] In short, the TPP seeks to severely limit national sovereignty and the ability of states to protect communities from the onslaught of transnational corporations.

Food and agriculture in the TPP

Agricultural trade in the TPP has largely been viewed as a tug of war between the large agricultural producers. Australia and New Zealand, for instance, want increased access to US markets for sugar and dairy, a demand strongly opposed by the US sugar and dairy producers' lobbies. Australia and New Zealand are also pushing the US on the issue of food aid, arguing that it functions as an indirect export subsidy to US producers.[11] With the entry of Japan, tensions over agricultural negotiations have heightened. Japan is the largest food-importing nation in the world, but also has strong protections for key products such as rice, barley, sugar, beef, and dairy.

Photo by Caelie Frampton

For Australia, New Zealand, and the US, the liberalization of Japanese agriculture means access to one of the largest and most profitable food markets in the world. But this would spell disaster for Japan's agricultural sector, where 80 percent of all farms are smaller than two hectares. The TPP countries with food production still in the hands of millions of smallholders would almost certainly be crushed by cheap imports from countries with strong industrial agriculture sectors. Surely, some would benefit: mostly big industrial farms, corporate seed companies, agrochemical companies and large agricultural trading firms. Food producers—i.e., farmers not producing commodities for the industrial food, feed, and agrofuels complex—have been completely excluded from TPP negotiations.

For years, farmers' organizations and social movements such as La Vía Campesina have been able to keep agriculture out of WTO negotiations through lobbying and protest. A central goal of TPP negotiations is to circumvent the WTO deadlock and take agricultural liberalization even further. As Karen Hansen-Kuhn of the Institute for Agriculture and Trade Policy (IATP) notes, if implemented, the TPP "would expand protections for investors over consumers and farmers, and severely restrict governments' ability to use public policy to reshape food systems."[12] The TPP not only brings agriculture back in to multilateral trade negotiations, it does so with a vengeance.

TPP and the dismantling of Japanese agriculture

According to the Buddhist concept of *shindo-fuji*, a healthy body comes from healthy soil, so one must appreciate the environment one lives in. Japan has a strong food movement, rooted in *shindo-fuji*, promoting local production and consumption. However, agricultural imports have been on the rise since World War II, severely undermining Japanese food production: in 1965, Japan's food self-sufficiency rate was 73 percent, but by 2010, it had dropped to 39 percent.[13] Japanese food self-sufficiency—now one of the lowest among Organisation for Economic Co-operation and Development (OECD) countries—is often explained as merely the result of changes in dietary preferences. Often missing in this discussion, however, is the tremendous pressure the US put on Japan to accept surpluses of wheat, soybeans and corn following World War II.

The traditional Japanese diet—rice combined with locally produced vegetables and fish—constituted one of the biggest barriers to post-war US imports. To open up a market for US food products, Japanese diets had to change to include bread, meat, and dairy products. Through the US-funded "Nutrition Improvement Action" program, people were told, "Eating rice makes you stupid! Eat Bread!" School lunch menus were westernized and "American Trains" and "Kitchen Cars" crisscrossed the country to promote a western diet. Today, Japanese people consume 9.5 percent more wheat, 152 percent more animal products and 131 percent more fat than in the 1950s. According to the Japanese Ministry of Agriculture and Fisheries (MAFF), TPP would drop food self-sufficiency from 39 to 14 percent.[14] Rice production would be hit severely. This could destroy Japanese agriculture and its rural culture. Additionally, important land reform laws passed in the 1940s and 50s that safeguard farmers' right to land have come under attack. Under pressure from the private sector, the government passed a revised land law in June 2009 cancelling the principle of "land to the tiller," allowing non-farmers to own farmland and foreign capital to lease farmland. Deregulation under TPP would grant foreign investors further influence over national policies that protect farmers, farmland, and rural communities.

The opposition against TPP in Japan encompasses a wide range of groups,[15] from progressive to conservative forces such as the Japan Agriculture and Fishery Organization, the Japan Medical Association and others. As much as 94 percent of prefectural assemblies and 80 percent of local city assemblies have passed resolutions against TPP. In Hokkaido, the opposition encompasses almost all groups and organizations in the prefecture, including the finance community. Of the 13 political parties, seven are opposed to TPP and only one party is vocal about its support of TPP. Opposition transcends traditional political divisions, demonstrating that a broad political coalition against TPP is possible. To organize effectively, we must increase international solidarity among farmers, citizens' groups, and local communities. The farmers of Japan hope to build strong alliances with groups and farmers in other TPP negotiating countries to stop corporate interests from destroying our agriculture and eroding our work for food sovereignty.

Two, three, many Seattles: building resistance

When trade ministers met in November 1999 in Seattle to initiate a new round of WTO trade and investment liberalization, they likely did not expect to be greeted by several thousand protesters "dancing, chanting, and conversing in a cold Seattle downpour."[16] The "Battle of Seattle" marked a watershed in the WTO's short history: outside the negotiations, global civil society made its voice heard on international trade issues like never before; inside, Global South countries strongly rejected a framework biased in favor of the most powerful nations, producers, and corporations. A member of the Zimbabwe delegation commented: "If it keeps going like this, we'll have to join the protesters outside."[17]

After Seattle, notes Pritchard, "the issue of how the WTO should relate to civil society became an issue of great concern to the organization."[18] A few years later, in mid-2003, the WTO's Doha Development Round Ministerial in Cancún ended in a similar breakdown. Differences over the regulation of food and agriculture—and the powerful role of farmers' organizations protesting the impact of free trade on rural livelihoods—figured prominently in the meeting's failure.[19] Like the WTO and other FTAs, the TPP is an attempt to bypass democratic processes and dismantle social and environmental protections that impede unbridled corporate profit. But peasant movements and civil society organizations have built up an unprecedented capacity for transnational mobilization over the last two decades. Successful resistance to TPP will depend upon the effective mobilization of those movements and alliances, building on the experiences and lessons learned from Seattle, Cancún, and broader struggles for democracy and food sovereignty.

NOTES

1   Julian E. Barnes, "US Plans Naval Shift Toward Asia," *The Wall Street Journal*, June 1, 2012, http://online.wsj.com/article/SB10001424052702303552104577439943137674490.html.

2   "US Warship in Southeast Asia Gives Punch to US Asian Pivot," *The Times of India*, April 18, 2013, http://timesofindia.indiatimes.com/world/rest-of-world/US-warship-in-southeast-Asia-gives-punch-to-US-Asian-pivot/articleshow/19611261.cms.

3   Julian E. Barnes, "US Plans Naval Shift Toward Asia," *op. cit.*

4   Agricultural Policy Advisory Committee (APAC) members: http://www.ustr.gov/about-us/advisory-committees/agricultural-policy-advisory-committee-apac, and Agricultural Technical Advisory Committee (ATAC) members: http://www.ustr.gov/about-us/intergovernmental-affairs/advisory-committees/agricultural-technical-advisory-committee-tra.

5   Shuji Hisano, "What Does the U.S. Agribusiness Industry Demand of Japan in the TPP Negotiations?" Working Paper No. 127, Graduate School of Economics, Kyoto University, February 2013, http://www.econ.kyoto-u.ac.jp/~chousa/WP/127.pdf.

6   "'Fast Track' Enables Bad Public Policy," Citizens Trade Campaign, 2013, http://www.citizenstrade.org/ctc/wp-content/uploads/2013/03/FastTrackFactsheet.pdf.

7   "Democratic Revolt Against TPP and Fast Track," Citizens Trade Campaign, June 11, 2013, http://www.citizenstrade.org/ctc/blog/2013/06/11/democratic-revolt-against-tpp-and-fast-track/.

8   Jimmy H. Koo, "Table Comparing the Patent Law Regimes - TPP vs. Canada, Mexico and NAFTA," http://infojustice.org/wp-content/uploads/2012/08/Patents-TPP-vs-Canada-Mexico-NAFTA-08162012.pdf

9   "Leaked document reveals Trans-Pacific Partnership would give corporations power over sovereign states," Citizen Action Monitor, June 6, 2013, http://citizenactionmonitor.wordpress.com/2013/06/06/leaked-document-reveals-trans-pacific-partnership-would-give-corporations-power-over-sovereign-states/.

10 "US firm to launch NAFTA challenge to Quebec fracking ban," *The Globe and Mail*, Nov. 15, 2012, http://www.theglobeandmail.com/globe-investor/us-firm-to-launch-nafta-challenge-to-quebec-fracking-ban/article5337929/.

11 Ian F. Fergusson et al., *The Trans-Pacific Partnership Negotiations and Issues for Congress*, Congressional Research Service, June 17, 2013, http://www.fas.org/sgp/crs/row/R42694.pdf.

12 "Who's at the Table? Demanding answers on agriculture in the Trans-Pacific Partnership," Institute for Agriculture and Trade Policy, February 2013, http://www.iatp.org/files/2013_02_28_TPP_KHK_0.pdf.

13 Japan Ministry of Agriculture, Forestry and Fisheries, http://www.maff.go.jp/j/zyukyu/zikyu_ritu/012.html.

14 Japan Ministry of Agriculture, Forestry, and Fisheries, http://www.maff.go.jp/j/council/seisaku/syokuryo/110202/pdf/refdata5.pdf.

15 "Japanese Movement Against TPP Growing," The Real News Network, May 7, 2013, http://therealnews.com/t2/index.php?option=com_content&task=view&id=31&ltemid=74&jumival=10178.

16   Jackie Smith, "Globalizing Resistance: The Battle of Seattle and the Future of Social Movements," *Mobilization: An International Journal*, 2001, 6(1): 1-20.

17   Allard 1999, 11, cited in Bill Pritchard, "The Long Hangover from the Second Food Regime: A world-historical interpretation of the collapse of the WTO Doha Round," *Agriculture and Human Values*, 2009, 26:297–307.

18   Bill Pritchard, "The Long Hangover from the Second Food Regime," *op. cit.*

19   Peter Rosset, *Food is Different: Why the WTO Should Get Out of Agriculture* (London and New York: Zed Books, 2006).

4. THE GREEN REVOLUTION: DEBT AND DEGRADATION

CIRCLE OF POISON: PESTICIDES IN A HUNGRY WORLD

David Weir and Mark Schapiro, 1981[i]

The export of banned pesticides from the industrial countries to the Third World is a scandal of global proportions. Massive advertising campaigns by multinational pesticide corporations— Dow, Shell, Chevron—have turned the Third World into not only a booming growth market for pesticides, but also a dumping ground. Dozens of pesticides too dangerous for unrestricted use in the United States are shipped to underdeveloped countries. There, lack of regulation, illiteracy, and repressive working conditions can turn even a "safe" pesticide into a deadly weapon. According to the World Health Organization (WHO), pesticides poison someone in underdeveloped countries *every minute.*[1]

But we are victims too. Pesticide exports create a circle of poison, disabling workers in American chemical plants and later returning to us in the food we import. Drinking a morning coffee or enjoying a luncheon salad, the American consumer is eating pesticides banned or restricted in the United States but legally shipped to the Third World. The United States is among the world's top food importers, and 10 percent of our imported food is officially rated as contaminated.[2] Although the Food and Drug Administration (FDA) is supposed to protect us from such hazards, during one 15-month period, the General Accounting Office (GAO) discovered that half of all the imported food identified by the FDA as pesticide-contaminated was marketed without any warning to consumers or penalty to importers.[3]

At least 20 percent of US pesticide exports are products that are banned, heavily restricted, or have never been registered for use here.[4] Many have not been independently evaluated for their impacts on human health or the environment. Other pesticides are familiar poisons, widely known to cause cancer, birth defects, and genetic mutations. Yet, the Federal Insecticide, Fungicide, and Rodenticide Act explicitly states that banned or unregistered pesticides are legal for export. In the United States, a mere dozen multinational corporations dominate the $7-billion-a-year pesticide market.

Pesticides: a pound per person

Worldwide pesticide sales are exploding. The amount of pesticides exported from the US has almost doubled over the last fifteen years.[5] The industry now produces 4 billion pounds of pesticides each year—more than one pound for every person on earth.[6] Almost all are produced in the industrial countries, but 20 percent are exported to the Third World.[7]

---

i   Adapted from David Weir and Mark Schapiro, *Circle of Poison: Pesticides and People in a Hungry World* (San Francisco: Food First Books, 1981).

And the percentage exported is likely to increase rapidly: the GAO predicts that during the decade ending in 1984, the use of pesticides in Africa, for example, will more than quintuple.[8] As the US pesticide market is "approaching saturation.. US pesticide producers have been directing their attention toward the export potential... exports have almost doubled since 1965 and currently account for 30 percent of total domestic pesticide production," the trade publication *Chemical Economics Newsletter* noted.[9]

Corporate executives justify the pesticide explosion with what sounds like a reasonable explanation: the hungry world needs our pesticides in its fight against famine. But their words ring hollow: in Third World fields, most pesticides are applied to luxury export crops, not to food staples the local people will eat. Instead of helping the poor to eat better, technology is overexposing them to chemicals that cause cancer, birth defects, sterility, and nerve damage.

"Blind" schedules, not "as needed"

The crisis is not just about the export of banned pesticides. A key problem in both the industrial countries and the Third World is the massive overuse of pesticides resulting from their indiscriminate application. Pesticides are routinely applied according to schedules preset by the corporate sellers, not measured in precise response to actual pest threats in a specific field. By conservative estimate, US farmers could cut insecticide use by 35 to 50 percent with no effect on crop production, simply by treating only when necessary rather than by schedule.[10] In Central America, researchers calculate that pesticide use, especially parathion, is 40 percent higher than necessary to achieve optimal profits.[11]

In the United States, the result of pesticide overuse is the unnecessary poisoning of farmworkers and farmers—about 14,000 a year according to the Environmental Protection Agency (EPA).[12] But if pesticides are not used safely here—where most people can read warning labels, where a huge government agency (the EPA) oversees pesticide regulation, and where farmworker unions are fighting to protect the health of their members—can we expect these poisons to be used safely in the Third World?

An inappropriate technology

In Third World countries, one or two officials often carry responsibility equivalent to that of the entire EPA in the US. Workers are seldom told how the pesticides could hurt them. Most cannot read. And even if they could, labels on banned pesticides often do not carry the warnings required in the United States. Frequently repacked or simply scooped out into old cans, peasants who have little experience with manmade poisons often handle deadly pesticides like harmless white powder.

But perhaps even more critical is this question: can pesticides—poisons, by definition—be used safely in societies where workers have no right to organize, no right to strike, no right to refuse to carry the pesticides into the fields? In the Philippines at least one plantation owner has reportedly sprayed pesticides on workers trying to organize a strike.[13] And in Central America, says entomologist Lou Falcon, who has worked there for many years, "The people who work in the fields are treated like half-humans, slaves really. When an airplane flies over to spray, they can leave if they want to. But they won't be paid their seven cents a day or whatever. They often live in huts in the middle of the field, so their homes, their children, and their food all get contaminated."[14]

Yet the President's Hazardous Substances Export Policy Task Force predicts that the export of banned pesticides is likely to increase as manufacturers unload these products on countries hooked on the agrochemical habit. "Continued new discoveries of carcinogenic and other damaging effects of many substances are probable over the next few years," predicts the task force. "In some cases, certain firms may be left with stocks of materials which can no longer be sold in the United States, and the incentive to recover some of their investment by selling the product abroad may be considerable."[15]

The genetic boomerang

The pesticide explosion also has a second built-in boomerang. Besides the widespread contamination of imported food, the overuse of hazardous pesticides has created a global race of insect pests that are resistant to pesticides. The number of pesticide-resistant insect species doubled in just 12 years—from 182 in 1965 to 364 in 1977, according to the UN Food and Agriculture Organization. So more and more pesticides, including new, more potent ones, are needed every year just to maintain present yields.

Government silence

Few Third World countries have either adequate pesticide regulations or the capacity to enforce them. As a result, the multinational pesticide producers have a free hand. Central America, for instance, has been turned into "a sort of experimental grounds for pesticide manufacturing companies," concludes the detailed study cited earlier.[16] Most Third World governments are reluctant to disclose their poisoning statistics, incomplete as they might be. Robert Chambers, who supervised the GAO's investigation of pesticides, cites three reasons the pesticide poisonings are often hushed up.

"One is tourism," he explains. "It doesn't look good to have press reports about contaminated food. Two, no government wants to admit it was poisoning its own people. Would you admit you were allowing dangerous conditions in your country with President Carter's emphasis on human rights? Three, the countries are worried that if they report poisonings, the FDA will start to check their food exports to the United States and find illegal residues. This could have a severe adverse impact on their export earnings."[17]

Pesticides to feed the hungry?

"We see nothing wrong with helping the hungry world eat," says an executive of the Velsicol Chemical Corporation, defending his company's overseas sales of Phosvel after it was banned in the United States.[18] And many would agree with his logic: since we need pesticides to produce more food for the hungry, pesticide dangers are a necessary evil—part of the price of averting famine. "Men will not starve because there are hazards in killing pests" is the way a Rohm and Haas official makes the same point.[19]

But in the course of our investigation, we came to a startling conclusion: over half, and in some countries up to 70 percent, of the pesticides used in underdeveloped countries are applied to crops destined for export to consumers in Europe, Japan, and the United States. The poor and hungry may labor in the fields, exposed daily to pesticide poisoning, but they do not get to eat many of the crops protected by pesticides.

In Central America, a staggering 70 percent of the total value of agricultural production—mainly coffee, cocoa, and cotton—is exported, despite w despread hunger and malnutrition there.[20] Cotton is one of the biggest pesticide users. In tiny El Salvador, cotton production absorbs one-fifth of all the deadly parathion used in the world.[21] Twenty-four hundred pounds of insecticides are used each year on every square mile of cotton fields in the country.[22] Yet cotton contributes to the global food supply only in processed cattle feed for Latin America's burgeoning beef production, almost half of which is exported to the United States and Europe.[23] The meat remaining for local consumption is eaten by the rich and the middle classes, not by the hungry.

Herbicides like 2,4,5-T and D (the basic ingredients of the infamous Agent Orange) are also used to help clear huge amounts of forest for grazing land in Latin America. The herbicide 2,4,5-T leaves residues of its contaminant, dioxin, in soil and water. Dioxin, one of the deadliest poisons ever developed, shows up later as birth defects, skin rashes, and miscarriages. In Indonesia, estate-style farms growing export crops—coconuts, coffee, sugar cane, and rubber—consume 20 times the quantity of pesticides used by the smallholders growing food for local markets. This, despite the fact that small holders cultivate seven times more acreage than the estates.[24]

Some might argue that although export crops do not directly feed hungry people, at least the foreign exchange earned benefits them indirectly: it is used to import economic necessities for development. But even the most superficial look at development in most Third World countries belies this assumption. Foreign exchange earned by agricultural exports does not return to improve the lives of the workers through better wages, housing, medical care, or schools. Instead, the foreign exchange is most often plowed into luxury consumer goods, urban industrialization, tourist facilities, and showy office buildings—all geared to the budgets and tastes of the top ten or 20 percent living in the cities.

More food and yet more hunger

While it is true that most pesticides in the Third World are used on luxury export crops, in the last 20 years Third World farmers growing basic food crops—especially rice and wheat—have also been encouraged to use ever greater quantities of pesticides. As part of the Green Revolution, hybrid seeds were developed that produce higher yields, given the correct amount of fertilizer and water; but the hybrids are much more susceptible to pests. Bred in the laboratory and in test fields in a foreign setting over only a few years, these "miracle seeds" do not have the pest-resistance characteristic of traditional seeds, bred over thousands of years in the same locality in which they are used.[25] To make up for this vulnerability, the new seeds must be protected with more pesticides.

Throughout much of the Third World, international lending agencies and government development programs have encouraged the use of these new seeds, often making their use a condition for receiving farm credit.[26] Once Third World farmers begin using the new, more vulnerable seeds, they have no choice but to vastly increase their use of pesticides.

Few dispute that the new seeds and their accompanying inputs (fertilizers and pesticides) have increased grain production, notably in Asia. But growing more food doesn't necessarily mean alleviating hunger. What we have learned is that food production can increase while the poor majority becomes even hungrier.

Take the Philippines. It is the home of the prestigious International Rice Research Institute, which helped instigate the Green Revolution in Asia. During the 1970s, use of the new seeds spread throughout the country. Accompanying their proliferation, pesticide imports leapt four-fold between 1972 and 1978.[27] As a result of the new seeds and new inputs, rice production almost doubled in the Philippines in little more than a decade. Indeed, in the late 1970s, the Philippines became a rice exporter. But has this production success reduced the hunger of the Philippine poor? No. According to studies by the Asian Development Bank and the WHO, Filipinos are now the worst fed people in all of Asia, with the exception only of war-torn Kampuchea.[28]

How can there be more food produced and yet greater hunger? The answer is that the Green Revolution strategy for producing more food forces more and more people off the land. Mechanization robs them of work. Dependency on irrigation, pesticides, and fertilizers—all required by the new seeds—favors the wealthier, literate farmers who have access to credit and political pull. Without land to produce food or money to buy it, people go hungry no matter how much their country produces.

This dramatic transformation is documented in the International Labor Organization's (ILO) study of rural poverty. After studying seven Asian countries, comprising 70 percent of the rural population in non-socialist underdeveloped countries, the ILO reported that the rural poor have become measurably poorer than they were ten or 20 years ago. The study concludes: "The increase in poverty has been associated not with a fall but with a rise in cereal production per head, the main component of the diet of the poor."[29]

Another ILO study of the Green Revolution points to vast increases in wheat yields in the Punjab district of India in the 1960s. Yet simultaneously, the portion of the rural population living below the poverty line increased from 18 to 23 percent.[30] Economic prosperity has not simply missed these people, the study concludes. "Their ability to supply their own basic needs has been gradually but unrelentingly reduced."[31]

NOTES

1   US State Department, *Proceedings of the U.S. Strategy Conference on Pesticide Management*, US State Report, 1979, 33..

2   Committee on Government Operations, Commerce, Consumer, and Monetary Affairs Subcommittee, *Report on Export of Products Banned by U.S. Regulatory Agencies*, H.R. Report No. 95-1686, 1978, 28.

3   *Ibid.*

4   US General Accounting Office, *Better Regulation of Pesticide Exports and Pesticide residues in Imported Foods is Essential,*" Report no. CED-79-43 at iii, 1979, 39.

5   Thomas O'Toole, "Over Forty Percent of World's Food is Lost to Pests," *Washington Post*, March 6, 1977.

6   Douglas Starr, "'Pesticide Poisoning Alarming,' Says FAO," *Christian Science Monitor*, February 1, 1978.

7   Ibid.; and Francis Moore Lappé and Joseph Collins, *Food First: Beyond the Myth of Scarcity* (New York: Ballantine Books, 1979), 64.

8   U.S. General Accounting Office, *Better Regulation of Pesticide Exports and Pesticide Residues in Imported Food is Essential,*" 1.

9   Jeanie Ayres, "Pesticide Industry Overview," *Chemical Economics Newsletter*, January-February 1978, 1.

10 Frances Moore Lappé and Joseph Collins, *Food First: Beyond the Myth of Scarcity* (Boston: Houghton-Mifflin, 1977), 41.

11 Instituto Centro-Americano de Investigación y Tecnología Industrial (ICAITI), *An Environmental and Economic Study of the Consequences of Pesticide Use in Central America Cotton Production*, Final Report, 1977, 149, 155, 161.

12 Frances Moore Lappé and Joseph Collins, *Food First: Beyond the Myth of Scarcity, op. cit.*, 67.

13 Osawa Yasuo, "Banana Plantation Workers Strike in the Philipines," *New Asia News*, May 1980, 7.

14 Dr. Lou Falcon, telephone interview with authors, May 21, 1979.

15 UN Food and Agricultural Organization, *Agriculture: Toward 2000* (Rome: U.N. Food and Agricultural Organization, 1979), 82.

16 ICAITI, *An Environmental and Economic Study of the Consequences of Pesticide Use in Central America Cotton Production*, 1976, 29.

17 Robert Chambers, GAO, personal interview with authors, March 17, 1980.

18 Richard Blewitt, vice-president of public relations, telephone interview with Terry Jacobs, Center for Investigative Reporting, July 31, 1979.

19 US State Department, *Proceedings of the U.S. Strategy Conference on Pesticide Management*, 30.

20 ICAITI, *An Environmental and Economic Study of the Consequences of Pesticide Use in Central America Cotton Production, op. cit.*, 26.

21   O'Toole, "Over Forty Percent of the World's Food is Lost to Pests," *op. cit.*

22   *Ibid.*

23   Lappé and Collins, *Food First: Beyond the Myth of Scarcity, op. cit.*, 289.

24   "Basic Supply and Marketing Data for Agro-Pesticides in Indonesia," ARSAP/Pesticides, FAO (Bangkok), January 1980, 15-16.

25   National Academy of Sciences, Committee on Genetic Vulnerability of Major Crops, *Genetic Vulnerability of Major Crops,* report, Washington, DC, 1972.

26   Benton Rhoades, personal interview with authors, March 21, 1980.

27   FAO, "Basic Supply and Marketing Data for Agro-Pesticides in Indonesia," 30.

28   Ho Kwon Ping, "The Mortgaged New Society," *Far Eastern Economic Review,* June 29, 1979, citing Asian Development Bank and World Health Organization reports.

29   Frances Moore Lappé and Joseph Collins, *Food First, Beyond the Myth of Scarcity, op. cit.*, 146.

30   ILO (International Labor Office), "Third World Seen Losing War on Rural Poverty," *Information,* February 1980, 8.

31   *Ibid.*

FARMER SUICIDES IN INDIA'S BREADBASKET

Bryan Newman, 2006[i]

India's tremendous middle-class growth and the much-celebrated boom of its IT sector over-shadow the dark despair of debt-driven farmer suicides in the countryside. Between 1993 and 2003, as many as 100,000 indebted Indian farmers took their own lives.[1] Many of these farmers died consuming the very same pesticides they used on their fields. This shocking message was carried to an audience of several thousands at the January 2007 World Social Forum in Nairobi, Kenya by Dr. Vandana Shiva, Director of the Research Foundation for Science, Technology and Natural Resource Policy, based in New Delhi.

Why are so many of India's farmers committing suicide even as rice and wheat are being stock-piled in national storage facilities?

The cradle of India's Green Revolution is the Punjab state. As India teetered on the brink of famine and rural chaos in the late 1960s, Punjab was singled out as ground zero for the largest agricultural experiment in the country's history. This experiment, designed to radically increase food production for the newly independent nation, came to be known as the "Green Revolution." As the mythic story goes, by the end of this Green Revolution, the state of Punjab had not only filled India's empty granaries, but had achieved a level of modernity and economic prosperity far exceeding its rural counterparts elsewhere in the nation.

In fact, the relative success or failure of the Green Revolution is fiercely debated in Punjab today by peasant tillers, large farmers, activists, economists, estate planners, and environmentalists. These actors see radically different patterns of "progress" and "crisis," "success" and "failure" (and sometimes both at the same time), depending largely on what criteria they include in their analysis of the Green Revolution.

The limitations of the Green Revolution in Punjab

The image of Punjab's proud, strong Sikh people and its rich, fertile plains, irrigated by vigorous Himalayan streams seems completely inconsistent with the dark despair of the state's current agrarian crisis. This discrepancy is all the more shocking in light of Punjab's celebrated place in agricultural history.

Those who speak of the Green Revolution's success look largely to the huge yield increases of rice and wheat that accompanied the introduction of "high-yielding" seeds in Punjab in the 1960s and 70s. Green Revolution critics do not dispute that rice and wheat fields have been increased through its implementation. What they do dispute is the extreme fixation on yields of

i   Adapted from Bryan Newman, "Indian Farmer Suicides: A Lesson for Africa's Farmers," Food First Backgrounder, Vol. 12, No. 4, Winter 2006.

these two crops, to the detriment of a more all-encompassing economic and social analysis of the impact of the Green Revolution.

The argument these critics make is that the Green Revolution's architects were inherently incapable of dealing with issues other than yields of wheat and rice. The planners ignored issues as wide-reaching as land distribution, ecological sustainability, and the long-term economic costs of an input-intensive agriculture. "Alternative" methods of increasing yields were not considered. Thus, as the argument goes, the introduction of Green Revolution technologies into Punjab, while succeeding in its original mission of growing significantly more food for the rest of India, has brought about economic, environmental, and social disasters that were unforeseen or overlooked by the Green Revolution's original architects. Many observers, both beyond Punjab and within, claim the present rash of suicides committed by deeply indebted farmers across the state is the result of two decades of recurring socioeconomic and environmental disaster.

Punjab's agrarian crisis can be roughly divided into three separate, but intimately interconnected, areas: 1) rampant and widespread debt among farmers due to shrinking markets, stagnating state-set support prices, reduced crop yields, and increasing production costs; 2) social inequalities exacerbated by the exclusionary policies of the Green Revolution; and 3) ecological breakdown in both soil and water systems.

Introduction of the Green Revolution into Punjab

The Green Revolution arose out of the Cold War era during a time of agrarian unrest throughout Asia. Well into the 1960s, the US was concerned that a communist revolution could succeed in India as it had in China, for India's massive peasant population was hungry, disillusioned, and angry, much like the peasantry of its neighbor to the north had been before the rise of Mao Zedong. Terrified over the prospect of a "Red India," Washington soon adopted the Green Revolution strategy of increasing food-grain yields as a way of pacifying India's fiery countryside.

The epicenter of this emerging agro-technological Green Revolution was not in the US, but halfway across the world in the Philippines, where scientists at the Ford and Rockefeller Foundation-funded International Rice Research Institute (IRRI) developed a package of new synthetic fertilizers and what they called "high-yielding varieties" of rice and wheat, seeds that increased yields under intensive irrigation with these new fertilizers. Indian activist Dr. Vandana Shiva explains, "It was not that native crop varieties were low yielding inherently. The problem with indigenous seeds was that they could not be used to consume high doses of chemicals. The Green Revolution seeds were designed to overcome the limits placed on chemically intensive agriculture by the indigenous seeds."[2]

The seeds of the Green Revolution had an intensely symbiotic relationship with the new fertilizers. When used together, along with increased irrigation, the results were certainly impressive. Yet to actually achieve these results in rural India, a "selective" approach to development "among farmers and among districts" proposed by a delegation of American agronomists in 1959 was solidified by their successors into the model of "building on the strong," or "building on the best."[3] In this case, the "best" meant that the largest farmers in terms of acreage, in the most well-endowed agricultural regions, would be trained and supported in the Green Revolution package. Punjab, despite being a relatively dry state overall, had a network of irrigation canals and enough larger-scale farmers to be chosen as a test case.

It did not take long for the new technologies to catch on in Punjab. Between 1960 and 1979, total statewide yields in wheat increased by 124 percent, while rice yields shot up by 175 percent.[4] India's grain storage facilities began to fill up with Punjabi grains. In the central Ludhiana district, Punjab's "showcase" zone of Green Revolution successes, farmers using new high-yielding varieties (HYVs) farmers almost immediately saw higher incomes from the new seeds, earning about 1,240 rupees per acre, compared to the roughly 750 rupees per acre they were earning previously with traditional varieties—an increase that stood even after taking into account the much higher input costs of the new varieties.[5]

However, total statewide yield does not reflect the yields of the majority of Punjab's farmers. For those with marginal, small- and medium-sized landholdings, the costly new inputs—fertilizers, pesticides, tubewell irrigation, etc.—priced the Green Revolution far beyond their means. A survey conducted in 1967 revealed that 65 percent of Punjabi farmers owned 15 acres or less, yet their holdings accounted for only 34 percent of the total farmland in the state. The minority large farmers—those holding 20 acres or more—owned the rest. And while the majority of Punjab's farmers worked only ten acres or less, the economics of the Green Revolution were such that only those farmers owning at least 20 acres were in a position to purchase the new inputs.[6]

As the Green Revolution evolved, cotton was incorporated, as were new developments in biotechnology and larger trends in global agribusiness. Nevertheless, top-down, technologically focused development remained. Yield became the primary, even exclusive, method of judging the Green Revolutions success. "Yield" could be increased cleanly and simply, without addressing social or environmental spheres at all. Furthermore, it was precisely because "yield" on its own does not address these spheres that the Green Revolution was unable to see its own dark side.

Today, the question that must be asked is whether or not feeding India is even an issue of increasing yield. India now stores a 38-million-ton food-grain surplus.[7] India stands, along with China, as one of the world's two largest markets for biotechnologies aimed at increasing production. This paradox is perhaps most striking when one looks at the infamous events of 2001. In that year, starvation deaths were reported in more than a dozen Indian states, a tragedy unheard of since the 1960s,[8] and yet this occurred at the same time that the government proposed dumping its mammoth surplus into the sea to make room for the next year's surplus.[9]

Simple arithmetic shows that despite an overwhelming 320 million malnourished or hungry citizens, with a 38-million-ton surplus of grain, India currently has within her grasp the resources to feed all of her billion-plus people. Nevertheless, as the events of 2001 show, a surplus is of little use without the infrastructure and political will to distribute it.

The debt trap and social inequality

The Public Distribution System (PDS) was launched in the early 1960s as a means to prevent the famines that had long decimated India. Yet today the PDS is more than a stopgap against famine; it provides regular food grain assistance to over 80 million families in India, and accounts for one-third of the nation's food-grain trade.[10] Despite its continuing relevance, the Indian government is currently in the process of dismantling the PDS as part of an increasingly liberalized agricultural economy that is reducing tariffs on imports, promoting genetically engineered seeds, and embracing transnational agribusiness.

These structural adjustments exacerbate access to affordable food by the people who need it. And they do not acknowledge that nearly three in every four Indians is a farmer. World Trade Organization (WTO) pressure to accept—free of tariffs—imports of food-grains and edible oils from countries including the US undercuts the price that small and mid-sized marginal Indian farmers receive for their crops. Further, bioengineered seeds require that already debt-ridden farmers purchase even more costly inputs.

With the severely weakened PDS buying less and less subsidized domestic food-grains, the nationalized Food Corporation of India (FCI) has lost its biggest customer. For Punjabi farmers, this has meant that their biggest customer, the FCI, is often no longer interested in buying their crops. Prices are often too low to offset the cost of inputs that went into production; the high production costs that initially priced small and medium farmers out of industrial agriculture are now overwhelming larger ones as well.

These low prices are in many ways the result of the low, Minimum Support Price (MSP) set by the government. Other factors also contribute to the debt crisis. Some argue that Punjab's excess production has led to a glut, which deflates the grain prices paid to farmers. Others argue that falling yields, due to soils damaged by years of chemical fertilizer and pesticide use, have meant that farmers' incomes cannot keep up with input costs.[11] The majority of the available evidence points to smaller Punjabi farmers being proportionally more affected by debt woes than larger ones, which exposes the undeniable connection between social inequality and debt accumulation in rural Punjab.

Given that today's agricultural economy favors large producers, small farmers have almost no ability to secure credit through conventional banks, allowing usury moneylenders to step in. High interest rates, combined with the low annual income of the small farmer, has created a vicious "debt trap." Once caught in this trap, the small farmer must sell or mortgage his land, an "extreme" step taken by about 14 percent of small farmers and by a few entire villages.

Ecological disaster

Traditional and sustainable agricultural knowledge was abandoned with the introduction of the Green Revolution. Instead of intercropping nitrogen-fixing legumes with cereals, synthetic fertilizers and pesticides are applied to monocrops of HYVs of rice and wheat. In addition to high levels of synthetic inputs, these HYVs also required dramatically more water inputs to actually produce greater yields.

Increased yields came at the expense of heavy pesticide use and excessive irrigation, soil infertility, and HYV pest and disease susceptibility. And there are associated health problems and increased financial costs of even further inputs to maintain high yields.

Debt and despair

A cursory glance might make it difficult to see the direct links between the Green Revolution and this epidemic of farmer suicides. Suicide can be viewed as an individual decision made by a single person driven to despair out of a complex web of motivations. Direct connections between that decision and the specific, historical moment are often difficult to make. Yet seen in another light, the issue of farmer suicide is indivisible from each and every one of Punjab's current environmental, economic, and social crises. The particulars of these crises—the "specific ecological moments" of falling water tables or dying soils for example—are then crucial points for understanding the interconnections. The totality of Punjab's agricultural crises can be seen in its true magnitude by linking water shortages, high input costs, crushing debt, and finally farmer suicide.

Farmer suicide in the Punjab region is by no means a completely understood or well-documented phenomenon. However, there is strong reason to believe that farmer suicide is a far wider problem than the Punjab government formally acknowledges. As one of the few outsiders to study this problem at length, Dutch researcher Tom Deiters explains, "considering [that] the official government data on suicides is collected from criminal records, this gives reason to believe that the government figures are grossly underestimated."[12] Deiters notes that suicide goes on the books as a felony in India. This fact has led many to argue that most suicides in the state go unreported simply because doing so would implicate the deceased as a criminal for all time. Therefore little is known about the thoughts and voices of many of Punjab's individual suicide victims. However, the deceased have, with the collective weight of their final acts on earth, issued an audible challenge to the way in which Punjab's agriculture is being industrialized. It is a challenge to the wisdom of the free market. And ultimately, it is a challenge to the very notion of "development" itself.

NOTES

1   Pankaj Mishra, "The Myth of the New India," *The New York Times,* July 6, 2006.

2   Vandana Shiva, *The Violence of the Green Revolution: Third World Agriculture, Ecology and Politics* (Zed Books, 1991), 36.

3   Vandana Shiva, *The Violence of the Green Revolution: Third World Agriculture, Ecology and Politics, op. cit.,* 45.

4   Anya McGuirk and Yair Mundlak, *Incentives and Constraints in the Transformation of Punjab Agriculture* (Research Feport 87, International Food Policy Research Institute; 1991), 19.

5   Francine Frankel, in *Food, Population, Employment: The Impact of the Green Revolution*, ed. Thomas T. Poleman and Donald K. Freebairn (Praeger Publishers, 1973), 129.

6   Francine Frankel, *Food, Population, Employment: The Impact of the Green Revolution, op. cit.,* 130-131.

7   Devinder Sharma, "Farmer's Suicides," *Znet South Asia*, January 24, 2004.

8   Raj Patel and Anders Riel Müeller, "Shining India? Economic liberalization and rural poverty in the 1990's," Food First Policy Brief No. 10, May 2004, 4.

9   Devinder Sharma, "India Shines!!!!!?" *Countercurrents.org*, February 10, 2004.

10   Devinder Sharma, "Farmer's Suicides," *op. cit.*

11   "Punjab Seeks Hike of Rs 100 Per Quintal in MSP of Wheat," New Kerala Online Newspaper, February 8, 2006, http://www.newkerala.com/news2.php?action=fullnews&id=5234.

12   Tom Dieters, email communication with author.

TEN REASONS WHY AGRA WILL NOT SOLVE POVERTY AND HUNGER IN AFRICA

Eric Holt-Giménez, Miguel A. Altieri, and Peter Rosset, 2006[i]

The Rockefeller Foundation and the Bill and Melinda Gates Foundation recently announced a joint $150 million Alliance for a Green Revolution in Africa (AGRA), provoking immediate criticisms that the proposal fails to take into account the failures of the original Green Revolution. The creators of AGRA claim the initiative will bring benefits to the continent's impoverished farmers, who—they assert—until now have been bypassed by the first Green Revolution. A day later, probably in an orchestrated move, Jacques Diouf, Director General of the UN's Food and Agriculture Organization (FAO), called for support for a "second Green Revolution" to feed the world's growing population. UN Secretary General Kofi Annan also weighed in to support the initiative.[1]

The AGRA plan is remarkable given that, according to a World Bank evaluation, the Consultative Group for International Agricultural Research (CGIAR)[2]—which brings together the key Green Revolution research institutions—has invested 40 to 45 percent of its $350 million per year budget in Africa over the last 25 years.[3] If these public funds were not invested in a Green Revolution for Africa, then where were they spent? If they were spent on the Green Revolution, then why does Africa need another one? Either the Green Revolution's institutions don't work, or the Green Revolution itself doesn't work—or both. The Green Revolution did not "bypass" Africa. It failed. Because this new philanthropic effort ignores, misinterprets, and misrepresents the harsh lessons of the first Green Revolution's multiple failures, it will likely worsen the problem. These are ten reasons why.

1. The Green Revolution deepens the divide between rich and poor farmers.

In the 1960s, at the beginning of the first Green Revolution, the Rockefeller and Ford Foundations promoted industrial-style agriculture in the Global South through technology "packages" that included modern varieties (MVs) of seeds, fertilizer, pesticides, and irrigation. The high cost of these purchased inputs deepened the divide between large farmers and smallholders because the latter could not afford the technology. In both Mexico and India, seminal studies revealed that the Green Revolution's expensive packages favored a minority of economically privileged farmers, put the majority smallholders at a disadvantage, and led to the concentration of land and resources.[4]

---

i   Adapted from Eric Holt-Giménez, Miguel A. Altieri, and Peter Rosset, *Ten Reasons Why the Rockefeller and the Bill and Melinda Gates Foundations' Alliance for Another Green Revolution Will Not Solve the Problems of Poverty and Hunger in Sub-Saharan Africa.* Food First Policy Brief, No. 12, October 2006. See original for full notes and references.

A study reviewing every research report published on the Green Revolution over a 30-year period all over the world—more than 300 in all—showed that 80 percent of those with conclusions on equity found that inequality increased.[5] Rural development requires the redistribution of land and resources, a fair and stable market, and sound agroecological management in order to be sustainable. This is especially true for sub-Saharan African countries like Ethiopia, Sudan, Somalia, and Mali, where the area of unused, good quality farmland is many times greater than the area actually farmed. It is also true for Zimbabwe and South Africa, where the majority of farmers have been excluded from access to minimally acceptable farmland. Most farmers in sub-Saharan Africa cultivate a small area of land. These farmers are highly vulnerable to debt and will likely find themselves on the wrong side of the divide when land begins to concentrate following the further introduction of Green Revolution technologies.

2. Over time, Green Revolution technologies degrade tropical agroecosystems and expose vulnerable farmers to increased environmental risk.

While Green Revolution MV seeds out-produced local varieties in good years under optimal conditions, they produced less than local varieties in bad years and over time did not perform well in the marginal environments where the poor live. This is because these so-called high-yielding varieties are actually *high-feeding varieties* that over time mine the fragile tropical and hillside soils—where the majority of the world's poor farmers cultivate their grains—of their natural fertility, requiring higher and higher applications of fertilizer.[6] This eventually degrades those soils, leading to extensive erosion. Given the end of cheap oil and the inevitable explosion of fertilizer costs, what kind of future does the Green Revolution really offer to poor farmers? The Green Revolution's genetically uniform crops also proved more susceptible to pests and diseases. To protect these crops, copious amounts of increasingly less effective and less selective pesticides are injected into the biosphere at considerable environmental and human costs.

Green Revolution packages required heavy irrigation. The Indian government subsidized the digging of some 21 million tubewells that, according to Tushar Shah, head of the International Water Management Institute, bring 200 cubic kilometers of water to the surface every year.[7] Over the last decades, tubewells have pumped many water tables dry, forcing vast areas to return to traditional, dryland farming or give up farming altogether.[8] According to India's hydrologists, nearly a fifth of the subcontinent is withdrawing more water than is being replaced by rain. In the Punjab—home of the Green Revolution—nearly 80 percent of groundwater is now "overexploited or critical."[9] This drawdown may be irreversible. Because most of these grains are exported, the hydrological result of the Green Revolution packages is the sacrifice of India's ancient aquifers to the voracity of the international grain trade, a situation sure to become more critical given predicted climate change.

3. The Green Revolution leads to the loss of agrobiodiversity, the basis for livelihood security and environmental sustainability.

The agricultural systems created by the Green Revolution are shockingly dependent on a small handful of varieties for its major crops. For example, in the US two decades ago, 60 to 70 percent of the total bean acreage was planted with two to three bean varieties, 72 percent of the potato acreage with four varieties, and 53 percent with three cotton varieties. As the industrial model was introduced into the developing world, agricultural diversity has been eroded as monoculture has started to dominate. For example, in Bangladesh, the promotion of Green Revolution rice led to a loss of diversity, including nearly 7,000 traditional rice varieties and many fish species. Similarly, in the Philippines, the introduction of HYV Rice displaced more than 300 traditional rice varieties that had provided farmers with stable yields under low levels of technology and environmental uncertainty.

Researchers have repeatedly warned about the extreme vulnerability associated with this genetic uniformity. Perhaps the most striking example of vulnerability associated with homogenous uniform agriculture was the collapse of Irish potato production in 1845, where the uniform stock of potatoes was highly susceptible to the blight, *Phytopthora infestans*. Banana monoculture plantations in Costa Rica have been repeatedly and seriously jeopardized by diseases such as *Fusarium oxysporum* and yellow sigatoka. In the US, in the early 1970s, high-yielding corn hybrids comprised about 70 percent of all the corn varieties; a 15-percent loss of the entire crop by leaf blight occurred in that decade. Uniform commercial potato production in western industrial nations is currently threatened by late potato blight, the same fungus that caused the potato famine in Ireland. Late blight is jeopardizing the $160 billion potato industry in the US

Kenyan farmer (Photo by Neil Palmer)

and is causing losses of up to 30 percent in Global South potato areas, especially in those where potato diversity has been lost.[10]

The net effect of the Green Revolution package is depletion of natural fertility, increasing pest damage, drying up of aquifers, and reduction of agrobiodiversity. As such, the Green Revolution increases environmental risk and exacerbates the economic vulnerability of poor farmers.

4. Hunger is not primarily due to a lack of food, but rather due to the fact that hungry people are too poor to buy the food that is available.

Nobel laureate Amartya Sen has shown that famine is fundamentally a problem of democracy, poverty, and food distribution. While the architects of AGRA dutifully recite the Green Revolution's often-trumpeted claims to success in raising agricultural yields, there is little understanding of the causes of hunger, or of the Green Revolution's colossal failure to effectively reduce poverty or hunger.

Nearly half of the African continent's 750 million people subsist on less than $1 a day—nearly twice as many as a quarter century ago.[11] They are too poor to buy the food that is available but often poorly distributed, or they lack the land and resources to grow it themselves. AGRA claims that by raising yields, it will help the region's 180 million smallholders feed themselves and the rest of the sub-Saharan poor.[12] But a good food production-population ratio does not necessarily indicate that famine will not occur. Famines have occurred in Asia during periods of high agricultural output and were due to speculative stockpiling, unemployment, and low purchasing power—not food shortages.

While the Indian subcontinent went from being a chronic food importer to a massive grain exporter, this did not keep 200 million Indians from going hungry in 1995 while the country exported $625 million worth of wheat and flour and 5 million metric tons of rice. Even as recently as 2001, starvation deaths were reported in more than a dozen Indian states, despite the fact that India ranks near the top of agricultural exporters in the Global South.[13] India's current 26-million-ton grain surplus could easily feed its 320 million hungry people, but it does not.[14] Why? Because starving villagers are too poor to buy the food produced in their own countryside.

Serious questions are raised when we look at the number of hungry people in the world in 1970 and 1990, spanning the two decades of major Green Revolution advances.[15] At first glance it looks as though great progress was made, with food production up and hunger down. The total food available per person in the world rose by 11 percent over those two decades, while the estimated number of hungry people fell from 942 million to 786 million—a 16 percent drop. This was apparent progress, for which those behind the Green Revolution were understandably happy to take the credit. But these figures merit a closer look. If you eliminate China from the analysis, the number of hungry people in the rest of the world actually increased by more than 11 percent, from 536 to 597 million. In South America, for example, while per capita food supplies rose almost 8 percent, the number of hungry people also went up, by 19 percent. It is essential to be clear on one point: it is not increased population that made for more hungry people—total food available per person actually increased—but rather the failure to address unequal access to food and food-producing resources.

5. Without addressing structural inequities, approaches relying on high-input technologies fail.

The growing hunger in Africa is largely due to the increased impoverishment of the rural people who once grew food, but who have now left farming. Today's African farmers could easily produce far more food than they do, but they don't because they cannot get credit to cover production costs, nor can they find buyers or obtain fair prices to give them a minimal profit margin. Under such circumstances, what difference will a new "technology package" make?

Rural Africa has been devastated by 25 years of corporate globalization's free trade and anti-peasant policies, imposed on the continent's governments by the World Bank, the International Monetary Fund (IMF), the World Trade Organization (WTO), the US, and the EU.[ii] Food crop marketing boards, though flawed, once guaranteed African farmers minimum prices and held food reserves for emergencies, and rural development banks gave farmers credit to produce food. The forced privatization of these boards and banks has left farmers without financing to grow food or buyers for their produce. Free trade agreements have made it easier for private traders—the only buyers and sellers of food who are left—to import subsidized food from the US and the EU than to negotiate with thousands of local farmers. This amounts to "dumping," which drives local farm prices below the costs of production and drives local farmers out of business.[iii] These are the very aspects of agricultural development that are ignored or undermined by the Green Revolution.

6. The private sector alone will not solve the problems of production, marketing, and distribution.

The first Green Revolution was introduced through the massive institutional support systems of the Indian and Mexican development states. Government agricultural ministries provided training, credit, research, extension, marketing, processing, and distribution services to farmers who adopted Green Revolution technology. These heavy state subsidies created a market for private sector entry into the seed, fertilizer, machinery, and trade activities in the Green Revolution. Few of these services are remotely available today.[iv]

---

ii   The World Bank is the largest development assistance provider to Africa in the world. The Bank's private sector lending arm, the International Finance Corporation (IFC), is the largest multilateral source of financing for private sector projects in Africa (http://www.ifc.org/ifcext/about.nsf/Content/Regions). This aid has contributed to the crippling debt burdens facing most African countries today. This debt forces them to focus on export crops—rather than food—to obtain the dollars they need to pay interest on these loans.

iii Not only was the Rockefeller Foundation misguided about the true causes of hunger when they initiated the first Green Revolution, but they assumed that progress and development in traditional agriculture inevitably required the replacement of local crop varieties by improved ones, which in order to perform required agrochemicals. They also assumed that the economic and technological integration of small farming systems into the global system is a positive step that enables increased production, income, and social wellbeing.

iv   Indeed, it made the private sector quite rich.

Today, structural adjustment programs have forced governments in the Global South to slash their basic services and gut their agricultural ministries.[16] There are next to no professional or technical staff for national agricultural research and extension. There are no trucks to carry technicians to the field (and no budget for gasoline, even if there were). Agricultural extension is reserved for large plantations that can pay for private technicians. The Rockefeller Foundation's notion that small rural shopkeepers will somehow provide farmers with the agronomic technical assistance needed to maintain complex integrated soil management programs, crop improvement, or stable marketing environments is ludicrous. At best, the salesman will assist a handful of foreign companies to sell chemicals that are expensive, unnecessary, damaging, and dangerous fertilizers, pesticides, and herbicides, and cheap foreign grains that will further undercut local farmers in their home markets.

7. The introduction of genetic engineering will make smallholder systems more environmentally vulnerable.

AGRA's directors openly admit that their conventional crop-breeding approach will pave the way for genetic engineering (GE) technology. Both the Gates[17] and the Rockefeller Foundations[18] are actively financing projects in genetic engineering (Bill Gates also has substantial private investments in GE).[19] However, GE increases the risks of environmental failure on smallholder farms.

The expansion of transgenic maize and soybean monocultures in Africa will not only narrow the genetic base of agriculture, but will also cause environmental risks. There are many widely accepted environmental risks associated with the rapid deployment and widespread commercialization of GE crops.[20] When transgenic varieties are used in the complex, diverse, and risk-prone cropping systems of peasant farmers, the risks are much greater than in large, wealthy farmer systems, or farming systems in Northern countries. The widespread crop failures reported for transgenics due to stem splitting, boll drop, etc., pose economic risks that can affect poor farmers much more severely than wealthy farmers. Also, the high costs of transgenics introduce an additional anti-poor bias into the system.

The most common transgenic varieties available today are those that tolerate proprietary brands of herbicides and those that contain insecticide genes. Herbicide-tolerant crops make little sense to peasant farmers who plant diverse mixtures of crop and fodder species, as such chemicals would destroy key components of their cropping systems. Transgenic plants that produce their own insecticides, usually using the "Bt" gene, closely follow the pesticide paradigm. This paradigm is rapidly failing due to pest resistance to insecticides. Instead of the failed "one pest-one chemical" model, genetic engineering emphasizes a "one pest-one gene" approach, shown over and over again in laboratory trials to fail, as test species rapidly adapt and develop resistance to the insecticide present in the plant. Bt crops violate the basic and widely accepted principle of "integrated pest management" (IPM), which is that reliance on any single pest management technology tends to trigger shifts in pest species or the evolution of resistance through one or more mechanisms.

In the US, the Environmental Protection Agency has mandated that farmers set aside a certain proportion of their area as a "refuge," where non-Bt varieties are to be planted in order to slow down the rate of evolution by insects of resistance. It is impossible for poor, small farmers in the Global South to set aside precious land for such refuges, meaning that resistance to Bt could occur much more rapidly in these places.

8. The introduction of GE crops into smallholder agriculture will likely lead to farmer indebtedness.

The expansion of GE crops in the Global South is driven by powerful transnational corporations that are desperately attempting to expand their markets in the Global South in the face of growing public rejection of GE foods in the industrialized world. While touted as the latest "silver bullet" in the war against hunger, GE crops will likely impoverish poor farmers by making them dependent on expensive external inputs.

Genetically engineered crops create opportunities for transnational corporations to control and profit from every step of the smallholder production processes. Smallholders will lose their agroecological flexibility in fertilizing, controlling weeds, or managing pests because these production steps will all be contained within the genetic information of the GE seeds distributed to them. Contamination of non-GE crops by GE neighbors is impossible to control on the small plots cultivated by African farmers. The problem with introducing transgenic crops into high-diversity regions is that the spread of characteristics of genetically altered grain to local varieties favored by small farmers could dilute the natural sustainability of these races. Once GE is introduced into a region dominated by smallholders, all farmers will eventually have to adopt or else pay heavy fines to seed companies for "stealing" the genetic material that crosses over into their fields.[v] Under these circumstances, smallholders' dependence on GE will lead to the enrichment of transnational seed, fertilizer, and herbicide companies—not the end of hunger.

---

v "To date, Monsanto has filed 90 lawsuits against American farmers. The lawsuits involve 147 farmers and 39 small businesses or farm companies, and have been directed at farmers residing in half of the states in the US. The odds are clearly stacked against the farmer: Monsanto has an annual budget of $10 million and a staff of 75 devoted *solely* to investigating and prosecuting farmers. The largest recorded judgment made thus far in favor of Monsanto as a result of a farmer lawsuit is $3,052,800.00. Total recorded judgments granted to Monsanto for lawsuits amount to $15,253,602.82. Farmers have paid a mean of $412,259.54 for cases with recorded judgments." (Introduction, "Monsanto vs. JS Farmers," Center for Food Safety, 2004, http://www.centerforfoodsafety.org/Monsantovsusfarmersreport.cfm).

9. AGRA's assertion that "there is no alternative" ignores the many successful agroecological approaches to development that have grown in the wake of the Green Revolution's failures.

There are many successful agroecological options and economic alternatives for sustainable production that have grown up in response to the failures of the Green Revolution.[vi] Across Africa, Latin America, and Asia, farmer-to-farmer movements, farmer-led research teams, and farmer field schools have already discovered how to raise yields, distribute benefits, protect soils, conserve water, and enhance agrobiodiversity on hundreds of thousands of smallholdings in spite of the Green Revolution.[vii] A survey of 45 sustainable agricultural products/initiatives spread across 17 African countries covering some 730,000 households revealed that agroecological approaches substantially improved food production and household food security. In 95 percent of these projects, cereal yields improved by 50 to 100 percent. Total farm food production increased in all projects. The additional positive impacts on natural, social, and human capital are also helping to build the asset space to sustain these improvements in the future.[21] This analysis indicates that sustainable agriculture can deliver large increases in food production in Africa.

There is no question that small farmers in Africa can produce all of their needed food and surpluses for market. The evidence is conclusive: new approaches and technologies spearheaded by farmers around Africa are already making a sufficient contribution to food security at the household, national, and regional levels. A variety of agroecological and participatory approaches in many countries show very positive outcomes even under adverse conditions. With appropriate support, the spread of these approaches to thousands of other farm households can contribute to food sovereignty rather than corporate dependency. This will require substantial policy and institutional changes, as well as strategic philanthropic support from visionaries who will dare to put their millions in the hands of progressive social movements. Sadly, the two Foundations have chosen to ignore them and push their own pro-corporate agenda.

10. AGRA's "alliance" does not allow peasant farmers to be the principal actors in agricultural improvement.

The Rockefeller and Gates Foundations consulted with the world's largest seed and fertilizer companies, with Big Philanthropy, and with multilateral development agencies, but have yet to let peasant farmer organizations give their views on the kind of agricultural development they believe will most benefit them.

---

vi See for example: Miguel A. Altieri, *Agroecology: The Science of Sustainable Agriculture* (Boulder: Westview Press, 1995) and Miguel A. Altieri and Clara I. Nicholls, "Agroecology and the Search for a Truly Sustainable Agriculture," Mexico: United Nations Environment Programme, 2005, http://agroeco.org/doc/agroecology-engl-PNUMA.pdf.

vii See, for example, Eric Holt-Giménez, *Campesino a Campesino: Voices from Latin America's Farmer to Farmer Movement for Sustainable Agriculture* (Oakland, CA: Food First Books, 2006).

Through La Vía Campesina, peasant and small farmer organizations from Africa and around the world are debating and formulating the policy changes needed to truly reverse the policy-driven collapse of peasant agriculture in Africa and other continents. These policies—including a step back from free-trade extremism and market fundamentalism; increased supports for family farmers; improved access to farmland, water, and local seats for the poor; and ecological farming methods—are together called food sovereignty.[22] Their February 2007 World Forum for Food Sovereignty in Mali, which includes African consumer and environmental groups as well, marks a key point in this process.[23] Without such changes, no farming technology—especially chemical and genetic-engineering based—can truly address hunger. In contrast to the Gates/Rockefeller approach, creating such a favorable policy environment for family agriculture will make it possible for the hungry to feed themselves using sustainable, ecologically sound farming methods, create rural employment, *and* produce a surplus, which is critical for the food security of local populations.

The food sovereignty approach is increasingly being taken seriously by other sectors, such as organizations representing consumers, urban poor, indigenous peoples, trade unions, environmentalists, and human rights activists, and by researchers and other experts. If the Gates and Rockefeller Foundations truly want to end hunger and poverty in rural Africa, then they should put their millions in the service of the struggle by peasant and farmer organizations and their allies to truly achieve food sovereignty.

NOTES

1   GRAIN, "Another silver bullet for Africa?" September 22, 2006, http://www.grain.org/articles/?id=19.

2   Consultative Group on International Agricultural Research, http://www.cgiar.org.

3   World Bank, *The CGIAR at 31: An Independent Meta-Evaluation of the Consultative Group on International Agricultural Research*, The World Bank, 2004, 220.

4   Francine Frankel, "Politics of the Green Revolution: Shifting Patterns of Peasant Participation in India and Pakistan" in *Food, Population, Employment: The Impact of the Green Revolution*, ed. Thomas T. Poleman and Donald K. Freebairn (Praeger, 1973); Cynthia Hewitt de Alcántara, *Modernizing Mexican Agriculture* (Geneva: United Nations Research Institute for Social Development, 1976).

5   Donald K. Freebairn, "Did the Green Revolution Concentrate Incomes? A Quantitative Study of Research Reports," *World Development* 23, no. 2 (1995): 265-279.

6   Stephen R. Gliessman, *Agroecology: Ecological Processes in Sustainable Agriculture* (Chelsea, MI: Ann Arbor Press, 1998).

7   Fred Pearce, "Asian farmers sucking the continent dry,' *The New Scientist*, August 28, 2004.

8   Devinder Sharma, "The Green Revolution turns sour," *The New Scientist,* July 8, 2000.

9   Somini Sengupta, "Thirsty Giants: India Digs Deeper, But Wells are Drying Up," *The New York Times,* September 30, 2006.

10 Lori Ann Thrupp, "Linking biodiversity and agriculture: Challenges and opportunities for sustainable food security," World Resources Institute, 1997.

11 "Africa Regional Brief Overview," The World Bank, last modified January 2008, http://web.world-bank.org/WBSITE/EXTERNAL/COUNTRIES/AFRICAEXT/0,,menuPK:258651~pagePK:146732~piP-K:64003010~theSitePK:258644,00.html.

12 Rockefeller Foundation, "Africa's Turn: A New Green Revolution for the 21st Century," 2006.

13 Raj Patel and Anders Riel Muller, "Shining India? Economic liberalization and rural poverty in the 1990s," Food First Policy Brief, May 2004.

14 Devinder Sharma, "The Green Revolution turns sour," *op. cit.*

15 Frances Moore Lappé, Joseph Collins, and Peter Rosset, with Luis Esparza, *World Hunger: Twelve Myths,* 2nd edition (New York and London: Grove Press and Earthscan, 1998).

16 Peter M. Rosset, *Food is Different: Why We Must Get the WTO Out of Agriculture* (London: Zed Books, 2006); Aaron deGrassi and Peter Rosset, "Public Research: which public is that?" *Seedling,* July 2003, 18-22.

17 "Bill & Melinda Gates Foundation," http://www.gatesfoundation.org.

18 "The Rockefeller Foundation: Building greater resilience and more inclusive economies," http://www.rockfound.org.

19 Al Krebs, "Bill and Melinda Gates Do African Agriculture," *Counterpunch,* September 13, 2006, http://www.counterpunch.org/2006/09/13/bill-and-melinda-gates-do-african-agriculture/.

20 Miguel A. Altieri, "Linking ecologists and traditional farmers in the search for sustainable agri-culture," *Frontiers in Ecology and the Environment* 2 (2004): 35-42; Miguel A. Altieri and Clara I. Nicholls, "Agroecology and the Search for a Truly Sustainable Agriculture," PNUMA, 2005; Miguel A. Altieri and Peter Rosset, "Strengthening the case for why biotechnology will not help the devel-oping world: Response to McGloughlin," *AgBioForum* 2 (1999): 226-236; Miguel A. Altieri and Peter Rosset, "Ten reasons why biotechnology will not ensure food security, protect the environment and reduce poverty in the developing world," *AgBioForum* 2 (1999): 155-162; Independent Science Panel on GM, Final Report, June 15, 2003.

21 Jules Pretty, "Can sustainable agriculture feed Africa? New evidence on progress, processes and impacts," *Environment, Development and Sustainability* 1 (2004): 253-274.

22 Vía Campesina et al.,"People's Food Sovereignty Statement," http://www.peoplesfoodsovereignty.org.

23 http://nyeleni.org/

5. AGROECOLOGY: GROWING KNOWLEDGE FROM THE GRASSROOTS

ON THE BENEFITS OF SMALL FARMS

Peter Rosset, 1999[i]

For more than a century, pundits have confidently predicted the demise of the small farm, labeling it as backward, unproductive, and inefficient—an obstacle to be overcome in the pursuit of economic development. But this is wrong. Far from being stuck in the past, small-farm agriculture provides a productive, efficient, and ecological vision for the future.

Small-farm productivity

How many times have we heard that large farms are more *productive* than small farms, and that we need to consolidate landholdings to take advantage of that great productivity and efficiency? The actual data show the opposite—small farms produce far more per acre than large farms.

One reason for the low levels of production on large farms is that they tend to be *monocultures*. The highest yield of a single crop is often obtained by planting it alone on a field. But while that may produce a lot of one crop, it generates nothing else of use to the farmer. In fact, the bare ground between crop rows invites weed infestation. The weeds then make the farmer invest labor in weeding or money in herbicide.

Large farmers tend to plant monocultures because they are the simplest to manage with heavy machinery. Small farmers, especially in the Third World, are much more likely to plant crop mixtures—intercropping—where other crops occupy the empty space between the rows. They usually combine or rotate crops and livestock, with manure serving to replenish soil fertility.

Such integrated farming systems produce far more per unit area than do monocultures. Though the yield per unit area of one crop—corn, for example—may be lower on a small farm than on a large monoculture farm, the total production per unit area, often comprising more than a dozen crops and various animal products, can be far higher.

This holds true whether we are talking about an industrial country like the United States, or any country in the Third World. In the United States, the smallest farms—those of 27 acres or less—have more than ten times greater dollar output per acre than larger farms. While in the US this is largely because smaller farms tend to specialize in high-value crops like vegetables and flowers, it also reflects relatively more attention devoted to the farm, and more diverse farming systems.

Small farms in economic development

More bushels of grain are not the only goal of most farm production; farm resources must also generate wealth for the overall improvement of rural life—including better housing, education,

i   Adapted from Peter Rosset, "On the Benefits of Small Farms," Food First Backgrounder, Vol. 6, No. 4, Winter 1999.

health services, transportation, local business diversification, and more recreational and cultural opportunities.

Here in the United States, the question was asked more than a half-century ago: what does the growth of large-scale, industrial agriculture mean for rural towns and communities? Walter Goldschmidt's classic 1940s study of California's San Joaquin Valley, *As You Sow: Three Studies in the Social Consequences of Agribusiness*, compared areas dominated by large corporate farms with those still characterized by smaller, family farms.

In farming communities dominated by large corporate farms, nearby towns died off. Mechanization meant fewer local people were employed, and absentee ownership meant farm families themselves were no longer to be found. In these corporate-farm towns, the income earned in agriculture was drained off into larger cities to support distant enterprises, while in towns surrounded by family farms, the income circulated among local business establishments, generating jobs and community prosperity. Where family farms predominated, there were more local businesses, paved streets and sidewalks, schools, parks, churches, clubs, and newspapers, as well as better services, higher employment, and more civic participation. Recent studies confirm that Goldschmidt's findings remain true.

If we turn toward the Third World, we find similar local benefits derived from a small farm economy. The Landless Workers Movement (MST) is a grassroots organization in Brazil that helps landless laborers to organize occupations of idle land belonging to wealthy landlords. When the movement began in the mid-1980s, the mostly conservative mayors of rural towns were violently opposed to MST land occupations in surrounding areas. In recent times, their attitude has changed.

A small farmer in Cuba

Most of their towns are very depressed economically, and occupations can give local economies a much-needed boost. Typical occupations consist of 1,000 to 3,000 families, who turn idle land into productive farms. They sell their produce in the marketplaces of the local towns and buy their supplies from local merchants. Not surprisingly, these towns with nearby MST settlements are better off economically than other similar towns, and many mayors now petition the MST to carry out occupations nearby.

Local and regional economic development benefits from a small farm economy, as do the life and prosperity of rural towns. Can we recreate a small-farm economy in places where it has been lost, to improve the well-being of the poor?

Recreating a small-farm economy

Recent history shows that the redistribution of land to landless and land-poor rural families can be a very effective way to improve rural wellbeing. We can examine the outcome of every land reform program carried out in the Third World since World War II, being careful to distinguish between genuine land reforms—when quality land was really distributed to the poor and the power of the rural oligarchy to distort and "capture" policies was broken—and "fake land reforms"—when the poor were relegated to the poorest, most remote soils. In every case of genuine land reform, real, measurable poverty reduction and improvement in human welfare has invariably been the result.

Japan, South Korea, Taiwan, Cuba, and China are all good examples. In contrast, countries with reforms that gave only poor quality land to beneficiaries, or failed to alter the rural power structures that work against the poor, failed to make a major dent in rural poverty. Mexico and the Philippines are typical cases of the latter.

More recently, Ibase, a research center in Brazil, studied the impact on government coffers of legalizing MST-style settlements versus the services used by equal numbers of people migrating to urban areas. When the landless poor occupy land and force the government to legalize their holdings, it implies costs: compensation of the former landowner, legal expenses, credit for the new farmers, and others. Nevertheless, the total cost to the state to maintain the same number of people in an urban shantytown—including the services and infrastructure they use—exceeds in just one month the yearly cost of legalizing land occupations.

Another way of looking at it is in terms of the cost of creating a new job. Estimates of the cost of creating a job in the commercial sector of Brazil range from two to 20 times more than the cost of establishing an unemployed head of household on farmland through agrarian reform. Land reform beneficiaries in Brazil have an annual income equivalent to 3.7 minimum wages, while still landless laborers average only 0.7 of the minimum. Infant mortality among families of beneficiaries has dropped to half of the national average.

This provides a powerful argument that using land reform to create a small-farm economy is not only good for local economic development but is also more effective social policy than allowing business-as-usual to keep driving the poor out of rural areas and into burgeoning cities.

National development and "bubble-up" economics

A relatively equitable, small farmer-based rural economy provides the basis for strong national economic development. The post-war experiences of Japan, South Korea, and Taiwan demonstrate how equitable land distribution fuels economic development. At the end of the war, circumstances including devastation and foreign occupation conspired to create the conditions for "radical" land reforms in each country, breaking the economic stranglehold of the landholding class over rural economies. Combined with trade protection to keep farm prices high and targeted investment in rural areas, small farmers rapidly achieved a high level of purchasing power, which guaranteed domestic markets for fledgling industries.

The post-war economic "miracles" of these three countries were each fueled at the start by these internal markets centered in rural areas, long before the much heralded "export orientation" policies which much later on pushed those industries to compete in the global economy. This was real triumph for "bubble-up" economics, in which redistribution of productive assets to the poorest strata of society created the economic basis for rapid development. It stands in stark contrast to the failure of "trickle-down" economics to achieve much of anything in the same time period in areas of US dominance, such as much of Latin America, and to the Asian financial crisis, which happened after many of the original policies have been discontinued.

Good stewards of natural resources

The benefits of small farms also extend into the ecological sphere. Where large, industrial-style farms impose a scorched-earth mentality on resource management—no trees, no wildlife, endless monocultures—small farmers can be very effective stewards of natural resources and the soil. To begin with, small farmers utilize a broad array of resources and have a vested interest in their sustainability. Their farming systems are diverse, incorporating and preserving significant functional biodiversity within the farm. By preserving biodiversity, open space, and trees, and by reducing land degradation, small farms provide valuable ecosystem services to the larger society.

In the United States, small farmers devote 17 percent of their area to woodland, compared to only 5 percent on large farms, and they keep nearly twice as much of their land in "soil improving uses," including cover crops and green manures. In the Third World, peasant farmers show a tremendous ability to prevent and even reverse land degradation, including soil erosion.

Compared to the ecological wasteland of a modern export plantation, the small farm landscape contains a myriad array of biodiversity. The forest areas from which wild foods on leaf litter are extracted; the woodlot; the farm itself with inter-cropping, agroforestry, and large and small livestock; the fishpond; and the backyard garden all allow for the preservation of hundreds if not thousands of wild and cultivated species. Simultaneously, the commitment of family members to maintaining soil fertility on the family farm means an active interest in long-term sustainability not found on large farms owned by absentee investors.

The small-farm path

To the productive, economic, and environmental benefits of small farm agriculture, we can add the continuance of cultural traditions and of the rural way of life. If we are truly concerned about rural peoples and ecosystems, then we must preserve and promote small, family farm agriculture.

Now is the time to educate the world's policymakers about the genuine value of small farm agriculture.

AGROECOLOGY: A PATH TO REALIZING THE RIGHT TO FOOD

Olivier De Schutter, UN Special Rapporteur on the Right to Food, 2011[i]

Agriculture is at a crossroads. For almost 40 years, neither the private sector nor governments have invested in agricultural research. In recent years, agrofood companies have increased direct and vertical capital investments to lower costs and ensure the long-term viability of supplies. The global food price crisis of 2007–2008 is now pushing governments to act. However, these efforts to combat hunger and malnutrition will fail if they do not improve livelihoods for the poorest—particularly small-scale farmers—in developing countries. Simply pouring money into agriculture will not be sufficient; we need to transition to low-carbon, resource-preserving agriculture. The question is *how*?

Agroecology can help achieve this goal by significantly improving agricultural productivity in poor, food-deficit countries, while preserving ecosystems and improving livelihoods.

A diagnosis

The global food-price crisis has led to calls for increasing production. One estimate is that there is a need for a 70 percent increase in overall agricultural production by 2050.[1] This assumes meat consumption will continue to increase from 82.2 pounds per person per year in 2000 to over 114.4 pounds per person per year by 2050, with 50 percent of total cereal production going to increasing meat production.[2] Feeding cereals to animals instead of people will consume the annual caloric needs of over 3.5 billion people.[3] Agrofuels are also diverting cereal crops for energy.

Today the main cause of hunger is poverty—not a shortage of food. Increasing incomes of the poorest is essential to ending hunger. We need to invest in agriculture, not only to meet growing needs, but also to reduce rural poverty. Because poverty remains so heavily concentrated in rural areas, GDP growth in agriculture is at least twice as effective in reducing poverty as GDP growth in other sectors.[4] Only by supporting small farmers can we help break the vicious cycle that leads from rural poverty to expansion of urban slums.

The loss of biodiversity, unsustainable use of water, and pollution of soils and water all compromise the continuing ability of natural resources to support agriculture. Climate change—with more frequent and extreme weather events such as droughts and floods and less predictable rainfall—is already impairing the ability of certain regions to feed themselves and destabilizing

i   Adapted from Olivier De Schutter, "Agroecology: A Path to Realizing the Right to Food," Food First Backgrounder, Vol. 17, No. 2, Summer 2011.

markets. By 2080, 600 million additional people could be at risk of hunger as a direct result of climate change.[5]

Industrial agriculture contributes to climate change, accounting for at least 13 to 15 percent of global, manmade greenhouse gas (GHG) emissions.[ii] In fact, the intensity of GHG in industrial agriculture increases faster than its productivity. While agricultural emissions of methane and nitrous oxide grew by 17 percent between 1990 and 2005, cereal yields increased by only 6 percent.[7] Industrial agriculture is becoming *more* carbon-intensive. With no change in policy, the GHG emissions from agriculture could rise by 40 percent by 2030.[8]

Agroecology: a solution to the crisis?

Agroecology is now recognized as a way to address these challenges among an increasingly wide range of scientific experts[9] and international agencies such as the UN Food and Agriculture Organization (FAO), Biodiversity International, and the United Nations Environment Programme (UNEP). Agroecology is the "application of ecological science to the study, design, and management of sustainable agroecosystems."[10] It improves agricultural systems by mimicking natural processes, thus enhancing beneficial biological interactions and synergies among the components of agrobiodiversity. Common principles of agroecology include recycling nutrients and energy on-farm rather than relying on external inputs; integrating crops and livestock; diversifying species and genetic resources; and focusing on interactions and productivity across agricultural systems rather than growing large plots of single crops.

Agroecology is highly knowledge-intensive, based on techniques that are not delivered top-down, but rather developed through farmers' knowledge and experimentation. The diversity of species involved in agroecological practices (including animals) requires diversifying farm tasks.

Agroecology techniques have been developed and successfully tested in many regions.[11] Integrated nutrient management limits the need to import inorganic and organic sources of nutrients and reduces nutrient losses by controlling erosion. Agroforestry incorporates multifunctional trees into agricultural systems. For example, in Tanzania, 350,000 hectares of land have been rehabilitated through agroforestry in the western provinces of Shinyanga and Tabora.[12] Similar large-scale projects are underway in other countries, including Malawi, Mozambique, and Zambia.

Water harvesting in drylands restores formerly abandoned and degraded lands to cultivation and improves the water productivity of crops. In West Africa, stone barriers built alongside fields decelerate and stop runoff water during the rainy season, thus improving water retention, replenishing water tables, and reducing soil erosion. Water retention capacity is multiplied five to ten times, the biomass production multiplies by ten to 15 times, and livestock can feed on grass that grows along the stone barriers.[13]

---

ii Editors' note: More recent figures place agriculture's contributions to climate change closer to 50 percent, looking at "food production more broadly to also include emissions from land-use change and deforestation, as well as the processing, packaging, transport and sale of agricultural products." See Rani Molla, "How Much of World's Greenhouse-Gas Emissions Come From Agriculture?" *The Wall Street Journal*, Sept. 29, 2014, http://blogs.wsj.com/numbers/how-much-of-worlds-greenhouse-gas-emissions-come-from-agriculture-1782/.

Integration of livestock, including dairy cattle, pigs, and poultry, into farming systems provides protein for the family while fertilizing soils. Some farmers incorporate fish, shrimp, and other aquatic resources into their farms in irrigated rice fields and fishponds. These approaches introduce agricultural biodiversity—the diversity of crops, livestock, agroforestry, fish, pollinators, insects, soil biota, and other components that occur in and around production systems—to achieve sustainable, diversified, and productive farms.

Agroecology's productivity

Agroecological techniques can significantly improve yields. Jules Pretty et al. compared the impacts of 286 recent sustainable agriculture projects in 57 poor countries covering 37 million hectares (3 percent of the cultivated area in developing countries). They found that agroecology increased productivity on 12.6 million farms, with an average crop increase of 79 percent,[iii] while improving the supply of critical environmental services.[14] Significantly, there was a 116 percent increase for all African projects and a 128 percent increase for the projects in East Africa.[15]

Agroecology's ability to increase incomes for small-scale farmers

One advantage of agroecology is the reliance on locally produced inputs. Many African soils are nutrient-poor and heavily degraded. But supplying nutrients to the soil does not require expensive commercial fertilizers. In fact, applying on-site livestock manure or growing green manures on degraded soils is often better. Farmers can also plant trees that take nitrogen out of the air and "fix" it in their leaves and subsequently incorporate it into the soil. A tree such as *Faidherbia albida*, a nitrogen-fixing acacia species indigenous to Africa and widespread throughout the continent, performs such a function.[16]

The use of nitrogen-fixing trees avoids dependence on synthetic fertilizers, the price of which has been increasingly high and volatile over the past few years, exceeding the price of food commodities even when food prices reached a peak in July 2008. This allows whatever financial assets a household has to be used on other essentials such as education or medicine.

Agroecology diminishes dependence on external inputs, and thus on subsidies and loans, commercial fertilizers, and pesticides. Diversified farming systems produce their own fertilizers plus their own pest control, thus diminishing the need for pesticides.[17] The availability of locally adapted seeds, planting materials, and livestock breeds also has multiple advantages for farmers, while providing a diversity of major crops such as maize, rice, millet, sorghum, potato, and cassava. This is particularly beneficial for small-scale farmers (especially women) who have low or no access to credit, lack capital, or cannot afford commercial fertilizer.

---

iii Note: The 79 percent figure is for the 360 reliable yield comparisons from 198 projects. There was a wide range in results, with 25 percent of projects reporting a 100 percent increase or more.

The contribution of agroecology to rural development

Agroecology contributes to rural development because it is more labor-intensive and most effectively practiced on relatively small plots of land. While governments have generally prioritized labor-saving policies, increasing employment in rural areas of developing countries where underemployment is currently massive and demographic growth remains high may make agroecology advantageous and might decrease rural-to-urban migration.

Agroecological approaches are fully compatible with gradually mechanizing farms. The need to produce equipment for conservation agricultural techniques such as no-till and direct seeding could create jobs in the manufacturing sector. This is particularly true in Africa, which still imports most of its equipment. But increasingly, African countries manufacture simple equipment such as jab planters, animal-drawn planters, and knife rollers.

Small-scale agroecological agriculture can be especially beneficial to other economic sectors if it is broad-based and increases incomes of farming households—not just enriching large landowners who rely on large-scale, heavily mechanized plantations. Increased incomes in rural areas will raise demand for locally traded goods or services, especially if agricultural growth is widely spread across large segments of a very poor population.[18]

Agroecology contributes to improving nutrition

Green Revolution approaches in the past have focused primarily on boosting cereal crops (rice, wheat, and maize) in order to avoid famines. However, these crops are mainly a source of carbohydrates, containing relatively little protein and few of the other nutrients essential for adequate diets. The shift from diversified cropping systems to industrial cereal-based farming contributed to micronutrient malnutrition in many developing countries;[19] of the over 80,000 plant species available to humans, only three (maize, wheat, and rice) supply the bulk of our protein and energy needs.[20] Nutritionists increasingly insist on more diverse agroecosystems to ensure a more diversified, nutrient-rich diet.

The diversity of species on agroecological farms, as well as in urban or suburban agriculture, is an important asset in this regard. Indigenous fruits contribute on average about 42 percent of the natural food basket that rural households rely on in southern Africa.[21] Not only is this an important source of vitamins and other micronutrients, it may also be critical for sustenance during lean seasons. Nutritional diversity is of particular importance to children and women.

Agroecology and climate change

Agroecology supports the health of our ecosystems by providing habitat for wild plants, supporting genetic diversity and pollination, and supplying and regulating water. It also improves resilience to climate change. Climate change means more extreme weather-related events. The use of agroecological techniques can significantly cushion the negative impacts of such events. Following Hurricane Mitch in Central America in 1998, farming plots cropped with simple agroecological methods had on average 40 percent more topsoil, higher field moisture, less erosion, and lower economic losses than similar plots on farms not using agroecology. On average, agroecological plots lost 18 percent less arable land to landslides than conventional plots, had a 49 percent lower incidence of landslides, and had 69 percent less gully erosion.[22]

With more frequent and severe droughts and floods expected, agroecological farming techniques are better equipped to handle them. The agroforestry program developed in Malawi protected farmers from crop failure after droughts, thanks to the improved soil filtration it allowed.[23] On-farm experiments in Ethiopia, India, Brazil, and the Netherlands demonstrated that the physical properties of organic farm soils improved drought resistance in crops.[24] In addition, agroecology's diversity of species and farm activities mitigates risks of extreme weather events, as well as those posed by the invasion of new pests, weeds, and diseases sure to result from global warming.

Agroecology also puts agriculture on a path to sustainability by delinking food production from our reliance on fossil energy (oil and gas). And it contributes to mitigating climate change, both by increasing carbon sinks in soil organic matter and above-ground biomass, and by reducing GHGs through direct and indirect energy use. The Intergovernmental Panel on Climate Change (IPCC) has estimated the global technical mitigation potential for agriculture to be 5.5 to six Gt of CO_2-equivalent per year by 2030.[25] Eighty-nine percent of this can come from carbon sequestration in soils by storing carbon as soil organic matter (humus); nine percent from methane reduction in rice production and livestock/manure management; and two percent from nitrous oxide reduction through better crop land management.[26]

Scaling up agroecology

We urgently need to reorient agricultural development towards systems that use fewer external inputs linked to fossil energies and that use plants, trees, and animals in combination, mimicking nature instead of industrial processes.

Governments have a key role to play. A shift toward sustainable agriculture entails transition costs, since it requires that farmers learn new techniques. A successful transition largely depends on the farmers themselves taking the lead. Governments should encourage learning from farmer to farmer, in farmer field schools, or through farmers' movements such as the *Campesino a Campesino* movement in Central America and Cuba.[27] Farmer field schools have been shown to significantly reduce pesticide use, as chemical inputs are replaced by knowledge. Large-scale studies in Indonesia, Vietnam, and Bangladesh recorded 35 to 92 percent reductions in insecticide use in rice, and 34 to 66 percent reductions in pesticide use in combination with four to 14 percent better yields recorded in cotton production in China, India, and Pakistan after farmers were trained in agroecology.[28]

The participation of food-insecure groups in formulating policies that affect them should become a crucial element of all food security policies, from design to assessment of results and decisions on research priorities. This is key to enforcing the right to food. Agroecology offers the best chance of improving the situation of millions of food-insecure peasants.

NOTES

1   Jennifer A. Burney et al., "Greenhouse gas mitigation by agricultural intensification," *Proceedings of the National Academy of Sciences* 107 (2010): 12052-12057.

2   FAO, "World Agriculture Towards 2030/2050," 2006.

3   UNEP, "The Environmental Food Crisis," 2009, 27, based on figures from FAO, "Livestock's long shadow," 2006.

4   World Bank, *World Development Report 2008: Agriculture for Development,* Washington, DC, 2007: 6.

5   UNDP, *Human Development Report 2007/2008. Fighting Climate Change: Human solidarity in a divided world,* 2007, 90.

6   Alexander Kasterine and David Vanzetti, "The Effectiveness, Efficiency, and Equity of Market-Based and Voluntary Measures to Mitigate Greenhouse Gas Emissions from the Agri-food Sector," (paper presented at the UN Conference on Trade and Development, 2010).

7   Ulrich Hoffman, *Assuring Food Security in Developing Countries under the Challenges of Climate Change: Key Trade and Development Issues of a Profound Transformation of Agriculture,* United Nations Conference on Trade and Development Discussion Paper No. 201, November 2010: 5.

8   Pete Smith et al., "Agriculture," in *Climate Change 2007: Mitigation, Contribution of WG III to the Fourth Assessment Report of the Intergovernmental Panel on Climate Change,* IPCC, 2007.

9   Beverly D. McIntyre et al., eds., *The International Assessment of Agricultural Knowledge, Science and Technology for Development: Summary for Decision-Makers Report of the Global Report* (Washington, DC: Island Press, 2009).

10   Miguel A. Altieri, *Agroecology: The Science of Sustainable Agriculture* (Boulder, Colorado: Westview Press, 2007).

11   Jules Pretty, "Agricultural sustainability: concepts, principles and evidence," *Philosophical Transactions of the Royal Society B* 363 (2008): 447-465.

12   Charlie Pye-Smith, "A Rural Revival in Tanzania: How agroforestry is helping farmers to restore the woodlands in Shinyanga Region," ICRAF Trees for Change no. 7, Nairobi: World Agroforestry Center, 2010: 15.

13   Amadou M. Diop, "Management of Organic Inputs to Increase Food Production in Senegal," in *Agroecological innovations, increasing food production with participatory development,* ed. Norman Uphoff (London: Earthscan, 2001), 252.

14   Jules Pretty et al., "Resource-conserving agriculture increases yields in developing countries," *Environmental Science and Technology* 40 (2006): 1114-1119.

15   UNCTAD and UNEP, *Organic Agriculture and Food Security in Africa, UNEP-UNCTAD Capacity Building Task Force on Trade, Environment and Development (UNCTAD/DITC/TED/2007/15),* United Nations, New York and Geneva, 2008: 16.

16   World Agroforestry Center, "Creating an Evergreen Agriculture in Africa for food security and environmental resilience," Nairobi, 2009, http://www.worldagroforestry.org/downloads/publications/PDFs/B09008.PDF.

17   Miguel Altieri and Clara Nicholls, *Biodiversity and pest management in agroecosystems,* 2nd ed. (Binghamton, NY: CRC Press, 2004).

18   Luc Christiansan, Liorel Demery and Jesper Kuhl, "The (evolving) role of agriculture in poverty reduction—An empirical perspective," *Journal of Development Economics,* forthcoming, 2011.

19   Montague.W. Demment et al., "Providing micronutrients through food based solutions: A key to human and national development," *J. Nutrition* 133 (2003): 3879-3885.

20   Emile A. Frison et al., "Agricultural biodiversity, nutrition and health: making a difference to hunger and nutrition in the developing world," *Food Nutrition Bulletin* 27 (2006): 167-179.

21   Bruce M. Campbell et al., "Local level valuation of Savannah resources: A case study from Zimbabwe," *Economic Botany* 51 (1997): 57-77.

22   Eric Holt-Giménez, "Measuring Farmers' Agroecological Resistance After Hurricane Mitch in Nicaragua: A Case Study in Participatory, Sustainable Land Management Impact Monitoring," *Agriculture, Ecosystems and the Environment* 93, (2002): 87-105.

23   Festus K. Akinnifesi et al., "Fertiliser trees for sustainable food security in the maize based production systems of East and Southern Africa: A review," *Agronomy for Sustainable Developmen* 30 (2010): 615-629.

24   Fetal Eyhord et al., "The viability of cotton-based organic agriculture systems in India," *International Journal of Agricultural Sustainability* 5 (2007): 25-38. ; John Landers, "Tropical Crop-Livestock Systems in Conservation Agriculture: The Brazilian experience," Integrated Crop Management 5, FAO, 2007.

25   IPCC, 2007: section 8.4.3.

26   Ulrich Hoffman, *Assuring Food Security in Developing Countries under the Challenges of Climate Change: Key Trade and Development Issues of a Profound Transformation of Agriculture, op. cit.,* 11.

27   Eric Holt-Giménez, *Campesino a Campesino: Voices from Latin America's Farmer to Farmer Movement for Sustainable Agriculture* (Oakland, CA: Food First Books, 2005); Peter Rosset et al., "The Campesino to Campesino agroecology movement of ANAP in Cuba," *Journal of Peasant Studies* 38 (2011): 1-33.

28   Henk Van den Burg and Janice Jiggins, "Investing in Farmers: The impacts of farmer field schools in relation to integrated pest management," *World Development* 35 (2007): 663-686.

THE CAMPESINO A CAMPESINO MOVEMENT: LINKING SUSTAINABLE AGRICULTURE AND SOCIAL CHANGE

Eric Holt-Giménez, 2006[i]

I think we should not fall in the trap of seeing the development of agroecology by just looking at the physical aspects of the farm or just at the economics. Agroecology is not just a collection of practices. Agroecology is a way of life... We can't have an agroecological change without a campesino movement.

—Nelda Martinez, Nicaragua

For 30 years, the *Campesino a Campesino* Movement (MCAC), now with several hundred thousand farmer-promoters, has helped farming families in the rural villages of Latin America improve their livelihoods and conserve their natural resources. The promoters of MCAC have shown that, given the chance to generate and share agroecological knowledge freely amongst themselves, smallholders are perfectly capable of developing sustainable agriculture, even under highly adverse conditions. The capacity to develop agriculture locally is not only the key to sustainable agricultural development; for campesinos it is a matter of survival. This explains in a very fundamental way why the movement has spread as widely as it has: It works!

However, the MCAC's experience still leaves us with the question: if sustainable agriculture is so great, why aren't all campesinos doing it? What keeps it from scaling up? Why is it still the exception rather than the rule?

The transition to sustainable agriculture ultimately depends on a combination of efforts between farmers and economic and social institutions: markets, banks, government ministries, agricultural research institutions, farmers' organizations, churches, and nongovernmental/nonprofit organizations (NGOs). Each of these institutions—including the market—has its own strengths and weaknesses, and each responds to the political agendas of the actors who are able to use it. Scaling up the successes of any experience in sustainable agriculture, including MCAC, therefore entails not simply farmers teaching other farmers to farm sustainably, but a political project that engages the power of these institutions to permit, facilitate, and support sustainable farming.

---

i   Adapted from Eric Holt-Giménez, "Movimiento Campesino a Campesino: Linking Sustainable Agriculture and Social Change," Food First Backgrounder, Vol. 12, No. 1, Winter/Spring 2006. This Backgrounder is based on the book *Campesino a Campesino: Voices from Latin America's Farmer to Farmer Movement for Sustainable Agriculture* (Oakland, CA: Food First Books, 2006).

Smallholders have relatively little control over the institutions shaping agriculture. If MCAC has provided them any influence at all, it is because the movement's successes expose the glaring failures of conventional agricultural development. Though they may still be just "islands of sustainability," MCAC's farmers have tremendous social and political potential, simply because conventional agriculture has failed to produce anything better—for campesinos, for the environment, or for the food security of the millions of poor rural and urban dwellers in Latin America. However, without structurally enabling institutional changes, a few hundred thousand agroecological smallholders will not tip the balance away from conventional to sustainable agriculture.

Campesino a Campesino's extensive knowledge networks have been highly successful in generating and spreading sustainable agricultural practices on the ground. In effect, MCAC has decentralized the practice of agricultural development. This is both a measure of and an explanation for its successes. If agriculture is to be sustainable, it must not only be based on the ecology of the specific agroecosystem where it is being practiced; it must evolve from the social structures and cultures in which the system itself is embedded. But if sustainable agriculture is to become the norm rather than the exception, then these embedded, agroecological experiences must scale out, geographically; and up, into the institutions that shape agriculture's social, economic, and political terrain; and in, into the culture of agriculture itself. To go to scale, Campesino a Campesino must not only be effective on the ground; it needs cultural, social, and political power to affect the structures and policies that hold back the development of sustainable agriculture.

As evidenced by the appearance of sustainable projects across Latin America, sustainability, equity, social justice, and the conservation of ecological and cultural diversity are now part of the discussion among development institutions. However, they are far from replacing the emphasis on monetary return of national, multilateral, or regional development programs. In this context, sustainable development, whether through state intervention, multilateral projects, or the "invisible hand" of the global market, is still fundamentally focused on sustaining economic growth to pay off foreign debt. In this logic, strategies that address local and national food security, sustainable livelihoods, social and economic justice, and the conservation of ecological and cultural diversity are at best secondary to export production aimed at that payment.

Changing the superstructure of economic development to favor sustainable agriculture implies the political, economic, and social transformation of the societies that produce that superstructure. The transition to sustainable agriculture requires social change. This includes massive education and mobilization of citizens who live in First World countries where economic institutions hold the debt incurred by Third World leaders who were counting on economic growth to pay back loans. Today many Third World countries are bankrupt, and exporting agricultural goods is simply delaying the inevitable default on these usury loans.

Though the MCAC has been highly effective in supporting local projects and developing sustainable practices on the ground, it has had little impact on the policy context for sustainable agriculture. Despite a far-flung network of hundreds of NGOs, the supporting institutions have generally not lobbied, pressured, or otherwise organized around policy issues in a significant way. Lobbying is only effective to the extent that it represents and articulates significant political and social force. In the Latin American countryside, "lobbying" often means mobilizing hundreds or thousands of campesinos in marches, protests, invasions, or occupations. Presently, neither the NGOs nor the advocacy groups promoting sustainable agriculture have the capacity to do this. Some farmer organizations do mobilize around agrarian issues, particularly on access to land. However, once peasants receive land, support for the sustainable use of the land is rarely, if ever, the subject of protest or mobilization.

A focus on the socioeconomic policies limiting sustainable agriculture, and the ability to create social pressure, are necessary conditions for MCAC to become an effective movement for social change. The campesinos in MCAC will need to become as knowledgeable regarding the structural conditions for sustainable agriculture as they are in the practices of sustainable agriculture itself.

MCAC's promoters are very aware of globalization. Their information, however, is patchy, and their understanding of where and how they may resist is unclear and limited. There is every reason to believe that promoters in the Movement could become literate in understanding and teaching farmers to incorporate political-economic information about industry, policy, markets, and finance into their existing networks for sharing agroecological knowledge. With support from NGOs, promoters could develop farmer-to-farmer methods for incorporating structural information into MCAC's body of agroecological knowledge—much as the Landless Workers Movement (MST) attempts to do in Brazil. Structural issues including food sovereignty, agroecological agriculture versus genetically modified crops, farmers' rights versus intellectual property rights, and other themes could be included in MCAC workshops, cross-visits, and regional gatherings.

The missing link between practical sustainable farming techniques and structural knowledge could be bridged by linking advocacy groups and farmers' unions and federations to sustainable agricultural development NGOs. Advocacy groups could provide training and information regarding structural issues, NGOs could help promoters develop appropriate methodologies, and MCAC's farmer-to-farmer networks could take care of spreading structural knowledge. As was the case with agroecological knowledge, it would probably only be a matter of time before these networks began to generate information as well. Experiences in preserving agrobiodiversity in the face of transgenic contamination, resistance to colonization by the soy-beef industry, or the creation of local and regional markets for food sovereignty, could all be easily shared alongside the agricultural innovations that constantly emerge and spread within MCAC.

Just as the expansion of farmers' agroecological knowledge created a demand for services and sustainable agriculture, the expansion of structural knowledge among campesinos will build a demand for agroecological advocacy to pressure for institutional changes.

How this demand is met will depend largely on smallholders and the possibilities for complementary capacities with farmer organizations, NGOs, and advocacy groups, and will likely vary widely from place to place. For example, promoters might pressure farmer organizations for agroecological policy advocacy or for greater representation on the boards of directors in order to ensure that their agroecological demands form an integral part of the organization's political agenda.

Or, they might seek more direct linkages with advocacy groups for direct action. Then again, they might demand more political accountability from the funding institutions and NGOs that bring them agricultural products, pressuring them to take proactive positions on structural reforms for sustainable agriculture. Peasants might pressure agricultural research institutions for greater accountability and transparency as well. After all, the biodiverse crops of smallholders provide the basic genetic material to these institutions to begin with. Smallholders might decide to organize locally in opposing multinational seed companies and research institutions to keep their countries GMO-free. They might demand that governments set up programs to channel and match remittances to finance and market sustainably farmed products.

Integrated transnational advocacy networks

The Campesino a Campesino Movement has used agroecology and horizontal learning networks to link campesino communities across village, municipal, and national boundaries. These networks occur in a larger structural context of national and transnational movements for social justice and environmental sustainability. The MCAC's networks have practice and demographic weight, but no political influence. The advocacy networks can exert significant political influence but lack a social base for lasting change. The divide between sustainability as advocated by activists, and sustainable agriculture as actually practiced on the ground by MCAC, reflects the social and political marginalization of both campesinos and activists. Overcoming the marginalization between alternative politics and the struggles of everyday life in the countryside depends on linking the two. Successful social movements are formed by integrating activism with livelihoods. These integrated movements create the deep, sustained social pressure that produces political will—the key to changing the financial, governmental, and market structures that presently work against sustainability.

THE ORGANIC FARMING MOVEMENT IN CUBA

Fernando Funes, 2002[i]

In recent decades, organic farming has been growing in importance, and today it is recognized as a strong international movement. The main purpose of this movement is the search for an alternative to the conventional "Green Revolution" model of agriculture. Initially, the Green Revolution had great impact on agricultural yields, but soon it revealed its fragility, vulnerability, and riskiness for the environment, human health, and agroecosystems, and led to little socioeconomic security for the poorest farmers. There is now great concern around the world about the environmental problems resulting from the industrial agriculture model, which have included erosion, salinity, and infertility in a large portion of our agricultural soils; the loss of biodiversity; growing deforestation; and socioeconomic problems in rural regions, including mass migration to cities.

In recent decades, especially in the 1990s, the organic movement in Cuba has grown, and great advances have been achieved through its practical application, not only in our agricultural systems, but also in our nation's conception of environmentally based development. The Cuban state has been supportive, through the establishment of specialized institutions, legislation, research, teaching and extension, and through productive practice. According to Patricia Lane, today's Cuban development model has the potential to transform our country into one of the first sustainable societies of the twenty-first century.[1]

Agriculture during the revolutionary period

After the triumph of the Cuban Revolution in 1959, land was distributed to more than 200,000 peasant families through the Agrarian Reform Laws of 1959 and 1963, while 70 percent of the *latifundio* lands (large landholdings) were passed over to state control. At the same time, great efforts were initiated in the areas of education, culture, health, and economic development. Rural towns, highways, and roads were built, along with rural electrification, as health services, schools, universities, and scientific centers were created throughout the country.

The main objectives of the revolutionary agricultural sector were: to meet the food requirements of the population; to generate export earnings; to provide raw materials for industry; and to eradicate poverty and unsanitary conditions in the countryside. In the early days of the revolutionary period, agricultural diversification and a greater emphasis on a nature-friendly type of agriculture were advocated.

However, the notion of agricultural progress soon succumbed to the demands and tendencies of

---

i   Adapted from Fernando Funes, "The Organic Farming Movement in Cuba," in *Sustainable Agriculture and Resistance,* edited by Fernando Funes, Luis Garcia, Martin Bourque, Nilda Perez, and Peter Rosset (Oakland, CA: Food First Books, 2002), 1-26.

the period, with a shift toward conventional agriculture. The blueprint for this shift came from the global strategy of the industrialized countries, including the socialist bloc in Eastern Europe. Although there were marked improvements compared to conditions faced in earlier periods, the modern agricultural model eventually showed signs of economic, ecological, and social problems, such as monocropping, deforestation, erosion, rural-urban migration, and excessive dependence on external inputs (fertilizers, pesticides, animal feed concentrates, farm machinery, and irrigation equipment).

Nevertheless, the powerful social transformations brought by the Revolution prevented thousands of farmers from being driven into poverty by the bankruptcies that normally plague input-squandering conventional agriculture, contrary to the experiences of other underdeveloped or developing countries. In the first three decades of this period, the favorable terms of trade Cuba received from socialist countries, especially the Soviet Union, made such heavy investment in this agricultural model possible.[2]

During this period, small farmers from across the country formed the National Association of Small Farmers (ANAP), and many joined Agricultural Production Cooperatives (CPAs) or Credit and Service Cooperatives (CCS), while maintaining crop diversification and integrated farming practices on their lands. Valuable farming traditions survived as small farmers continued to use animal traction and intuitively practiced agroecological sciences, which kept the management and economics of their farms on a sustainable basis, using very few or no external inputs.

Sustainable agriculture in Cuba

Recent changes in Cuban agriculture

In the 1970s, the Cuban government became aware of some of the problems of the dominant agricultural model—and began to introduce changes that would lead to an agricultural system that used fewer inputs and was more rational and in keeping with the current situation. Policies were initiated to substitute for imported inputs and raw materials, and to stimulate financial and material savings in all sectors, and a new emphasis was placed on profitability and self-sufficiency.

In addition, research centers changed their objectives and strategies to focus on programs with a more rational and sustainable basis. In this period, the world energy crisis and the rising prices of imported fuels, fertilizers, feed concentrates, pesticides, and other manufactured products had a negative impact on Cuba's agricultural economy. The 1980s saw growing research, development, and extension of methods to substitute for imported inputs.[3]

The solid research system that was founded in the 1960s was strengthened in the Ministry of Agriculture (MINAG), with 17 research centers and 38 experimental stations (795 researchers and 168 PhDs in different fields); in the Ministry of Higher Education (MES), with its network of research centers and universities; in the Ministry of Education (MINED); and in the other institutions that carry out agroecological research today.

The "special period" in Cuba

In 1989, an acute crisis began suddenly with the collapse of the European socialist countries and the disintegration of the Soviet Union. We must keep in mind that in any event Cuba is not blessed with abundant capital nor with sufficient domestic energy supplies. Prior to 1989, more than 85 percent of our trade was with socialist countries in Europe, and a little more than 10 percent with capitalist countries. Cuba imported two-thirds of its foodstuffs, almost all of its fuel, and 50 percent of its machinery and spare parts from socialist countries. With the crisis, Cuba's purchasing capacity was reduced to 40 percent, fuel importation to a third, fertilizers to 25 percent, pesticides to 40 percent, and animal feed concentrates to 30 percent. All agricultural activities were seriously affected. Suddenly, $8 billion a year disappeared from Cuban trade.

Between 1989 and 1993, the Cuban GNP fell from $19.3 to $10 billion. Imports were reduced by 75 percent, including most foodstuffs, spare parts, agrochemicals, and industrial equipment. Many industries were forced to close, and public transportation and electric plants worked at minimum capacity.[4] Unexpectedly, a "modern" and industrialized agricultural system had to face the challenge to increase food production while maintaining production for export, all with a more than 50 percent drop in the availability of inputs.

To face the crisis, the Cuban government put economic austerity measures and emergency changes into practice, such as: a new domestic economic policy, an opening to foreign investment, the liberalization of the rules governing the possession of dollars by Cuban citizens, and the granting of licenses for private work in various sectors. Together with structural reorganization, new agricultural techniques developed in recent decades received their first extensive implementation, as a variety of measures were introduced, including:

- Decentralization of the state farm sector through new organizational forms and production structures

- Land distribution to encourage production of different crops in various regions of the country

- Reduction of specialization in agricultural production

- Production of biological pest controls and biofertilizers

- Renewed use of animal traction

- Promotion of urban, family, and community gardening movements

- Opening of farmers' markets under "supply and demand" conditions

The objective of agrarian policy during this "special period" was to move to a low-external-input form of agriculture, while at the same time boosting production. This required a greater level of organization of Cuban research and agricultural extension structures, a better flow of information, and a reduced emphasis on technologies requiring a lot of capital and/or energy.

Simultaneously, the United States tightened the economic blockade of Cuba. In 1992, the Torricelli bill was approved, barring shipments to Cuba of food and medical supplies by overseas subsidiaries of US companies, and later the Helms-Burton Act (1996) restricted foreign investment in Cuba. These laws have been strengthened by a variety of amendments, multiplying the effects of the blockade, which took on increasingly cruel and extreme characteristics.

In spite of everything, Cuba has managed to maintain high scores on most social indicators. The literacy rate in Cuba is still above 95 percent; education is free and compulsory until age 16; the average level of schooling is the ninth grade; and of 11 million inhabitants, more than half a million are university graduates. Infant mortality is 6.4/1,000 live births. There are approximately 60 doctors for every 10,000 inhabitants, and average life expectancy is still above 75 years. For every 100 economically active Cubans, 96 have jobs.[5] Women make up 43 percent of the workforce, employed principally in education, health care, and in the scientific and technical sectors. While Cuba accounts for only 2 percent of the Latin American population, it has 12 percent of its scientific workers.[6]

Many sectors of agricultural production have been recovering in recent years, especially roots and tubers and fresh vegetables (which reached historic production levels in 1999), and national forest cover, which currently surpasses 21 percent of the national land area.[7] Urban agriculture has made an important contribution to food security. Significant progress has been achieved with programs for small-scale rice and medicinal plant production, the use of animal traction has been rediscovered, farmers' markets are growing rapidly, and MINAG and other state entities have opened other 'fixed price ceiling" marketplaces which offer affordable food prices.

The organic farming movement in Cuba

The extraordinary work of the movement's precursors mentioned earlier—and subsequent generations that together with thousands of peasants and farmers imparted their knowledge, ideas, and experiences—have forged today's Cuban organic farming movement and its basic principles. In the 1970s and 1980s, many Cuban scientists and farmers started searching for alternatives to high-input agriculture. Several research centers adopted this line of work, and a consciousness was gradually created that Cuba could reduce the use of imported inputs, making agricultural systems more sustainable from economic and environmental viewpoints.

In light of the historical background and the recent transformations initiated by the Cuban state, in 1992 a group of professors and researchers, mainly from the Ministry of Higher Education, aware of the need to promote alternatives to conventional agriculture, joined together at the Agrarian University of Havana (UNAH—at that time called the Advanced Institute of Agricultural Sciences of Havana, or ISCAH) to discuss agroecological ideas. They organized the First National Conference on Organic Agriculture, held in May 1993 at the National Institute of Agricultural Sciences (INCA), with the participation of more than 100 Cuban delegates and 40 from abroad, and founded the Formative Group of the Cuban Organic Farming Association (ACAO). Its principle objectives were to:

- develop a national consciousness of the need for an agricultural system in harmony with both humans and nature, while producing sufficient, affordable, and healthy food in an economically viable manner;

- develop local agroecological projects, and promote the education and training of the people involved in this new paradigm of rural development;

- stimulate agroecological research and teaching, and the recovery of the principles on which traditional production systems have been based;

- coordinate technical assistance to farmers and promote the establishment of organic and natural agricultural production systems;

- encourage the exchange of experiences with foreign organizations (with emphasis on the Latin American tropics and subtropics), and with specialists in sustainable agriculture and rural development; and

- promote and publicize the importance of marketing organic products.

In December 1999, ACAO was awarded the Right Livelihood Award, also known as the "Alternative Nobel Prize," in a solemn session of the Swedish Parliament, for its work disseminating and promoting organic agriculture. This came in recognition of all of ACAO's work in organic farming, though it is also a testimony to the thousands of Cuban men and women who are developing and implementing organic practices day by day, as another way of resisting the tightening of the economic blockade that our country has suffered for more than 40 years.

The present and future challenge

Organic farming and agroecology do not just represent a change of technological models, but of the very way in which we conceive of agriculture. This process automatically means a change in social consciousness, in tune with local reality.

Organic agriculture and agroecology make sense in the Cuban socioeconomic context, since as a rule this type of agriculture maintains a revolutionary worldview. Its principles run counter to the vicious globalization promoted by neoliberalism, and are more in favor of a socially just and solidarious, more human globalization, without dependency on transnational corporations and in favor of self-sufficiency. Agroecology does not harm the environment, reduces the role of middlemen and intermediaries, develops the consciousness of farmers, and applies knowledge rather than crude technological recipes. It is an ally of nature and considers the farmer as a cultural and not just productive unit.

From a social viewpoint, Cuba is ideally situated to demonstrate the full possibilities of organic farming and to achieve truly sustainable agricultural systems.[8] The favorable conditions present in Cuba include:

- A strong demand for agricultural products

- Plenty of qualified personnel linked to agricultural activities

- A population experienced in community work

- Administrative and social structures that support food self-sufficiency

- Official mass media willing to sponsor publicity campaigns for the peoples' benefit

- Research results that are compatible with the new model

- The return of many people to the countryside in recent years

- Organizations dedicated to the creation of an agroecological culture

Organic farming is generally attained through a gradual conversion process, rather than through drastic changes and a sudden rupture with previous productive systems throughout a country, as occurred in Cuba due to the economic crisis. Yet due to these circumstances, Cuba has the conditions to continue perfecting agroecological production with fewer inputs, attuned to the specific conditions of each region, crop, productive purpose, and technological and economic conditions.

Research and development programs must continue to demonstrate the vast potential of organic farming and agroecology, develop ever more effective methodologies for extension, increase the number of publications, improve and support training, and search for ways to increase foreign collaboration. Finally, we must not lose the commitment and dynamic of work among people who are conscious of the importance of this paradigmatic shift in agriculture, especially with the threat that the new paradigm will face when imported chemical inputs become widely available again, given that there still are many farmers who use organic methods out of necessity rather than conviction.

NOTES

1   Patricia Lane, *El modelo cubano de desarrollo sostenible,* Seminario Internacional Medio Ambiente y
     Sociedad, Havana, 1997.

2   Fernando Funes and M. Monzote, "Perspectivas de la Agricultura Organica en Cuba," (paper
     presented at Consejo Tecnico Asesor del MINAG, 1999).

3   Fernando Funes, "Experiencias Cubanas en agroecologia," *Agricultura Organica* 3 (1997).

4   E. Espinosa, "La economía Cubana en los 1990s: De la crisis a la recuperación," *Carta Cuba,*
     Facultad Latino Americana de Ciencias Sociales, (Havana: MINAG, 1997).

5   I. Francisco, "Trabajan 96.2 de cada cien cubanos laboralmente activos, *Granma, 36:253:3,* 2000.

6   Wayne Ellwood, "Cuba: The facts," *The New Internationalists* 301 (1998): 24-25.

7   O. Pelaez, "Trabajan por acelerar programas de reforestación, *Granma* 36 (2000): 258.

8   M. Monzote and Fernando Funes, *Agricultura y Educación Ambiental,* Primera Convención
     Internacional sobre Medio Ambiente y Desarrollo, Memorias Congreso de Educación Ambiental para
     el Desarrollo Sostenible, Havana, 1997.

6. FOOD SOVEREIGNTY: POWER OF THE PEASANTS

THE ORIGINS AND POTENTIAL OF FOOD SOVEREIGNTY

Hannah Wittman, Annette Desmarais, and Nettie Wiebe, 2010[i]

The global food crisis of 2007–08, marked by skyrocketing food prices, urban food riots, and the continued displacement of the rural poor, was a clear indication that the dominant model of agricultural development has not succeeded in eradicating poverty or world hunger. In desperation, in Haiti, Bangladesh, Egypt, West and Central Africa, and countless other locations, hundreds of thousands of people took to the streets demanding affordable food. Behind these highly visible events lurks the very real and ongoing human suffering caused by the lack of that key necessity for all human life—food.

The stunted growth and high mortality rates of hungry children and the ill health and lost potential of malnourished adults are clear and tragic results of the chronic food shortages suffered by an increasing number of people. A growing number of households and communities fear for tomorrow's meals, even though there may be enough food for today. And even for those of us whose cupboards are well stocked and who have adequate incomes to pay our grocery bills, there are grounds for unease about the content, safety, and origins of our food and the long-term sustainability of our food system. Hence, the security, cost, safety, and nutrition of food and the future of food production itself are everyone's concern.

What are the possible solutions to this crisis?

Some proponents of neoliberal globalization would have us believe that the crisis is the result of shortages and market failures. They assure us that the best way to keep up with the growing population is to prevent national governments from intervening in the market, focus on scientific high-tech approaches, increase production with the adoption of genetically modified seeds (GMOs), and further liberalize agriculture and food. But despite having powerful advocates and enforcers, such as the World Bank, the International Monetary Fund (IMF), and the World Trade Organization (WTO) on their side, these solutions reveal a spectacular failure when it comes to reducing poverty and eradicating hunger.

As an alternative to the neoliberal model, peasants, small-scale farmers, farmworkers, and indigenous communities organized in the transnational agrarian movement La Vía Campesina argue that the current—and linked—food, economic, and environmental crises are in fact the direct result of decades of destructive economic policies based on the globalization of a neoliberal, industrial, capital-intensive, and corporate-led model of agriculture.[1] La Vía Campesina,

---

i   Adapted from Hannah Wittman, Annette Desmarais, and Nettie Wiebe, "The Origins and Potential of Food Sovereignty," in *Food Sovereignty: Reconnecting Food, Nature and Community* (Blackpoint: Fernwood and Oakland: Food First Books, 2010), 1–12.

formed in 1993 and now representing 148 organizations from 69 countries, has become one of the strongest voices of radical opposition to the globalization of an industrial and neoliberal model of agriculture, claiming that "the time for food sovereignty has come."

Initiating the food sovereignty concept

Food sovereignty as a concept evolved from the experience of, and critical analysis by, farming peoples, those most immediately affected by changes in national and international agricultural policy introduced throughout the 1980s and early 1990s. The results of the inclusion of agriculture in the General Agreement on Tariffs and Trade (GATT) negotiations, articulated in the WTO, brought into sharp relief communities' widespread loss of control over food markets, environments, land, and rural cultures. The term "food sovereignty" was coined to recognize the political and economic power dimension inherent in the food and agriculture debate and to take a proactive stance by naming it.

Food sovereignty—broadly defined as the right of nations and peoples to control their own food systems, including their own markets, production modes, food cultures, and environments—has emerged as a critical alternative to the dominant neoliberal model for agriculture and trade.

La Vía Campesina first discussed food sovereignty at its Second International Conference, held on April 18–21, 1996, in Tlaxcala, Mexico.[2] Peasant and farm leaders who gathered there no longer saw potential in the concept of "food security" to ensure local access to culturally appropriate and nutritious food. In common usage, food security describes "a situation that exists when all people, at all times, have physical, social, and economic access to sufficient, safe, and nutritious food that meets their dietary needs and food preferences for an active and healthy life."[3] This definition invites an interpretation towards food-related policies that emphasizes

La Vía Campesina march in Dakar, 2011 (Photo by Tanya Kerssen)

maximizing food production and enhancing food access opportunities, without particular attention to how, where, and by whom food is produced. This common definition is also uncritical of current patterns of food consumption and distribution.

Governments and agribusiness corporations have pursued food security by promoting increased agricultural trade liberalization and the concentration of food production in the hands of fewer, and larger, agribusiness corporations. Excess production is offloaded through "dumping," an international trade strategy that places food in targeted export markets at prices below the cost of production. This practice has had devastating effects on domestic agricultural systems, which cannot compete with the influx of subsidized commodities saturating local markets. International aid agencies that subscribe to the view that food insecurity is primarily the result of a lack of supply have also opted for variations of this "just produce and/or import more food from somewhere" strategy.

These contemporary policies aimed at food security offer no real possibility for changing the existing, inequitable, social, political, and economic structures and policies that peasant movements believe are the very causes of the social and environmental destruction in the countryside in both the North and the South. To counter these structures and policies, La Vía Campesina proposed a radical alternative, one "directly linked to democracy and justice," that puts the control of productive resources (land, water, seeds, and natural resources) in the hands of those who produce food.[4] The conference in Tlaxcala defined 11 principles of food sovereignty, all of which were then integrated into La Vía Campesina's Position on Food Sovereignty, presented at the World Food Summit in Rome in November 1996.[5] Subsequently, La Vía Campesina worked with other organizations and civil society actors to further elaborate the food sovereignty framework.

The scope of food sovereignty

The theory and practice of food sovereignty has the potential to foster dramatic and widespread change in agricultural, political, and social systems related to food by posing a radical challenge to the agroindustry model of food production. The transformation envisioned entails a changing relationship to food resulting from an integrated, democratized, localized food production model. It also entails a fundamental shift in values expressed in changed social and political relations. At an international workshop on food sovereignty, Jim Handy, a professor of history at the University of Saskatchewan, summarized the revolutionary implications of the seemingly simple idea of democratizing the food system:

> I would like to express my sense of awe at the enormity of the change that is envisioned through the concept of food sovereignty. Food sovereignty challenges not just a particular development model, doesn't just challenge a particularly abhorrent form of neoliberalism, doesn't just suggest a new set of rights. Rather, it envisions fundamental changes in the basis of modern society. Modern society was based on a set of exclusions and enclosures that were fundamental to the emergence and strengthening of capitalism. Those exclusions were felt primarily in the countryside and primarily in agriculture. Capitalism was dedicated to divorcing producers from any right over the goods they produce and encasing those goods in ever larger, ever

more disconnected, ever more monopolized, and ever more destructive markets. Food sovereignty challenges all of that because it demands that we rethink what was at the very center of this transition; it demands that we treat food not simply as a good, access to which and the production of which is determined by the market, it demands that we recognize the social connections inherent in producing food, consuming food, and sharing food. In the process it will change everything.[6]

Certainly, ideas about food sovereignty force us to rethink our relationships with food, agriculture, and the environment. But perhaps the most revolutionary aspect of food sovereignty is that it forces us to rethink our relationships with one another. The magnitude of this transformation hit home in a powerful way when, during its Fifth International Conference, La Vía Campesina launched a campaign with the slogan, "Food sovereignty means stopping violence against women."[ii] Because women play a key role in food production and procurement, food preparation, family food security, and food culture, the social and political transformation embedded in the food sovereignty concept specifically entails charged gender relations. Food sovereignty for communities and peoples cannot be achieved without ensuring equality, respect, and freedom from violence for women. As the Maputo Declaration stated: "If we do not eradicate violence towards women within our movement, we will not advance in our struggles, and if we do not create new gender relations, we will not be able to build a new society."[7]

The theoretical context of the food sovereignty struggle is framed by the changing relationship to food imposed by the industrialization of production and the globalization of agricultural trade. The globalized food system distances eaters from the people who produce food and from the places where food is produced—literally and conceptually. The more industrialized, processed, and distant food is, the less connected to and knowledgeable about it the consumer becomes. This paucity of knowledge changes our relationships to our meals, stripping meaning, cultural significance, and even appreciation from our daily food experiences. But it also undermines our capacity to make decisions about this key determinant of our lives and our economies. Hence the inextricable connection between food, culture, and democracy.

Broadening the struggle for food sovereignty

Food sovereignty has gained significant momentum as numerous local, national, and international social movements and NGOs have embraced it in efforts to shift agriculture and food policy.[8] Some of these initiatives involve recognizing the specific implications of food sovereignty for specific local and regional populations, as in the case of the European Platform for Food Sovereignty, Task Force Food Sovereignty in the Philippines, the People's Coalition on Food Sovereignty, and the People's Caravan for Food Sovereignty, which involves a coalition of Asian agricultural and peasant movements. For instance, the movement for indigenous food sovereignty in Western Canada, involving the rights of traditional populations to "hunt, gather, fish, grow, and eat"[9] must grapple with the competing demands of local agricultural populations to expand their own productive capacity. Similarly, urban food sovereignty networks seek ways

---

ii   From its inception women within La Vía Campesina have engaged in an ongoing struggle for gender equality, and have taken some exemplary steps to establish gender parity. The dynamics of this are discussed in depth in Annette Aurelie Desmarais, *La Vía Campesina: Globalization and the Power of Peasants* (London: Pluto Press, 2007).

to protect and to link local food systems to urban consumers, who increasingly recognize and demand access to local food.

The food sovereignty movement also seeks to influence policy change at an international level through global coalition building. The People's Food Sovereignty Network, mentioned earlier, is a powerful example of this. The International Planning Committee for Food Sovereignty (IPC)—a global network bringing together representatives of indigenous peoples, fisherfolk, farmers/ peasants, youth, women, and NGOs from many regions of the world—plays the key role of global coordination and communication. The IPC emerged in 2000 as a coalition of 52 civil society organizations (CSOs), including La Vía Campesina, to plan a collective approach to the 2002 World Food Summit: Five Years Later. It works to develop common positions within the network, which are then presented to international institutions and key meetings.

The IPC also helps to organize regional and international gatherings around food sovereignty, including an especially important event, the Nyéléni International Forum on Food Sovereignty, held in February 2007 in Nyéléni, Mali. Just over a decade after introducing food sovereignty in the international arena, La Vía Campesina worked as a member of the Nyéléni Forum steering committee, which included the Network of Farmers' and Producers' Organizations of West Africa, World Women's March, World Forum of Fish Harvesters and Fisherworkers, World Form of Fisher Peoples, Friends of the Earth International, and others involved in the IPC, to organize a global forum to deepen understandings of food sovereignty, enhance common actions and solidarity, and develop strategies for implementing food sovereignty at local and global levels. The event brought together 500 representatives of social movements, peasant movements, pastoralists, indigenous peoples, fishers, migrant workers, and NGOs from 80 countries based in the Global North and South, who vowed to continue to work together to build alliances at all levels and in so doing strengthen the global movement for food sovereignty.[10]

By most accounts, the Nyéléni Forum was highly successful. First, it effectively moved food sovereignty beyond the producers' perspective and production, to include consumers' associations and consumption, something that La Vía Campesina was anxious to do. Second, the forum reached consensus on a vision of food sovereignty that sees food as being integral to local cultures, closes the gap between production and consumption, is based on local knowledge, and seeks to democratize the food system. Third, the gathering provided a space where national and international coalitions were solidified. Finally, after Nyéléni, there was no doubt that we were now talking about a global food sovereignty movement that clearly understood the challenges ahead. As the Nyéléni documents stated,

> Food sovereignty is more than a right; in order to be able to apply policies that allow autonomy in food production it is necessary to have political conditions that exercise autonomy in all the territorial spaces: countries, regions, cities and rural communities. Food sovereignty is only possible if it takes place at the same time as political sovereignty of peoples.[11]

The discourse of food sovereignty has thus entered the official international stage. In addition to the FAO's support for the IPC, reports submitted by the former Special Rapporteur on the Right to Food to the United Nations Commission on Human Rights (now replaced by the Council on Human Rights) advocate food sovereignty as the path to ensure peoples' human rights to food and food security.[12] And, although he did not use the language of food sovereignty, the statement by Olivier De Schutter, the current Special Rapporteur on the Right to Food, stressed the need to consider alternative sustainable models of agricultural development to ensure the full realization of the right to food.[13] Key aspects of a sustainable model, he argued, are access to and secure tenure on land for the most vulnerable, regulation of transnational corporations, and reorientation of national and international policies—all of which are components of food sovereignty.

All of this local, national, and international grassroots activity and pressure for policy change has prompted a variety of responses from different levels of government and international bodies, some more proactive than others. In recognizing the need for policies that support social, economic, and environmental sustainability, numerous local mayors in several European nations have signed petitions endorsing a key element of food sovereignty: local production for local consumption. The Green Party in some European countries has held meetings on the subject to examine how it might help redefine European agricultural policy.

Several national governments have also integrated food sovereignty into their national constitutions and laws. For example, between 1999 and 2009, food sovereignty was included in national legislation promulgated by the governments of Venezuela, Mali, Bolivia, Ecuador, Nepal, and Senegal. Certainly, there is the question of the extent to which these countries will succeed in further articulating laws and creating the necessary structures and mechanisms to implement the kind of genuine food sovereignty that will transform existing agriculture and food systems. For our purposes, it is important to recognize that as a result of the strong mobilization and engagement of peasant organizations, NGOs, and urban-based movements, as well as the election of progressive political parties to power, these countries are in the process of creating—and in some cases already have opened—political spaces for debates within their borders about alternatives.[14]

Of course, social movements face some very real obstacles in their attempts to implement food sovereignty, as is clearly the case in Ecuador. With the constitution in hand, Ecuador's National Assembly began work on developing legislation to implement food sovereignty. After public consultations on February 17, 2009, the National Assembly passed its progressive Organic Law on the Food Sovereignty Regime. However, in March 2009, President Correa delivered a partial veto of the new law, citing concerns about the ban on GMOs, consequences of changes in land ownership structures, and issues related to the production of agrofuels.[iii] Newspapers reported that some social movements and government officials believe that the president acted under pressure from agribusiness.[15] In a telling gesture, during the same month, the Government of Ecuador withdrew its support for Acción Ecológica (Environmental Action), a major environmental organization that had been working on food sovereignty.[16]

Moreover, although the new constitution contains groundbreaking articles supporting environ-

iii Even before delivering his partial veto, President Correa had introduced a new agricultural law that initially was designed largely to benefit agribusiness interests (Denvir 2008, cited in S. Beauregard, "Food Policy for People: Incorporating Food Sovereignty Principles into State Governance." Senior Comprehensive Report, Urban and Environmental Policy Institute, Occidental College, Los Angeles, April 2009, departments.oxy.edu/uepi/uep/index.htm.)

mental sustainability, in January 2009, the National Assembly passed a new Mining Law to spur extraction in new areas by national and international companies. Many of Ecuador's social movements argue that this law undermines many of the constitution's guarantees, such as the rights to clean and safe water and a healthy environment—both important elements of food sovereignty. As Dosh and Klingerman state, the new law jeopardizes those aspects of the constitution's articles that "ascribed to the environment itself the rights to be respected, sustainably maintained, and regenerated."[17] Without a doubt, we need to observe and analyze carefully what happens in Ecuador, as those experiences hold important lessons for food sovereignty movements and national governments elsewhere.

Conclusion

The idea of food sovereignty was initially introduced by La Vía Campesina to express both the truth of power relations within the food domain and the hope for the democratic, widely dispersed, just distribution of those powers over food. The term itself opens the way for both critique and hope. This generous, provocative opening has been used to good effect—broadening, deepening, challenging, and exploring some key issues evoked by the concept of, and struggles for, food sovereignty.

It is fitting that the idea of food sovereignty was first seeded, metaphorically speaking, by those whose lives and livelihoods are on the front lines of the battle for control over the land, resources, and seeds necessary for food production. The ongoing experience of planting seeds; a long history of struggle for land, resources, and social space; and the critical, collective analysis of their immediate or imminent displacement have combined to lend peasants and small-scale farmers a particularly urgent perspective on the current food situation. Hence the leadership role that progressive agrarian movements, gathering as La Vía Campesina, have played in launching and living out the struggle for food sovereignty.

But just as most seeds require appropriate, living soils, water, and good weather to flourish, the concept of food sovereignty has "come alive" in an historical moment where many others are recognizing that the current food system is not only part of, but actively perpetuating, destructive environmental, social, and political dynamics. This awareness and critique is the living ground in which the struggle for food sovereignty is taking root. The solidarity of allies from all walks of life and many sectors of society around the world provides the needed tilth for food sovereignty initiatives. There is ample evidence that the food sovereignty concept is increasingly firmly rooted. It is engaging a wide spectrum of people on many levels. The roots are robust and growing, sometimes twisted and unpredictable in their reach, complexity, and refinement—but definitely both alive and life-giving.

Food sovereignty is a radical, provocative, transformative concept with multiple layers of meaning and application. As with the growing, harvesting, and reseeding of grains, achieving food sovereignty is an ongoing, regenerative work in progress.

NOTES

1   La Vía Campesina, "An Answer to the Global Good Crisis: Peasants and Small Farmers Can Feed the World!" Jakarta, Indonesia, May 1, 2008, www.viacampesina.org.

2   La Vía Campesina, "Proceedings from the II International Conference of the Vía Campesina," NCOS Publications, 1996.

3   FAO (Food and Agriculture Organization of the United Nations), *The State of Food Insecurity in the World 1999*, Rome: 2001.

4   La Vía Campesina, "Proceedings from the II International Conference of the Vía Campesina," *op. cit.*

5   La Vía Campesina, "The Right to Produce and Access to Lan," Position of the Vía Campesina on food sovereignty presented at the World Food Summit, Rome, November 13-17, 1996

6   Jim Handy, intervention at the international workshop entitled "Food Sovereignty: Theory, Praxis and Power," Saskatoon: University of Saskatchewan, November 17-18, 2007.

7   La Vía Campesina, "Declaration of Maputo: V International Conference of La Vía Campesina, Maputo, Mozambique," October 19-22, 2008.

8   Nouminren, "Draft Declaration of Food Sovereignty for the Japanese Farmers and Consumers," (position paper presented at Nyéléni 2007 by the Japanese Farmers and Consumers for Safe Food and Health, Selingué, Mali: February 23-27, 2006).

9   D. Morrison, "B.C. Food Systems Network Working Group on Indigenous Food Sovereignty: Final Activity Report," prepared for Provincial Health Services Authority—Community Food Action Initiative, Interior Health—Community Food Action Initiative and the B.C. Food Systems Network—Work Group on Indigenous Food Sovereignty, March 2008.

10 Nyéléni, proceedings of the Forum for Food Sovereignty held Selingué, Mali, February 23-27, 2007.

11 Nyéléni. Proceedings of the Forum for Food Sovereignty.

12 J. Ziegler, "Report Submitted by the Special Rapporteur on the Right to Food, Jean Ziegler, in accordance with Commission on Human Rights Resolution 2003/25," United Nations Commission on Human Rights, sixtieth session, February 9, 2004.

13 Olivier De Schutter, "The Right to Food and a Sustainable Global Food System," Special Rapporteur on the Right to Food to the 17th Session of the UN Commission on Sustainable Development, 2009.

14 S. Beauregard, "Food Policy for People: Incorporating Food Sovereignty Principles into State Governance," Senior Comprehensive Report, Urban and Environmental Policy Institute, Occidental College, Los Angeles: April 2009. Available at departments.oxy.edu/uepi/uep/index.htm.

15 El Universo, "Veto Parcial a Ley de Soberanía Alimentaria," March 21, 2009. Available at www.eluniverso.com.

16 El Universo, "Correa Dice que ONG se Meten en Asuntos de Política," March 11, 2009. Available at www.eluniverso.com.

17 P. Dosh and N. Kligerman, "Correa vs. Social Movements: Showdown in Ecuador," North American Congress on Latin America, September/October 2009, 3, www.nacla.org/node/6124

WOMEN'S AUTONOMY AND FOOD SOVEREIGNTY

Miriam Nobre, World March of Women, 2011[i]

Over the last ten years, World March of Women (WMW) has adopted a platform for food sovereignty and forged alliances with La Vía Campesina and other organizations that advance the concept. We understand food sovereignty to be the right of people, countries, and states to control their own agriculture and food systems. This entails protecting food production and food culture in a way that all persons can access adequate quantities of decent quality food. The challenge for urban women and women of the Global North is how to participate in this process with the same commitment as rural women and women of the Global South. The path to this goal begins with solidarity among women with different experiences and demands, continues through open debate, and culminates in action with respect to domestic work and caregiving—and action against the commodification of everyday life and of women's bodies.

Our starting point

The WMW is an international feminist movement uniting groups in over 60 countries around the continuous fights to change the world and the lives of women. The movement began in 2000 as a campaign against poverty and sexist violence. At that time, more than 5 million signatures were collected to support a platform of demands submitted to the United Nations on October 17, 2000. The first demand was to eliminate poverty by implementing national laws and strategies to ensure women would not be discriminated against in "their rights to access basic resources such as potable water, food production and distribution, in order to ensure food security for the population."[1] After this international action, the majority of participating groups decided to continue working together. They established a common agenda and greater political identity through national coordination, with an international action every five years. The international goals were translated into national contexts, where most countries developed platforms for their own demands.

The second international action was the "Women's Letter to Humanity," which traveled through 53 countries between March 8 and October 17, 2005. As the letter traveled, each participating country provided a cloth square to the Quilt of Solidarity, a visual representation of the letter. The letter is a statement expressing five core values: equality, liberty, solidarity, justice, and peace. It reads:

> A society's economy serves the women and men comprising that society. It is based on the production and exchange of socially useful wealth distributed among peoples, with the priority being satisfying collective needs, eliminating poverty, and ensuring the balance of collective and individual interests. It ensures food sovereignty.

i   Adapted from: Miriam Nobre, "Women's Autonomy and Food Sovereignty," in *Food Movements Unite! Strategies to Transform Our Food Systems*, ed. Eric Holt-Giménez (Oakland, CA: Food First Books, 2011), 293–306.

The letter was drafted over the course of several months before it was finally approved at the Fifth International Meeting of the WMW in Kigali, Rwanda. In 2005, the replacement of the term *food security*, used in 2000, with *food sovereignty* probably occurred due to open participation in the drafting process. The fact that rural women appropriated the principle of food sovereignty when La Vía Campesina proposed its emergence in the "Letter to Humanity" is an indication of the influence of grassroots organizations on the overall movement. As the letter and quilts traveled from country to country, small rural towns proved to be important stopping points and protest zones. Local groups from these areas were responsible for organizing activities around the letter and generating national recognition from other leaders. This shattered the traditional image of the feminist movement being led by urban women living in large urban centers. The new dynamic was reflected in the letter's demands, which emphasize rural women's concerns.

At the end of the letter's journey, we consolidated different countries' demands around common goals, identifying four fields of action: women's work, the common good, violence against women, and peace and demilitarization. These guided the WMW's international agenda from 2006 until 2010, when we reexamined them. At first, the term *common good* referred to the fight against the privatization of natural resources and to women's community rights to define the use of land, water, biodiversity, and food sovereignty. In 2008, this term was expanded to include education, health, common community knowledge, and the fight against its privatization.

Learning to work in alliances

In 2007, in conjunction with La Vía Campesina, Friends of the Earth International, and other organizations, we organized Nyéléni, the Forum for Food Sovereignty, in Selingué, Mali.

In one of the first workshops held by the WMW and La Vía Campesina, one of the women farmers challenged the group, saying, "The issue is that we have a core difference. We want to preserve our space and time in the kitchen and in the preparation of food, which is an expression of our culture and our knowledge, and prevent it from being replaced with junk food, and you want to stay far away from the kitchen."

From the beginning, we realized we operated on contradictory grounds; we value caregiving, which is made invisible by the patriarchal capitalist system, yet we do not want to do it alone. We want to share this work with men and, collectively, with social organizations in the state, with public policies that support caregiving. We want to stop society from overworking women so we have time to pursue our own interests, yet we also reject market solutions like fast, industrialized food.

We believed Nyéléni should focus on helping women from different sectors (farmers, fisherwomen, pastoralists, migrants, etc.) affirm themselves as political entities with their own analyses and demands. The most prevalent theme in our debates was women's right to land, water, seeds, and territory, and their role in the production, preparation, and distribution of food. The Nyéléni women's declaration agreed to "reject capitalist and patriarchal institutions that conceive of food, water, land, people's knowledge, and women's bodies as mere goods."

In 2008, the Seventh International Meeting of the WMW in Galicia, Spain, produced a mass demonstration in front of an international supermarket chain, an open forum for debate in the public market in the center of Vigo. Our Galician sisters evaluated the collective work of the WMW, La Vía Campesina, Friends of the Earth, and other ecological and consumer movements positively. Our achievements resulted in a demand that the concept of food sovereignty be incorporated into the constitution of the Autonomy of Galicia. The WMW encouraged participation in the local, responsible consuming cooperative. In 2010, a WMW Galician organization was at the forefront in a counter-summit questioning European Union fishing policies, drawing attention to the fierce exploitation of women working in the fishing industry.

Food sovereignty is a popular concept in Latin America, Africa, and Asia, but is less prevalent in North America and Europe. Globally, the concept still mobilizes more rural than urban women. To forge new alliances between rural and urban women, we must deal with the issues of: caregiving in society, referred to here as reproductive work, and the commodification of everyday life in relation to women's bodies, as defined by a system of patriarchy.

Politicizing reproductive work

Food sovereignty constructs a political agenda around reproduction that involves everyone, not only women. Reproduction, caregiving (of children, sick persons, seniors, and men), and assuring food, health, and general welfare are considered women's tasks. Even more than tasks, these are considered the core of a woman's identity. Being a woman means that one must always be ready to attend to others' physical and emotional needs—needs we all have throughout our lives.

The market production of goods and services is the only sphere in which policy debates and social movements tend to direct their economic demands. However, the production of goods would be impossible without work, and for this we must be fed, cared for, and materially and socially reproduced. In order to bring to light that which is hidden, we feminists talk about a sexual division of labor and two economic spheres, production *and* reproduction.

In general, the production sphere is considered masculine, and the reproduction sphere is considered feminine. But these spheres are not separate, and we seek to reveal the links hidden between them. For example, when structural adjustment programs demand governments cut social programs, the social work itself does not disappear but is shifted to the sector of non-wage work done by women in their families and communities. When companies function in the "just-in-time" logic, they hire women in times of harvest or for bulk orders, but then fire them when this period ends. Women's unemployment is not a problem, since women always have so much to do in the home anyway.

It is essential to understand the sphere of reproduction in its own logic, not as an inverted mirror of the sphere of production. For example, simply counting the time dedicated to caregiving does not reveal its full dimensions. To begin with, many activities are simultaneous, so the question is instead how women manage and prioritize the work (for example, watch the stove, help with the children's schoolwork). Further, more than the question of getting work done is the permanent disposition to get it done, from guessing the wants and needs of children and spouse, to predicting whether or not there will be enough sunshine during the day to wash and dry clothes.

The feminist economist Cristina Carrasco has analyzed the time and logic of caregiving, concluding it is irreconcilable with the time and logic of the market.[2] When the two interact, it is at a great cost to women. Women's work is the adjustable variable that maintains the margins of exploitation of labor in order to accumulate capital, i.e., profit. Contrary to the proposal of companies, states, and international institutions, we are not in search of the conciliatory policy between paid work and the family, but rather seek to overcome the logic of the market. This framework, largely contributed to by feminist economic theory, allows activists from women's movements to create and utilize increasingly complex analyses and moments of change. It allows us to ask: "How do we build rights and claims in terms of food sovereignty? And how do we succeed in winning these rights?"

Just as we have a long history of demanding services that support reproduction, such as daycare centers, school food, and public laundromats, we also have substantial experience in assuming collective processes in reproductive work. Women organizing into shopping groups or engaging in collective food preparation are common in the working history of the movement, even if this is not very visible. Throughout every long strike or massive layoff, one finds a group of women keeping working families fed.

In the political economy of resistance, there's always food collectively prepared by women, such as the *ollas comunes* (communal pots) in Honduran communities that are declared a coup-free zone. It is these same women who participate in the *ollas comunes* that in protests add the motto "No coup d'états or violence against women" (*Ni golpes de estado, ni golpes contra las mujeres*).

In Latin America, there are many accounts of women getting together in communal kitchens, buying groups, and milk-distribution groups. The majority of these groups are created in response to moments of crisis or extreme levels of poverty. With some exceptions, such as in Peru, these experiences are dispersed, and not considered by the feminist movement to be part of the collective history of the women's movement. This is because the nucleus of these organizations is a traditionally feminine activity and therefore considered a process which supports women's subordinate role. However, in the WMW, we believe that there is a big difference between being responsible for food production in individual homes, and the collective preparation of food. Women often begin organizing in precarious conditions in order to also attend to their responsibilities as mothers and later, as a result, break out of their traditional, subordinate roles. They occupy public space, negotiate with authorities, and question the established order in their communities and in their families.

Therefore, our challenge is how to make social movements understand the importance of social reproductive politics and act upon them. In other words, how do we raise awareness and change personal and collective practices *within* social movements? We must also determine how to lobby our governments to implement structural changes, such as the way in which cities, public transportation, and official work is organized.

We are women, not commodities!

When we began meeting with rural women fighting against genetically modified organisms (GMOs) and pesticides, we saw that the international companies that were advertising and lobbying to distribute GMOs were the same companies that produce synthetic hormones that promise eternal youth, or contraceptives that are beyond the control of women, such as injections or hormonal implants. We realized that the so-called "bioindustry" and the associations of industrial manufacturers of agricultural inputs, seeds, food processing, and drug manufacturing, have increasingly similar strategies. The use of nanotechnology in agriculture and cosmetics is yet one more example of the strategies used by these companies.

From our perspective, we should take into account how these strategies have developed and how they are organized in our daily lives, and consider how to find alternatives. At the center of these alternatives is a new understanding in the relationship between reproductive work and overcoming the alienation between our bodies. Making peace with our bodies—which are represented in the patriarchal system as fragile, sickly, unstable—is essential in feminism.

The exploitation of our work and our time in order to generate profits for the few creates suffering. We attempt to reduce the suffering with quick remedies. Medicines that regulate demeanor, such as antidepressants, ensure profits for the pharmaceutical industry. Our relationship with food is similar; we feed our anxiety with sugars and carbohydrates. GMOs, food additives, and vitamin supplements all turn basic nutrition into a collection of quick-fix remedies. We depend on doctors' and specialists' recommendations for our health. However, medicine, like all other sciences, operates within androcentric patterns. Women's bodies are only specifically considered in terms of pregnancy and birth. For example, the fact that women are more sensitive to agrotoxic contaminations due to the characteristics of their bodies is ignored.[3]

In terms of eating disorders, women are overrepresented in the population. This is not just a public health concern but also a theme for political debate about how our society relates to food, and the requirements and controls that take place upon and in women's bodies.[4] The imposition of a standard of beauty and the ideology of value as attributed by the gaze of others, especially men, makes women vulnerable to the cosmetics industry in plastic surgery (the most evident commodification of women's bodies). The "perfect" body can now be purchased, in order to find or keep a companion, sell oneself in the industry of prostitution, or even get a company job requiring "good appearance." What these motivations have in common is their distance from the personal right that is expressed in the motto "My body belongs to me" (*Meu corpo me pertenece*). Contrarily, they all respond to the imposed constraints and expectations on women in relation to a patriarchal society.

Women are questioning the relationships between commodification and their bodies, between themselves and others, and between women and nature. The homogenization of standards of feminine beauty is similar to the homogenization of crops found in industrial monocultures. We therefore search for other paradigms with which to organize our daily life and the production and reproduction of our society.

The current construction of the WMW regarding food sovereignty

Food sovereignty has been integral to WMW activity in several countries. In 2007, a WMW campaign for rural women's rights in India sought to strengthen their involvement in food production and agricultural work. In Turkey, WMW groups became involved in the campaign against the water privatization efforts spearheaded by the Coca-Cola Company. They are part of the national platform against GMOs, framing their food sovereignty goals from a feminist perspective. In Mali and Benin, women's associations act collectively in market choices. Their aspiration is to develop markets in West African countries that exist as an alternative to the free-market rationale. In Peru, women participated in a campaign for native seeds and defied water-privatization efforts.

The WMW Third International Action of 2010 recounted these experiences and opened up an international debate. In Belgium, a demonstration of over 6,000 women demanded, among other things, that women in agriculture be recognized as having social rights, whether they are farmers' wives or migrant laborers. In addition, they protested the North's economic policies, highlighting their consequences on the whole planet and especially on the Global South.

We wish to go beyond debate. In good feminist tradition, we believe collective experience breeds strong movements. We stress the importance of food and political organization. Food preparation is a class issue as well as a gender issue. Many middle-class women do not concern themselves with the labor required to feed everyone at public events. We all run the risk of replicating society's division between "professional" work (methodology and discourse) and manual labor (logistics and food). Our movement is assuming more and more collective responsibility for food preparation and distribution.

It is already obvious to food movements that they should prepare their own food, using agroecological products bought directly from small producers. However, the same cannot be said of movements led by women, who cook every day for their families or for the families for whom they work. The feminist movement provides them an escape from these responsibilities and time for themselves. The question is how can we maintain this respite while collectively assuming food-preparation responsibilities?

While 2,000 Brazilian sisters marched between March 8 and 18, 2010, 80 women marched in the kitchen, preparing meals and holding debates. Every day, a team of 20 women took turns washing up and participating in debates. The Brazilians arranged to spend one day of the march in the kitchen, to learn how to run it while also training in political debate. This proved challenging; not only was there limited experience among participants but limited resources as well. Still, our sisters acted respectfully, staying true to popular feminist education principles. They valued the group's diverse backgrounds, ages, and experience, as well as the absence of a chef. When the march arrived at the kitchen site, we were received by our Brazilian sisters with the slogan "The kitchen is the heart; without food there is no revolution" (*A cozinha é o coração; sem comida não há revolução*).

Overcoming obstacles to food sovereignty

We united behind the principle of food sovereignty first because our rural sisters in the WMW invited us to join their struggle for land and fair conditions to live and produce as farmers. Secondly, as allies of La Vía Campesina and Friends of the Earth, we understood the importance of uniting all groups dedicated to improving living conditions for both men and women. We also understand that food sovereignty allows us to expand the feminist movement's horizons. Furthermore, questioning the system of modern consumption from the starting point of what we eat brings us closer to our own bodies, which are alienated, mistreated, and reduced to mere commodities.

Food sovereignty opens doors to other issues. It urges us to address energy sovereignty, and sovereignty over the territory where we live. The concept of territory encompasses the right to land, water, biodiversity, and self-determination. We believe our bodies are our primary territory. To live in pleasure and harmony with one's body, free from the threat of physical violence or harmful consumption, is a political act. As we fight to defend our territory from GMOs, we fight to rid it of violence against women.

The strength of the food sovereignty movement comes from its linkages with other movements. Our contribution as a feminist movement is to link the goal of women's autonomy with the vision of sovereignty for all people.

NOTES

1   World March of Women, "Demands of the World March of Women in the Year 2000 in The World March of Women 1998-2008 A Decade of International Feminist Struggle," World March of Women (São Paulo: 2008), 55.

2   Cristina Carrasco, "Por uma economia não androcêntrica: debates e propostas a partir da economia feminista," in *Trabalho doméstico e de cuidados. Por outro paradigma de sustentabilidade da vida humana*, ed. Maria Lúcia Silveira and Neuza Tito, (São Paulo: SOF, 2008).

3   Boston Women's Health Book Collective, *Our Bodies—Ourselves* (New York: Simon & Schuster, 2000).

4   Mabel Arnayz and J. Comelles, eds. *No comerás. Narrativas sobre comida, cuerpo y género en el nuevo milenio* (Barcelona: Icaria, 2007).

FOOD SOVEREIGNTY IN PRACTICE IN THE BASQUE COUNTRY

EHNE Bizkaia (The Basque Farmers Union), 2013[i]

It has now been 20 years since La Vía Campesina coined the term food sovereignty, defining it as the right of all peoples to decide on their food systems from production to consumption, based on agroecology and organized for the construction of local and national sovereignty. EHNE Bizkaia—the Basque union of small farmers and ranchers—has been working to advance food sovereignty since La Vía Campesina's foundational congress in 1993. In *Euskal Herría* (the Basque Country) the struggle for food sovereignty is embedded in a broader struggle for political and cultural autonomy, drawing on a long history of Basque resistance against fascism and state-sponsored repression. A strong model of local cooperative food production thrives in the region, as part of a framework of community empowerment and solidarity economy.

When we talk about, define, and explain food sovereignty, many people see it as a utopia because it clearly means we have to go beyond the existing laws of the global market and the agroindustial model of production to construct a real alternative based on a clear political position that prioritizes people and the environment above the interests of multinational corporations. Years after defining the term, we now see clear examples that demonstrate that alternative market models based on collaboration, commitment, and mutual aid between producers and consumers is possible. The organizations that work to build this alternative model are using different tools, affirming a model of change, and showing us that we can do things differently.

One example is the Red Nekasarea, a project of EHNE Bizkaia, started in 2007 to establish direct links between production and consumption. In less than ten years, policies that favored big box stores and big infrastructure had covered 13 percent of the Basque Country under a layer of cement, leading to a dramatic loss of environment and livelihoods in the countryside. Something had to be done. In this context, we created a network of producers and consumers that were not only sellers and customers but also mutual aid groups in which everyone was equally responsible for the food system.

The change of vision needed to form these groups required a lot of work—primarily education—with the producers in order to understand that they needed to do things they hadn't done before, like spending time communicating with their group or distributing planned, weekly food baskets (*cestas*). Those who receive the food are not just "customers," but people who are actively concerned with the day-to-day work of the farmer and who collaborate in production at different times throughout the year. Though this model seemed utopian in 2007, today it provides 800 families with food baskets produced by 80 farmers who plan production based on

i   Adapted from EHNE Bizkaia, "Food Sovereignty in Practice in the Basque Country," Food First Backgrounder, Vol. 19, No. 3, Fall 2013.

mutual agreements with consumers. Coordinator of Red Nekasarea Isa Alvarez recalls, "Two years ago the Red Nekasarea was based more on the urban sector supporting the rural sector—consumers helping producers. Now with the economic crisis, we need to make this support go in both directions because there are a lot of people in the city who have economic difficulties and can't access food, so now the consumer groups are working to solve these problems."

It's important to point out that this network is not just creating an alternative consumption model, but really implies the creation of a whole new *economic* model. First, the monthly quota people pay for their food baskets is not viewed as a payment for food but as support for a village form of production. In exchange, the farmer delivers baskets of their seasonal produce; they do not produce just on demand, and Red Nekasareas's rules limit the size of participating farms. The idea is to create a network of collective groups that will multiply into many groups, not just consolidate into a few, large groups. One of the objectives is to regenerate the social structure of the agrarian sector: over the last few years, 50 young people have been able to start farming. As farmer-member Unai Aranguren affirms, "Given the economic crisis, our plan to forge agroecology as a source of change, along with the political understanding of the local population and the creation of networks between producers and consumers is bringing more and more people back to the countryside."

One of the clear examples from this network is something that happened last year with one of EHNE's farmers. A winter storm blew down farmer Joseba Koskorrotza's greenhouse, destroying his crop, leaving him with nothing to distribute to his Nekasarea group and ruining his chances for the following year's spring planting. For him, this was an economic disaster, made worse by the fact that he was unable to keep his commitments to the consumers in his group. Any other farmer in this situation would be ruined or at the very least would have to take out loans to stay afloat. But this case was very different.

The first thing that happened was that his food basket group came to his village on the weekends to help him rebuild his greenhouse so he could get back on his feet quickly. But even so, there was no produce to fill the food baskets. His fellow farmers in the Red Nekasarea didn't hesitate. There were 28 produce farmers in Red Nekasarea, and Joseba had 29 weekly food baskets to distribute, so each one of the producers donated a food basket each week to cover Josebas's group's needs while Joseba continued to charge for the cost of the produce. For the farmers, it was not a big deal to donate one basket, but for the one on the receiving end, it made the difference between success and failure. Claims Joseba:

> The spirit of solidarity that we thought was lost is there, but we have to put our fears and shame aside. That's when one realizes that if you get involved like this, in this network, it's not just to farm differently... it also means being part of a collective that is governed by other values—values that we thought were lost and that in difficult times make you see that you are not alone. It is when you understand that food sovereignty is more than just a new proposal for our relationship with the land... It's also a way of relating with our own community.

Examples like this may seem simple, but they are possible thanks to the preparation of all those involved and to a lot of communication. This helps tc weave relations of trust, which works better than any form of certification. All of this comes from knowing that the achievement of food sovereignty only comes through collective processes that are capable of rethinking the present system and building new forms, not just based on production but on relationships between people. This is the only way to attain the transformation proposed by food sovereignty.

7. FOOD WORKERS, FOOD JUSTICE

LINKING FOOD, LABOR, AND IMMIGRANT RIGHTS

Eric Holt-Giménez, Zoe Brent, and Annie Shattuck, 2010[i]

The food movement in the US is growing stronger, but too often the people who work in our food system are overlooked. Some 17 percent of all US jobs are in the food sector.[1] Many of these jobs are carried out by undocumented immigrant workers. Consequently, food workers are the lowest paid and most under-protected workers in the nation. Low wages and substandard working conditions subsidize the enormous profits of the food industry and put the triple burden of poverty, labor abuse, and food insecurity on those most vulnerable. The movement for food justice cannot thrive in a system where food workers are criminalized, exploited, and going hungry.

Labor in the corporate food system

In 2009, the US Bureau of Labor Statistics listed food preparation and serving-related occupations as the lowest paid of all occupational categories ($8.59 median wage), followed by farming, fishing, and forestry ($9.34 median wage). Twenty-five percent of grocery workers experience minimum wage violations.[2] On-the-job injuries are common. According to Oxfam, in 2004, farmworkers suffered the highest rates of toxic chemical injuries, with an estimated 300,000 pesticide poisonings yearly.[3]

A decline in union representation—from 35 percent to 12 percent since World War II—parallels the spread of poor labor conditions, dependence on undocumented labor, and corporate concentration.[4] Aggressive antiunion campaigns and recruitment of temporary or foreign workers hinder organizing efforts and keep labor costs painfully low. Real wages for meatpacking workers fell from $20 per hour in 1977 to $10.50 per hour in 2001, while consolidation of the beef packing industry increased drastically.[5] By 1999 the top four firms controlled 80 percent of the market—more than doubling in two decades.[6] Meanwhile, rates of undocumented workers have risen to an estimated 20 to 50 percent of the workforce.[7] Sadly, this kind of exploitation is not unique to meatpacking but is also common in the field, the store, and the restaurant.

In the field

The women and men who harvest, pack, process, and serve our food can't afford to feed their own families healthy food. Research conducted by the California Institute for Rural Studies (CIRS) in Fresno County, California—the state's breadbasket—found that 45 percent of farm workers surveyed were food insecure and 48 percent were on food stamps—more than double

i   Adapted from Eric Holt-Giménez, Zoe Brent, and Annie Shattuck, "Food Workers – Food Justice: Linking Food, Labor, and Immigrant Rights," Food First Backgrounder, Vol. 16, No. 2, Summer 2010.

the national average.[8] Since job opportunities and wage rates are key determinants of food security, it is safe to assume that food workers are among the most insecure. Their dependence on cheap, processed food as a source of needed calories results in high rates of obesity and diet-related illnesses. Another survey done by the CIRS in 1999 of farmworkers in six regions throughout California found that 81 percent of males and 76 percent of females were overweight, and 28 percent and 37 percent were obese, respectively.[9]

In the store

In food retail, permanent, economically secure jobs are being replaced with temporary contract work. Labor contractors provide large firms with short-term workers for low-wage, low-skilled jobs. Why? All personnel, insurance, and labor issues relating to those employees automatically become the responsibility of the contract agent. In this way, big corporations can wash their hands of responsibility for inhumane or unfair job conditions—even as they profit from exploited labor. As Safeway spokesman Susan Houghton stated when asked about the unfair and unhealthy labor conditions of Safeway's janitors, "We just contract with these companies to provide services... This is something you need to talk to the vendors about."[10] Workers bouncing from job to job are less likely to organize than unionized workers with job security and legal residency. This undermines labor rights and long-term economic security for all workers, encouraging a "race to the bottom" in the labor market.

In the restaurant

Jobs in the restaurant business have grown significantly faster than jobs in other sectors in the past decade, but the benefits of growth do not necessarily filter down to workers. At $2.13 an hour, the federal minimum wage for tipped workers has not changed in 19 years; in fact, it fell 37 percent in real terms since it was established in 1991. According to the National Employment Law Project, tipped workers have twice the poverty rate of other workers.[11]

Wages are only the tip of the iceberg. The Restaurant Opportunities Center (ROC) study of working conditions in five major cities found that some 90 percent of restaurant workers did not have health insurance or paid sick days, nearly 70 percent said they worked even when they were ill, and some 40 percent were not paid for overtime. Moreover, the few good jobs in the restaurant industry tend to go to white workers over people of color. The median income of white restaurant workers is 22 percent higher than for workers of color. The Center also found that white jobseekers are 25 percent more likely to get interviews than workers of color with similar qualifications.[12]

Immigration: the key issue, the false debate

Recent anti-immigrant legislation in the state of Arizona allows law officers to detain and arrest any person suspected of being undocumented. By criminalizing immigrants, the discriminatory law allows politicians to avoid addressing the causes of migration and the widespread abuses of immigrant labor, thus undermining the position of all workers—especially in the food system.

Current immigration law rewards labor abuses. Fines for violating the National Labor Relations Act (NRLA) are minimal. The Immigration Reform and Control Act of 1986 links one's legal status to one's job, criminalizing undocumented labor. As a result, firing and the threat of deportation are used to silence workers who speak out or attempt to organize. The use of undocumented labor is remarkably profitable for industry. In California—the richest agricultural state in the nation—undocumented immigrants' gross economic contribution through sales, income, and property taxes was $45,000 per person (including children) in 1994. Yet the workers were paid an average of $8,840 each. The difference is profit that goes directly to industry—primarily construction, agriculture, food processing, restaurants, and services.[13]

Little attention is paid to why people migrate in the first place. Free trade agreements allow the US to dump its surplus of subsidized grain abroad where it sells at prices well under the costs of production. Since 1994, the North American Free Trade Agreement (NAFTA) has bankrupted much of rural Mexico, driving over 2 million smallholders out of the countryside.[14] The very same companies that benefit from NAFTA also save on labor costs by actively recruiting those same smallholders as undocumented workers to fill underpaid jobs.[15] Research from the Pew Hispanic Center in 2006 indicates that some 24 percent of farmworkers, 12 percent of food preparation workers, and 27 percent of butchers and food processors are undocumented.[16]

Linking food justice with worker and immigrant rights

Addressing worker and immigrants' rights in the food system is a key step toward community food security and food sovereignty—the democratic control over our food systems.

Fixing federal and state policy is essential, but the grassroots are not waiting for leadership from above. Workers, farmers, and activists are already busy changing the labor landscape in the food system.

In the field

The Coalition of Immokalee Workers (CIW), in alliance with the student-led Fair Food Challenge, has successfully campaigned to end modern-day slavery in Florida's tomato fields. Their combined pressure convinced Taco Bell, McDonald's, Burger King, Whole Foods, and others to buy only from growers who agreed to pay another penny a pound to pickers.

Swanton Berry Farm of Davenport, California, the first organic farm to invite and sign a union contract with the United Farm Workers, provides a union wage, health benefits, subsidized housing, and stock options to career-oriented farmworkers.

In the store

Twenty-two percent of all grocery store workers belong to a union or are covered by union contracts, compared with 14 percent in other industries. The benefits of union contracts are striking. Unionized women earn on average 11.2 percent more than their nonunion counterparts. Young workers earn 12.4 percent more. Workers in chain stores are more likely to be unionized or covered by contracts than workers in independent grocery stores, but new independent models are emerging as well.[17]

The new People's Community Market, as well as Mandela Marketplace, both in Oakland, California, base their business models on worker-ownership and a community-service mission to bring fresh healthy produce and good jobs to low-income neighborhoods.

In the restaurant

ROC recommends an immediate increase in the minimum wage for tipped workers, paid sick days, and access to health insurance, as well as what they call "high road" practices to "assist and encourage employers to provide living wages, basic workplace benefits, and opportunities for advancement to restaurant workers." Such initiatives include rent and property tax incentives for employers who implement exceptional workplace practices, subsidies to employment-based health insurance, and collective health insurance provisions. The Center's worker-owned restaurant already follows "high road practices" while paying workers a genuine living wage.

ROC, CIW, and at least one United Food and Commercial Workers local are all members of a new coalition—the Food Chain Workers Alliance—fighting for fairness from farm to fork.

These are just a few examples of a growing movement beginning to link food and labor justice. In order to achieve a more equitable food system, the criminalization of workers, enforced inequality, and the use of immigration policy as a supply system for exploited labor all need to change. A fair deal for food workers is an essential part of the foundation of an equitable, sustainable food system. Understanding food justice as a labor issue—and labor as a food justice issue—is an important step in this direction.

NOTES

1 Marlon Beck et al., *Agribusiness Industry, 2006* (Washington, D.C.: Industrial College of the Armed Forces, 2006).

2 Annette Bernhardt et al., "Broken Laws, Unprotected Workers: Violations of Employment and Labor Laws in America's Cities," (Chicago: Center for Urban Economic Development, New York: National Employment Law Project, and Los Angeles: UCLA Institute for Research on Labor and Employment, 2009).

3 Oxfam, "Like Machines in the Fields: Workers without rights in American agriculture," *Trading Away Our Rights: Women Working in Global Supply Chains* (Boston: Oxfam America, 2004), 76.

4 David Bacon, "Unions at War," *San Francisco Bay Guardian*, August 10, 2005.

5 Chris Kutalik, "Immigrant Workers Buck Long Slide in Meatpacking Raids Follow as Backlash," LaborNotes, 2007, 335.

6 James M. MacDonald et al., "Consolidation in U.S. Meatpacking," Agricultural Economic Report, USDA (Washington, D.C.: USDA, 2000), 47.

7 Dell Champlin and Eric Hake, "Immigration as Industrial Strategy in American Meatpacking," *Review of Political Economy* 18, 1 (2006): 49–70.

8 Cathy Wirth et al., "Hunger in the Fields: Food Insecurity Among Farmworkers in Fresno County," California Institute for Rural Studies, November 2007, 36.

9   Don Vollarejo et al., "Suffering in Silence: A Report on the Health of California's Agricultural Workers," California Institute for Rural Studies, 2000, 38.

10   Rose Arrieta, "Janitors Challenge Grocery Chains on Health, Safety Standards," *Working in These Times*, Oct. 22, 2009, accessed Nov. 1, 2009, http://inthesetimes.com/working/entry/5073/janitors_challenge_grocery_chains_on_health_safety_standards.

11   Rajesh D. Nayak and Paul K. Sonn, "Restoring the Minimum Wage for America's Tipped Workers," (New York: National Employment Law Project, 2009), 28.

12   "Behind the Kitchen Door: A Summary of Restaurant Industry Studies in New York, Chicago, Metro Detroit, New Orleans, and Maine," Restaurant Opportunities Centers United, 2010,: 2.

13   Urban Institute 1994, cited in David Bacon, *Illegal People: How Globalization Creates Migration and Criminalizes Immigrants* (Boston: Beacon Press, 2008).

14   Joseph E. Stiglitz and Andrew Charlton, *Fair Trade for All: How Trade Can Promote Development* (New York: Oxford University Press, 2005).

15   "Blood, Sweat and Fear: Workers' Rights in U.S. Meat and Poultry Plants," (New York: Human Rights Watch, 2004); Stephanie E. Tanger, "Enforcing Corporate Responsibility for Violations of Workplace Immigration Laws: The Case of Meatpacking," *Harvard Latino Review* 59 (2006), 59–90; Dell Champlin and Eric Hake "Immigration as Industrial Strategy in American Meatpacking," *op. cit.*

16   Jeffrey S. Passel, "The Size and Characteristics of the Unauthorized Migrant Population in the U.S.: Estimates based on the March 2005 Current Population Survey," Hispanic Trends, Pew Research Center, 2006, 23.

17   Vicky Lovell et al., *The Benefits of Unionization for Workers in the Retail Food Industry* (Washington, D.C.: The Institute for Women's Policy Research, 2002), 38.

THE RESTAURANT OPPORTUNITIES CENTER

José Oliva, Restaurant Opportunities Centers United, 2011[i]

At age 13, I came to the United States with my parents after being exiled from my home country, Guatemala. Food has always been at the center of my story and my people's story.

My family's exile was a direct result of the powerful relationship between the United Fruit Company (UFC, now known as Chiquita Brands International, Inc.) with the US State Department. In 1954, the CIA sponsored a coup to depose Jacobo Arbenz Guzmán, Guatemala's democratically elected president. This was largely at the UFC's request after Arbenz nationalized lands belonging to them and redistributed them among Guatemala's landless peasants. The coup triggered a civil war that lasted 36 years and killed more than 200,000 people. My grandfather, Mario Gonzalez Orellana, was squarely on one side of that conflict, having served as Vice Minister of Economics for Arbenz. My mother had been raised with clear pro-democracy, anti-hunger values; I was born with that fire in my belly as well.

We were forced to flee Guatemala in 1985, when my parents began organizing anti-dictatorship student and labor protests. I remember watching bodies being pulled from the river that roared past my grandparents' house in Xela, my hometown. I was to leave all of the death and hunger behind—or so I thought.

We went to the Canadian embassy in Guatemala City and begged them to give us asylum. But they refused, saying they had a quota and it had already been filled. They directed us to the American embassy, saying "Don't ask for asylum. You'll never get it. Instead, say you're a teacher and you own a home. Apply for a tourist visa. Tell them you want to see Disney World." That is exactly what we did. Being the eldest of two boys, I pretended to be excited to go see Mickey Mouse, and we got the visa. The next day, we were on a plane to Orlando.

The change in setting could not have been starker. Instead of goons with guns, there were old ladies with shopping bags full of plastic trinkets. Instead of dead bodies being pulled out of rivers, there were miles and miles of restaurants and shopping malls. Instead of hungry people protesting the brutal military regime, there were happy, sunny sidewalks filled with people laughing and joking. This is the way life ought to be, I thought.

After several weeks in Orlando, my parents made the decision to move the family to Chicago, in part because of a very hostile, right-wing environment in South Florida. Soon after we arrived there, my mother found a job at an Italian restaurant called Giordano's, in one of Chicago's wealthy northern suburbs. I used to look inside through the restaurant's front window and think, "This is the job I want when I grow up." It was fancy and clean inside, and everyone was smiling. My mother didn't work there very long. She left one day and didn't go back. It wasn't until much

---

i   Adapted from José Olivia, "The Restaurant Opportunities Center," in *Food Movements Unite! Strategies to Transform Our Food Systems*, ed. Eric Holt-Giménez (Oakland, CA: Food First Books, 2011), 173–186.

later that she told me, "*Hijo*, if you only knew how they treated women in that place. It was like rubbing salt in a wound." She was working an average of 60 hours per week with no overtime pay, and was constantly harassed, along with most of the other women in the restaurant. She earned minimum wage doing salad prep. My father was having trouble finding work, so what she brought home was the total income for a family of four. I would find out for myself years later what the restaurant industry was truly like for immigrants and people of color.

My grandfather always thanked the Creator for tragedies, no matter how devastating. In the *Popol Vuh*—the Mayan Bible—destruction is a form of creation. So, my grandfather accepted pain and suffering as a necessity for change. The coup that overthrew his boss's government was no exception. It brought him a peaceful life in the country away from the 11 consecutive dictatorships that would follow. When we came to the United States, in exile and shame, I tried to remind myself of my grandfather's peace and wisdom in his exile.

Because of my parents' sacrifice and many lucky breaks, I graduated from high school and went on to college. Since we had come to the US on a tourist visa we'd overstayed, I was completely undocumented at that time. I could not apply for student loans, grants, or even scholarships. I had to pay for my classes and books out of my own pocket. I did what anyone else in my position would do: I got a job.

I found my first restaurant job when I was in high school, at a fast-food restaurant across the street from my house. My first day of work, I had to put on a giant chicken costume and walk around the block handing out flyers. My friends all recognized me (the suit had a huge open beak through which my face was plainly visible) and would walk behind me, kicking the suit's tail feathers. Apart from the brief humiliation, the job was hard. When I first burned myself in the kitchen (a second-degree burn) while dumping grease from a frying container, the manager shrugged and said, "It happens to all of us." He lifted his shirtsleeve to reveal several scars. During and after college, I worked at several other restaurants—Shoney's, Red Lobster, Francesca's—each considered "better" than the last. But for the workers, with the exception of a few "front of house" folks, the conditions were the same: minimum wages, no breaks, slips, falls, and burns. All I could think while working these jobs was, "There are more of us workers than managers. They can't possibly do all the work themselves. Why do we take so much abuse?"

ROC: Restaurant Opportunity Centers

On September 11, 2001, I was eating breakfast with my mother, watching the morning news, when there was an interruption in the broadcast, saying an airplane had crashed into the World Trade Center. The story that was to unfold was no exception to my grandfather's rule. The tragic events of that day led to the creation of a new actor in the restaurant industry: the Restaurant Opportunities Center of New York (ROC-NY). ROC would revolutionize both worker organizing and the restaurant industry.

Survivors from Windows on the World, the fine-dining restaurant on the World Trade Center's top floor, had banded together to create an organization with a groundbreaking model to change conditions in the industry. The restaurant workers from Windows hailed from all over the world, an intentional choice by the owner, who wanted staff that spoke every possible language so the tourists there always had someone to converse with. The staff members were like family, and all made a good living. ROC cofounder and former Windows worker Fekkak Mamdouh says that within one year of working at Windows, he was earning $50,000—more than he'd ever earned before. He would also meet with several other Muslim coworkers for daily prayers in the World Trade Center's North Tower stairway.

Seventy-three Windows workers perished on September 11, 2001. The other 300 were left jobless. But they didn't sit around and mope. Under the leadership of Mamdouh and Saru Jayaraman, who had started several other successful local and national organizations, they came up with a plan for changing the very nature of the industry. They knew it wasn't enough to find new jobs. Bad jobs dominated the industry; even if a few former Windows workers managed to find good jobs, the majority would be placed in the low-wage, no-benefits positions. They knew they had to change the industry's overall conditions.

They came up with a three-pronged strategy to create a new business model in the restaurant industry, one that ROC still uses today. Instead of the old "race to the bottom" model, it would lead to a new vision of "shared prosperity." The model's three prongs—research and policy; workplace justice; and promotion of the high road—are interdependent and intended to work as a synergetic wheel, energizing each other while engaging restaurant workers to create sustainability in their own industries.

Since its creation in 2002, ROC-NY has won nearly a dozen workplace justice victories against large fine-dining empires in the city. It has also developed groundbreaking research and a high-road association comprising several employers that provide benefits above and beyond what the law requires. This model's success in New York led the founders of ROC-NY to create ROC United in 2008. ROC United is a national organization composed of local ROCs in seven locations: Chicago, Los Angeles, New York, Miami, New Orleans, Detroit, and Washington, DC. All use the three-pronged model to improve conditions in their local restaurant industries.

A "dog-eat-dog" business

As ROC's founders knew well, the bad experiences my mother and I had had in the restaurant industry were far from isolated incidents. They were part of an entire business model. Workers call it the "dog-eat-dog" way of doing business. The key components of this business model are:

- **Contingent labor:** As a worker, there is little consistency in work scheduling. You may be on a schedule one week and off the next, never to be called back—not fired, just not on the schedule. You may have 60 hours of work one week and three the next, depending on the whims of managers, the ups and downs of business, or other factors over which workers have no control.

- **Informality:** Workers are often paid cash under the table, with no taxes withheld. No employee manual is ever provided. No rules, principles, or workplace policies are set; workers are kept uninformed and uncertain about their own rights.

- **A culture of legal violations:** Labor and employment law is routinely violated, and rates are systematically denied as a way of creating a culture of inevitability and futility.

- **A classic divide-and-conquer approach:** Employers hire immigrant workers and people of color for "back of house" jobs—as cooks, preps, and dishwashers, while hiring mostly native-born white workers for the "front of house" jobs such as bartender and waiter. Besides creating a huge wage gap, in which people of color make an average of $4 less per hour than their white counterparts, this tactic also pits immigrants against native-born workers, and white workers against workers of color.

These four employment practices are not new. What is new is their simultaneous deployment, not in the small mom-and-pop diners, but the trend-setting, fine-dining segment of the restaurant industry—which is mimicked by the rest of the industry. These employment practices are now finding their way to many other industries and sectors, in essence "restaurantizing" the workplace and creating a new race to the bottom for all workers. Moreover, in an economic setting in which unions only represent about 13 percent of the overall workforce, and where capital is globally mobile, the implementation of these four employment practices has compounded the situation of powerlessness—necessitating a new model for empowering workers.

A model from the past

The restaurant industry employs more than 10 million people, making it the largest private-sector employer in the nation. As such, it is a powerhouse of influence. The wages and standards it sets for workers have a heavy spillover effect on the rest of the US economy—especially the larger food industry. We've seen the spillover effect before in US history. At the turn of the last century, the auto industry was the largest private-sector employer in the nation, with over 6.5 million workers, and its low wages and harsh working conditions became the staple for the entire manufacturing sector. In 1933, according to a Federal Trade Commission report on the motor vehicle industry, the average wage for an autoworker was just over $1,000 per year, and by extension, the entire economy suffered. The low wages and dangerous working conditions dragged down the entire manufacturing sector and the economy overall. It was not until the United Auto Workers collectively bargained for better wages and conditions that an increase in spending, among other things, pulled the economy into recovery. As a matter of fact, the creation of the middle class of the 1950s and 60s was a direct result of the amplified voice employees had in the workplace.

ROC United's research has shown that, unlike the auto industry of days past, the restaurant industry is not a vehicle for the middle class—yet. However, we are at a crossroads. Restaurant owners can either buy into the old dog-eat-dog business model, or they can boldly embrace a "shared prosperity" model. The concept is simple: provide a healthy, locally grown, delicious meal and treat workers well; then they treat customers well, and everyone wins. Already, ROC United has won several victories, introducing a bill in Congress, developing groundbreaking research at the national level, and winning several more workplace justice campaigns.

A thriving business

Nationwide, and in each of the five regions studied by ROC United's recently released reports—New York City, Chicago, Metro Detroit, New Orleans, and the state of Maine—the restaurant industry is vibrant, resilient, and growing. In 2007, the restaurant industry contributed over $515 billion in revenue to the nation's gross domestic product. Perhaps the industry's most important contribution to the nation's economy is the thousands of job opportunities and career options it provides. Despite the current economic recession, the restaurant industry continues to grow nationwide. In each locality, restaurant employment growth has outpaced that of the local region's economy overall. Since formal credentials are not a requirement for the majority of restaurant jobs, the industry provides employment opportunities for new immigrants whose prior experience outside the US may not be recognized by other employers; for workers who have no formal qualifications; and for young people just starting out.

In all five locations studied, we found two roads to profitability in the restaurant industry—the "high road" and "low road." Restaurant employers who take the high road provide the best jobs in the industry, offering living wages, access to health benefits, and career advancement. Taking the low road to profitability, however, creates low-wage jobs with long hours, few benefits, and exposure to dangerous and often unlawful working conditions. Many restaurant employers in each of the five regions examined appear to be taking the low road, creating a predominantly low-wage industry in every region throughout the country, and making health and safety law violations commonplace.

While there are a few "good jobs" in the restaurant industry that offer living wages, the majority are "bad jobs," characterized by low wages, few benefits, and limited opportunities for upward mobility or increased income. According to the US Bureau of Labor Statistics (BLS), the national median hourly wage for food preparation and service workers in 2010 was only $9.54, including tips, which means that half of all restaurant workers nationwide actually earn less. In the same year, the federal poverty-line wage for a family of three was $8.86, meaning that more than half of all restaurant workers nationwide struggle in poverty.

At each location ROC studied, an overwhelming majority (over 90 percent) of restaurant workers surveyed reported that they do not have health insurance through their employers (see table below). In addition, earnings in the restaurant industry have lagged behind those of the entire rest of the private sector. In terms of annual earnings, restaurant workers around the country made only $12,868 on average in 2008, compared to $45,371 for the total private sector, according to the Quarterly Census of Employment and Wages of the Bureau of Labor Statistics. A substantial number of workers in each local study reported overtime and minimum wage violations, lack of health and safety training, and a failure to implement other health and safety measures in restaurant workplaces. In all five regions studied, we found that workers of color hold most of the industries "bad jobs," while white workers tend to disproportionately hold the few "good jobs." Last year, when I met two young African American workers stepping out into the humid night after a long shift in one of the Bourbon Street's greasy pizza joints, they wasted no time in telling me they make $4 an hour while the white women in the upscale oyster bar next door make $15 an hour with tips. "They'll never hire us over there. That's just the way it is," said Mickey, one of the two young men, as he lit up a smoke.

Workers also reported discriminatory hiring, promotion, and disciplinary practices. These challenges resulted in a three-dollar differential between white restaurant workers and workers of color in the five regions studied, with the median hourly wage of all white workers surveyed being

$14.70, and that of workers of color being $11.50.

In each locality, we found that restaurant employers who violated labor laws were also more likely to violate health and safety standards in the workplace—such as failing to provide health and safety training, or forcing workers to engage in practices that harm the health and safety of customers. The pervasiveness of accidents, coupled with the fact that so few restaurant workers have health insurance, can lead to escalating, uncompensated care costs incurred by public hospitals. In all five localities, more than one quarter (26.5 percent) of surveyed workers reported that they or a family member had visited the emergency room without being able to pay for their treatment.

Figure 2: Summary of Restaurant Workers' Experiences in Chicago, Metro Detroit, New Orleans, Maine, and New York City (Source: ROC United, 2010)

PERCENTAGE OF WORKERS SURVEYED IN ALL AREAS WHO...	
Did not have health insurance provided through their employer	90.1 percent
Did not have paid vacation days	78.0 percent
Did not have paid sick days	89.6 percent
Worked while sick	66.7 percent
Suffered from overtime violations	38.3 percent
Reported that their experience of being passed over for a promotion was based on race	30.9 percent
Reported having to do things under time pressure that might have harmed the health and safety of the consumer	24.4 percent
Reported that they or a family member had to go to the emergency room without being able to pay	26.5 percent
WAGE DIFFERENTIALS BY RACE	
Median wage of white workers	$14.70
Median wage of workers of color	$11.50

ROC research also sheds light on the hidden costs of low-wage jobs and low-road workplace practices to consumers, taxpayers, and the public at large. Violations of employment and health and safety laws place customers at risk and endanger the public.

Low wages and the lack of job security among restaurant workers leads to increased reliance on social-assistance programs, resulting in an indirect subsidy to employers engaging in low-road practices and fewer such public resources available to all in need. A key finding of our research was that whenever restaurant workers and high-road employers are hurt by low-road practices, so is the rest of society.

However, there is another path to profitability. It is possible to create good jobs while maintaining a successful business in the restaurant industry. Our interviews with employers revealed that as long as there is an enduring commitment to do so, it is possible to run a successful restaurant business while paying living wages, providing workplace benefits, ensuring adequate levels of staffing, providing necessary training, and creating career-advancement opportunities. In fact, in each locality, more than ten percent of the workers we surveyed reported earning a living wage (in some locations, more than 20 percent), and similar numbers reported receiving benefits, thereby demonstrating both the existence of good jobs and the industry's potential to serve as a positive force for job creation. Workers who earn higher wages are also more likely to receive benefits, ongoing training, and promotion, and are less likely to be exposed to poor and illegal workplace practices. For example, workers earning a living wage, calculated according to locality, were also much more likely to have health insurance than workers earning less than the state minimum wage.

The ROC model

The ROC model represents a new way to build power for workers through an entirely participatory process that surrounds the restaurant industry on all sides, using the three-pronged approach: research and policy, workplace justice, and promotion of the high road.

ROC engages in rigorous, statistically significant research on the restaurant industry that illustrates its workings in every market where a local ROC is located. The research utilizes a combination of surveys and interviews with a statistically representative sample of workers and employers who provide insight into the labor dynamics of their respective restaurant markets. But more importantly, the surveys allow us to meet workers and employers, develop relationships with them, and understand which issues run deep in the restaurant worker community.

Workers in local ROCs form policy committees that turn the issues workers care about into full-on policy campaigns aimed at improving the lives of all restaurant workers. Paid sick days, minimum wage, and other legislation would make conditions more tolerable for millions of restaurant workers.

In every restaurant market, there are ethically minded employers. They usually feel isolated and alone in the larger dog-eat-dog environment. The goal of the Restaurant Industry Roundtable is to bring these good folks together and allow them to share their best practices. The Roundtable demonstrates that another model is not only possible, but also profitable. Additionally, Roundtable restaurant owners will visit legislators side-by-side with workers to advocate for legislation the local ROC policy committee has chosen to work on.

ROC Restaurant Industry Roundtables have developed a code of conduct that dictates what the basic standards and working conditions ought to be in the restaurant industry. In order to be a member of a roundtable, a restaurant must comply with this code, and in return, ROC promotes that restaurant in an ethical-eating consumer guide, and on its website and in print materials.

This model is not just for the restaurant industry but for the entire food chain. What happens in the restaurant industry affects not only workers, but also everyone who eats.

Workers in the food movement

Meanwhile, there is another question that has seldom been asked: How does food affect workers? Food does not magically appear in Whole Foods or on the plate of your favorite slow-food restaurant. There is a trajectory from farm to fork that involves workers at every step. From seed to harvest, shipping, warehousing, butchering, or processing—from preparing to serving in a restaurant, or stocking and selling at the local grocery store—workers do it all for us, the consumers. Workers are a fundamental part of the food chain. And workers and consumers are not in separate, isolated silos. Workers are consumers and vice versa. From production to consumption, the working class is the driving engine of the global food system.

Just as we did in the 1930s, we can once again create a new middle class—one that is engaged, conscious, and aware of the food it eats. The only way we can do this is by bringing workers wholly into the food justice movement and ensuring the movement remains class conscious, allowing for critiques that go beyond our food to include the workers who make it. Food shaped my political understanding of the world and my family's place in this struggle. My hope is that food will create a world that does not require any more sacrifices from my family, or anyone else's.

SAKUMA BERRY FARMWORKERS ORGANIZE

Since their first walkout on July 10, 2013, berry pickers on Sakuma Brothers Farms in Burlington, Washington, have struck several times in protest of their sub-minimum wages, racial discrimination, poor living conditions, and workplace intimidation. In the face of these egregious labor violations, workers have remained steadfast in their ongoing fight to improve their conditions, and they have formed their own organization called "Families United for Justice" (*Familias Unidas por la Justicia*, FUJ).

It's a labor dispute, not a "cultural misunderstanding"

by Rosalinda Guillen and Leah Scrivener, 2013[i]

Specializing in berries, the Sakuma Brothers Farms sell a large portion of their crop to the Häagen-Dazs ice cream company. General Mills owns Häagen-Dazs, and Nestlé USA controls Häagen-Dazs's distribution in the United States. Both Nestlé USA's "Supplier Code" and General Mills' "Supplier Code of Conduct" outline strict standards on labor and require that their suppliers

- compensate their workers with pay and benefits that comply with applicable minimum wage and overtime requirements;

- provide workers with a safe, clean, and healthy work environment, "and where provided, safe housing conditions…maintained in accordance with the standards set by applicable codes and ordinances";

- shall not discriminate or harass their employees.

Both companies also state that they have the right to terminate contracts with any suppliers who do not comply with the labor code. Häagen-Dazs has contacted Sakuma Brothers Farms to ask for an explanation for the ongoing strikes and protests.

FUJ claims that Sakuma Brothers Farms has blatantly violated these standards. In addition to complaints of racist and sexist treatment at the hands of Sakuma Brothers Farms' labor contractors, workers believe that Sakuma Brothers Farms has systematically withheld wages over the years. Furthermore, they claim that supervisors have routinely threatened them into working through their rest breaks. Finally, the workers' cabins and bathrooms are over-crowded, filthy, and in disrepair.

In response to the work stoppages and outside pressure from the media and Skagit County residents, Sakuma's owners are participating in ongoing negotiations with FUJ, but have taken a hardline attitude, hiring high-powered corporate labor attorneys, consultants, communications

---

i   Food First, August 15, 2013, http://foodfirst.org/its-a-labor-dispute-not-a-cultural-misunderstanding/.

specialists, and security guards. In an attempt to sway public opinion (and avoid the legal implications of a formal strike), Sakuma Brothers frames the issue not as a labor dispute, but as a "cultural misunderstanding" due to "miscommunication."

As one of the workers put it: "I don't know what country you're from, but there's no way to misunderstand when you can't work for minimum wage, when your mattresses are so dirty and covered with bugs that you can't sleep, and when your boss calls you a stupid donkey."

It's clear that Sakuma would like to portray this as a "cultural misunderstanding" because the moment that they call it a "labor dispute," the US Department of Labor can get involved and cancel their request for H-2A guest workers. Sakuma Brothers Farms was expecting a crew of H-2A workers to arrive in early August, but the Department of Labor has put a temporary hold on their request, presumably because the current so-called "cultural misunderstanding" on Sakuma Brothers Farms looks suspiciously like a labor dispute.

The majority of the workers are indigenous Triqui and Mixteco people from Oaxaca, Mexico. Most of them are poor migrant workers who travel all over California during the wintertime, doing fieldwork wherever they can find it. Some of the families have been returning to Sakuma Brothers Farms for the past 13 years, and some of the families come from the same towns in Mexico, so their general familiarity and shared cultures have built the foundation for the powerful organizing that they have been able to do over the past five weeks.

The strikers, along with the support of local community protestors and favorable media coverage, have earned several important accomplishments. The work of FUJ has unified all of the

Farmworkers picking strawberries

workers at Sakuma Brothers Farms in their belief that they have rights and will fight for them.

In addition, as a result of the workers' pressure, on July 10, Sakuma Brothers Farms employers immediately agreed to rehire Federico Lopez (a farm worker who had initiated the first walk-out and was then fired to set an example). Recently, Sakuma Brothers Farms employers agreed to include the worker committee in management's process of determining the price per pound of berries picked. Additionally, Sakuma management agreed to transfer an abusive supervisor out of the work crew, and replaced him with a more reasonable one. And finally, they repurposed and cleaned some of the workers' cabins and bathrooms.

Despite these accomplishments, workers fear that they will not be permanent, since they have not been formalized in writing. The workers want to see concrete standards set in place to define their wages, their rights, and their protection from retaliation. But so far, negotiations have been moving along slowly, and Sakuma Brothers Farms' attorneys and ownership have been dragging their heels and have shown reluctance to make permanent changes.

FUJ believes that consumer pressure will likely be needed to influence the company to support workers' demands. They are urging supporters to make phone calls to Sakuma Brothers Farms, to Nestlé, and to General Mills to urge them to respect their labor codes of conduct.

Sakuma workers protest exploitative guest worker initiative

by Carly Finkle, 2013[ii]

Low wages and poor working conditions at Sakuma Brothers Farms in Washington State prompted over 200 seasonal farmworkers to go on a series of strikes earlier this summer, starting July 10th. They returned to work on July 26th after a series of negotiations, believing that the managers would continue to negotiate in good faith, but then resumed their strike when the company did not follow their agreements. The arrival of 170 H-2A guest workers contracted by Sakuma Brothers Farms is clearly an attempt to undermine the Sakuma farmworkers' bargaining power, displace local labor, and ultimately, depress wages.[1] The Sakuma farmworkers' demands reflect the need for drastic policy changes in labor and immigration law that extend far beyond the fields of Sakuma Brothers Farms.

The Senate has proposed plans to massively expand the national H-2A guest worker program in their immigration reform bill that Congress will debate this month. If passed, the program would funnel underpaid and exploited workers into agricultural jobs at the expense of workers' rights.

Seasonal farmworkers constitute a very marginalized workforce, in part due to their exemption from many basic labor protections. Further, over half of the 2 million farmworkers in the United States are undocumented immigrants, and the fear of deportation combined with the short length of seasonal employment often prevents migrant workers from reporting employer abuses and organizing collectively. State law in Washington state exempts all seasonal hand-harvest laborers who are paid on a piece-rate basis from minimum wage regulations.[2] Federal laws gov-

---

ii   Food First, September 4, 2013, http://foodfirst.org/sakuma-farms-workers-protest-exploitative-guest-worker-initiative/.

erning overtime pay, rights to collective bargaining, employer provision of healthcare, and many safety standards also exclude farmworkers.[3] The denial of these standard labor protections— afforded to almost all "unskilled" workers—further exploits an already vulnerable workforce.

In most markets, labor shortages force employers to improve wages and working conditions to attract workers. However, a study by Farmworker Justice shows that the presence of government-subsidized guest workers places downward pressure on an industry's wages and working conditions.[4] The H-2A wage in Washington State currently guarantees guest workers and all employees doing comparable work a wage of $12 per hour.[5] Under immigration reform, the guest worker wage for berry pickers would be set nationally at only $9.64, dramatically driving down wages for domestic farmworkers as well.[6] This will, of course, only aggravate the "labor shortage" problem.

The constant short-term entry of foreign employees also undermines a workforce's ability to bargain collectively.[7] Workers at Sakuma Brothers Farms fear that this is the management's primary motivation for applying for H-2A visas.[8] The Department of Labor temporarily suspended their approval of Sakuma Brothers Farms' application for guest workers in July due to the ongoing strike, but lifted the suspension when the workers agreed to return to the fields during negotiations, mistakenly assuming it signified an end to the labor dispute.[9] Guest workers often obstruct labor organizing because their contracts are tied to a single employer. Many are unable to speak out against abuses for fear of losing their jobs and being immediately deported.[10]

To be effective, immigration policies must be accompanied by comprehensive labor reforms to improve the protections, wages, and conditions of farmworkers. However, the current and proposed H-2A guest worker programs incentivize employers to keep wages and working conditions too low to attract local labor. This perceived labor shortage allows employers to apply for underpaid H-2A guest workers who are unable to organize and are unlikely to report abuses.[11] Workers at Sakuma farms insist that there would be no labor shortage if berry pickers were offered increased wages and decent working and living conditions.[12]

The first step toward solving the perceived labor shortage in the agricultural industry should not be to outsource labor through the guest worker program, but to increase domestic demand by paying fair wages and treating workers with the respect they deserve. In industries where labor shortages continue to exist, international workers issued H-2A visas should not be tied to a single employer, and workers must be granted more labor protections, including the right to organize.[13] The Sakuma farmworkers' struggle for respect, living wages, and fair working conditions must be taken up at a national level through immigration and labor reforms in order to address the inequalities that remain deeply entrenched in the US agricultural labor market.

NOTES

1   Shanna Sheridan, "Relations Sour Again Between Berry Farm and Workers," 790 KGMI, August 20, 2013, http://kgmi.com/local/relations-sour-again-between-berry-farm-and-workers; David Bacon, "Stand-off in the Strawberry Fields," Al Jazeera America, August 19, 2013, http://america.aljazeera.com/articles/2013/8/19/stand-off-in-thestrawberryfields.html.

2   "Wages for Agricultural Jobs," Washington State Department of Labor & Industries.,accessed August 1, 2013. http://www.lni.wa.gov/WorkplaceRights/Agriculture/Wages/default.asp.

3   "Health Care Reform Implications for Employers with Seasonal Employees," USI Affinity, September 29, 2010.

4   "No Way to Treat a Guest: Why the H-2A Agricultural Visa Program Fails U.S. and Foreign Workers," Farmworker Justice, accessed August 19, 2013, http://www.farmworkerjustice.org/sites/default/files/documents/7.2.a.6%20No%20Way%20To%20Treat%20A%20Guest%20H-2A%20Report.pdf.

5   Lornet Turnbull and Anna Boiko-Weyrauch, "Striking Farmworkers Afraid of Guest-Worker Program," *The Seattle Times*, July 25, 2013, http://seattletimes.com/html/localnews/2021456869_migrant-workersxml.html.

6   *Ibid.*

7   "Close to Slavery: Guestworker Programs in the United States," Southern Poverty Law Center, February 20, 2013, http://www.splcenter.org/get-informed/publications/close-to-slavery-guestworker-programs-in-the-united-states.

8   *Ibid.*

9   "Community to Community Development," Facebook, August 15, 2013, https://www.facebook.com/Community2Community.

10 *Ibid.*

11 *Ibid.*

12 *Ibid.*

13 "Immigration Policy Principles for Food Sovereignty," US Food Sovereignty Alliance, accessed August 13, 2013, http://usfoodsovereigntyalliance.org/immigration-policy-principles-for-food-sovereignty.

8. LAND GRABS, LAND REFORM, AND LAND JUSTICE

THE MST AND GRASSROOTS LAND REFORM IN BRAZIL

Angus Wright and Wendy Wolford, 2003[i]

Forty years ago, everyone in Brazil but the rich and the generals knew that Brazil needed an agrarian reform. It was the only thing that would bring this country around to use its land rationally, economically... We threw that chance away and went through years of dictatorship instead. What if Brazil had had its reform starting then? What kind of a country would we have been able to construct! Instead, we have all this violence, this waste. Now it is time. We shouldn't waste another forty years.

—Small businessman, Northern Brazil

Since the late 1970s, more than 1 million people in Brazil have transformed their lives. They have done so by organizing peaceful protests that have forced the Brazilian government to redistribute approximately 20 million acres of agricultural land to 350,000 families and to assist them further in creating new livelihoods. These people have vastly improved the quality of education and healthcare available to their families, achieving these gains by successfully challenging the institutions and some of the most powerful people of Brazil, a nation of 175 million people and one of the world's ten largest economies.

The social function of land

Although members of Brazil's Landless Workers Movement (*Movimemo dos Trabalbadores Rurais Sem-Terra*, MST) have often had to confront police, military troops, and the court system to gain land, the MST strategy of land occupations does not usually break the law but instead is based on forcing the government to comply with the law.

Brazil has for nearly five centuries been plagued by a radically unequal distribution of land. Wealthy landholders ruled the countryside with impunity, grabbing land through means fair means and foul, intimidating and even murdering those who stood in the way of their dominance of the land. They held sway over state legislatures and courts, and there were few who could challenge them. They were encouraged by their dominance and impunity to use the land wastefully, retarding the development of the economy and trapping millions of Brazilians in poverty. To combat this problem, successive Brazilian national governments beginning in the 19th century asserted the idea (which also had roots in the colonial legal tradition) that land, in order

---

i   Adapted from Angus Wright and Wendy Wolford, "Now It Is Time: The MST and Grassroots Land Reform in Brazil," Food First Backgrounder, Vol. 9, No. 2, Spring 2003.

to be legally claimed by an owner, had to "serve its social function." Brazilian governments repeatedly promised to make this concept meaningful by redistributing land to the poor, but the power of landholding families and their domestic and foreign allies has kept the governments from fulfilling their promises.

In the late 1970s, landless rural people realized that they might be able to achieve reform by occupying land and demanding that the government apply the "social function" principle. They were also often able to successfully challenge the titles held by wealthy landowners because so many of the titles were based on fraud. The key was organization. Land occupations needed to be carried out by enough people—usually several hundred or more—and enlist enough community support that the government and large landholders could not displace them except through embarrassingly large and politically costly jailings or massacres.

Catholic priests inspired by liberation theology (a movement within the Church emphasizing social justice) and lay political activists helped the landless organize these occupations. Once proven successful, occupations began to break out throughout Brazil, and by 1984, the landless were able to create a national organization, the MST. Significant agrarian reform had begun for the first time in Brazilian history.

The encampments

It is not easy to organize or maintain successful land occupations. The greatest motivator is the desperation of the rural poor, pressed to the wall by ongoing inequalities that continue to throw them off the land—inequalities exacerbated by the aggressive development of capital-intensive agricultural operations. MST organizers must identify enough people in an area ready to

MST assembly in Brasilia, 2007 (Photo by Wilson Dias/ABr)

take on the difficulties of an occupation. They must also keep a constant eye out for land that is held under terms that can be legally contested. When the landless first move onto a piece of land, they are usually thrown off it one or more times by gunmen employed by landowners or by police forces under landowner control. The landless set up camps on the land itself or nearby with shelters made of large sheets of black plastic—whatever materials may come to hand. They plant any ground available—often just small gardens—and usually must rely on support from the MST state and national offices, other settlements, labor unions, church groups, and sympathetic political organizations. It is difficult to maintain the morale of the families in the camps in the face of hunger, disease, and demoralizing delay.

It is essential to stay put until a court and/or the government's agrarian reform ministry makes a decision to grant land, a process that typically takes two to four years. In the meantime, landlords or police may attack the encampment repeatedly, abusing, beating, and imprisoning people. Several hundred MST leaders have been assassinated in these struggles. Even more rural leaders not affiliated with the MST have been murdered, as they do not enjoy the support and protection the MST affords. In spite of the problems, however, the people's deep hunger for land and the organizational skill of the MST have made it possible for people in thousands of encampments to succeed in getting land.

Making agrarian reform work

People in agrarian reform settlements say again and again that "the land is only a first step." They mean this in three ways. First, it is not easy for small farmers in Brazil (or anywhere) to succeed against government and corporate policies that favor large operations. Second, agrarian reform does not in itself solve many of the social and economic problems that rural poor people face. Third, the MST and most of its members see themselves as a revolutionary force leading the transformation of Brazil into a more just and prosperous nation.

Agrarian reform settlers carry into their communities most of the ingrained problems of their society as a whole: sexism, racism, and the tendency to rely on hierarchical, paternalistic, and personality-based relationships. The difference in MST settlements is that the organization and a large share of the settlers are deeply committed to fighting these old problems. The organization was founded in part on the educational ideas of Paulo Freire, who insisted that the awakening of critical consciousness and a sense of social responsibility are the foundations of learning and positive change. Settlers engage in formal and informal discussion of the problems and establish rules and understandings meant to create a more egalitarian society, both for Brazil and for each settlement. The MST trains thousands of elementary and secondary teachers and community organizers to help carry the vision of social equality forward.

Settlers must also struggle to make their landholdings productive and sustainable. The MST has trained hundreds of its own agronomists and technical advisors, and it pressures the government to provide more. The organization demands, with occasional and partial success, adequate production credit. They work with other family farmers to try to transform government policy favoring export and large-scale agriculture into policy that would favor feeding Brazilians and supporting small-scale agriculture.

In its earliest years, the MST was influenced by the idea that "modern," chemical-intensive agriculture was the most viable. Now, the organization has been educated by experience to see that the most successful small-scale farms are those that produce a diverse range of products for local markets and that conserve and enhance the productive quality of the land. The MST has adopted this sustainable model (agroecology) as its goal for all MST settlers, though both the organization and the settlers themselves recognize that most settlements are far from realizing this vision. Some settlements, however, have already become successful models of organic and agroecological production.

The MST has also played a significant role in redefining the debate over the fate of the Brazilian Amazon, insisting from the very beginning that agrarian reform on existing agricultural land is the solution for Brazil's rural poor, and that expansion of the frontier into forested land is not. Within the Amazon itself, the MST endeavors to stabilize agricultural settlements through the practice of agroecological and agroforestry models that end or reduce the need for settlers to clear new ground.

Now it is time

The million people—men, women, and children—who are members of the MST have faced down police, the military, and gangs of hired gunmen, suffering imprisonment, beatings, and sometimes death. Instead of waiting for the government to meet its longstanding promises to redistribute land, members of the MST have occupied land claimed by others, continuing the occupations until the government has met their immediate needs for land. And they continue to do so: at this writing more than 80,000 MST families who have not yet benefited from land distributions are occupying land in the continuing battle to make agrarian reform an enduring reality in Brazil. In addition, approximately 200,000 families who are not members of the MST have also received land in the agrarian reform sparked by the MST.

GRABBING POWER: THE NEW LAND STRUGGLES IN NORTHERN HONDURAS

Tanya M. Kerssen, 2013[i]

Compared to most Latin American countries, there are few English-language books about Honduras written for a popular audience. Even after the June 2009 coup that ousted president Manuel Zelaya and the massive popular movement that followed, Honduras languished in mainstream media obscurity, overshadowed by celebratory coverage of the Arab Spring. When the media did report on Honduras (or Central America in general), it generally portrayed the region as a hopeless "basket case" beset by gangs, crime, and a tragically unwinnable War on Drugs. These portrayals tell us little about the structural (political and economic) causes of poverty and violence. Nor do they show us how fiercely Hondurans are fighting to take back control of their local economies, protect their families from violence, and build democracy from the ground up.

While Honduran cities are growing rapidly, marked by highly precarious working and living conditions, the majority (74 percent) of the poor are *rural*: they are peasants (*campesinos*), landless workers, and indigenous and Afro-indigenous peoples.[1] As throughout Latin America, both rural and urban poverty are closely linked to the unequal distribution of land—with enormous landholdings (known as *latifundios*) on one hand and smallholdings (*minifundios*) on the other. In Honduras, approximately 70 percent of the farmers hold 10 percent of the land in minifundios while 1 percent of the farmers hold 25 percent of the land in massive estates.[2]

Over the last three decades, the poverty generated by Honduras's unequal land distribution has been magnified by climate change, rising food prices, and land grabs for corporate agribusiness and tourism development. While deepening both urban and rural vulnerability, these events also sparked new forms of grassroots organizing and political consciousness. Honduras is not a hopeless basket case. It is, like many countries and communities around the world, a place where hunger, poverty, and violence are rooted in a lack of genuine democracy—and not, as some would have it, a lack of foreign aid or economic growth. And that is precisely what Honduran peasant movements are fighting for: the democratization of land, food, and political power.

Situating Honduras in the global land grab

In the wake of the 2007–2008 global food, fuel, and financial crises, observers have called attention to a growing trend in large-scale farmland investments, particularly in poor countries of the Global South. While reliable figures are hard to come by, estimates range from around 56.6 million to 227 million hectares of grabbed land globally.[3] These land grabs erode local control, often reorienting production from meeting local needs to meeting global market demands for

---

i   Adapted from Tanya M. Kerssen, *Grabbing Power: The new struggles for land, food and democracy in Northern Honduras* (Oakland, CA: Food First Books, 2013).

food, feed, and fuel. The impact on land-based livelihoods—those of peasants and indigenous peoples whose survival hinges directly on access to land and nature—has been deeply devastating. The term "land grab" has now become a media buzzword, a catchall phrase for the new global wave of peasant dispossession.

New players have been identified (e.g. financial companies, pension funds, sovereign wealth funds) as the buyers of huge tracts of land. Compared to previous instances of land grabbing by colonial powers or agribusiness firms, these investors tend to be much more interested in the financial value of land (and of the resources on, under, or near it) than the value of its production. Pension funds, for instance—which have quickly become one of the largest institutional investors in land—"see long-term pay-offs from the rising value of farmland and the cash flow that will in the meantime come from crop sales, dairy herds or meat production."[4] The speculative nature of land acquisitions by a new set of global actors—in the context of the food, fuel, and financial crisis—is a defining feature of the new land grabs.[5]

As Borras et al. point out, however, prevailing approaches to the land grabbing question have tended to highlight certain regions and dimensions to the neglect of others. For instance, studies generally focus on the role of *foreign* companies and *foreign* governments (primarily China, India, South Korea, and the Gulf States) in the global land rush. This approach tends to miss or marginalize land grabs carried out by domestic and intra-regional capital, as well as the role of local elites and the state itself.[6] Analyses also tend to focus on "mega" deals, measured in terms of *numbers of hectares* grabbed, generally defining a land grab as an acquisition (lease or purchase) greater than 1,000 hectares.[7] In a recent presentation, GRAIN identifies land grabs as acquisitions of 10,000 hectares or more.[8]

From the point of view of rural people facing eviction and loss of livelihood, it matters little whether the deals in question are for 10,000 hectares or ten. The experience of displacement— whether gradual or sudden, small or large—is one of physical and structural violence, and the end result is community fragmentation and even cultural obliteration. As the agrarian scholar Samir Amin puts it, "We have reached a point at which, in order to open up a new area for capital expansion, it is necessary to destroy entire societies."[9]

Along with an emphasis on foreign-led mega-deals, the prevailing approach to land grabs has been Africa-centric. With cases like Ethiopia, where over 1 million hectares of Anuak indigenous lands have been leased to foreign investors (primarily Indian and Saudi), this regional focus clearly is not unwarranted.[10] But in looking at Latin America, where a different set of dynamics appears to be at work, there is evidence that land grabbing is occurring "to an extent wider than previously assumed."[11] The case of the Aguán Valley in northern Honduras, for instance, has been identified in a number of media articles and reports[12] as an emblematic case of land grabbing. And yet, it fits poorly within the model of land grabs outlined above for a number of reasons.

First, the main instance of land grabbing in the Aguán occurred nearly two decades ago, between 1990 and 1994, before the recent food, fuel, and financial crises that are widely viewed as triggering the new rush on land. Neoliberal land legislation in 1992 facilitated the process, reversing earlier agrarian reforms and unleashing new investment dynamics that were highly unfavorable to peasant farmers. In a short period, a few wealthy investors seized more than 21,000 hectares (over 70 percent) of peasant lands in the Lower Aguán Valley.

Second, while this would seem to meet the condition of a large-scale land grab, it was not a single transaction, but rather hundreds of small deals, in some cases for less than three hectares. Cumulatively, this flurry of land deals generated widespread peasant dispossession, and concentrated some of the country's best farmland and water resources into a few hands.

Third, the primary actors in the case of the Aguán were not foreign investment firms or transnational agribusiness, but Honduran elites. The biggest investor was Honduran businessman Miguel Facussé Barjum—known as the "richest man in Honduras"—who now controls most of the valley for corporate palm oil production. As part of the "ten families" (as they are commonly known) who now control the country's wealth, Facussé amassed his fortunes with the help of economic policies that liberalized trade and investments—first in manufacturing, and then in agriculture. These policies led to the consolidation of a globally oriented agroindustrial bourgeoisie.

This reconfiguration of class power set the stage for a new, intensified phase of agroindustrial expansion beginning in 2009. This phase began with the most all-encompassing and arguably the crudest "grab" of all: the grabbing of state power. The coup that overthrew president Manual Zelaya on June 28, 2009, can be read as the expression of a class process set into motion by neoliberal restructuring. The "new" land grabs in Honduras, then, look more like a deepening and intensification of a process already well underway. Put another way, the grabbing of state power is, at least in part, the *political consequence* of an earlier wave of land grabs.[ii] Thus, following the work of economic geographer David Harvey, I argue that neoliberal policies in Honduras should be viewed as a "political project to re-establish the conditions for capital accumulation and to restore the power of economic elites."[13]

Seen in this light, the Honduran case might help us to understand the potential future ramifications of current land grabbing elsewhere.

Neoliberalism and class power

Throughout the 20th century, Honduras was known as the quintessential "banana republic," dominated by US agribusiness (e.g. United Fruit) and US military and geopolitical objectives. As historian Walter LaFeber puts it:

> North American power had become so encompassing that US military forces and United Fruit could struggle against each other to see who was to control the Honduran government, then have the argument settled by the US Department of State.[14]

US capital thus dominated Honduran politics at the time, as well as the most fertile soils and

---

ii This was the case in Paraguay, for example, where the concentration of land for export soy production appears to have consolidated elite power leading up to the June 22, 2012, overthrow (dubbed a "constitutional" or "parliamentary" coup) of president Fernando Lugo (see Benjamin Dangl, "A Coup Over Land: The Resource War Behind Paraguay's Crisis," *Upside Down World*, July 16, 2012, accessed August 2012, http://upsidedownworld.org/main/paraguay-archives-44/3758-a-coup-over-land-the-resource-war-behind-paraguays-crisis).

the most lucrative export markets. Comparatively, the Honduran landed elite—which derived its power primarily from enormous ranches and cotton plantations in the south and west of the country—had much less influence. They were, in fact, "the economically poorest and politically weakest rural oligarchy in Central America."[15]

As Honduran historian Darío Euraque points out, however, the dominance of US capital in the North did not mean the complete absence of Honduran elites. After World War II, an incipient homegrown bourgeoisie, composed largely of Arab Palestinian immigrants, developed around the northern city of San Pedro Sula, in the heart of the banana-growing Sula Valley.[16] The ethnic composition of this elite class—with Arab surnames like Kattán, Canahuati, Facussé, Násser, Kafati, and Larach—was the result of government policies in the early 20th century that promoted foreign immigration as a means to social, cultural, and economic progress.[17] With the Ottoman Empire in decline, many Palestinian Arabs immigrated to Central America, concentrating in Honduras. While the government hoped these newcomers would develop agriculture, first generation Palestinian immigrants (who intended eventually to return home) rejected the government's land grants and instead gravitated towards commerce, quickly establishing themselves as a powerful merchant class and eventually investing in industry. By the late 1950s, wealthy Palestinian families—often referred to as "Turks" (*los turcos*)—already controlled 75 percent of investments in the import-export sector and about 50 percent of investments in manufacturing.[18]

This "emerging new class of wealth," however, tended to be excluded from political activity partly by their own choice and partly as a result of the unwelcoming attitudes of native Hondurans.[19] Structural adjustment policies of the 1990s, however, sparked a massive transfer of state resources to the Honduran private sector, granting north coast-based elites unprecedented access to global markets, investment capital, and political power. They expanded their power primarily through two boom sectors of the neoliberal period: manufacturing (*maquilas*) located in over a dozen Export Processing Zones (EPZs) and palm oil based in the Lower Aguán River Valley. A third elite-controlled sector, coastal tourism, flourished in the late 1990s as part of the effort to restructure northern Honduras along investment-friendly lines.

In addition, US-backed militarization in Central America, increasing sharply during the counterinsurgency wars of the 1980s, promoted elite interests by repressing labor unions and peasants associated with the "communist threat." Honduran business and military interests became increasingly intertwined—with one another and with the US—in the 1980s. The anticommunist Association for the Progress of Honduras (APROH) was founded in 1983, with membership comprising all of the country's major businessmen, to promote deregulation, trade liberalization, and a military approach to suppressing popular resistance movements.[20] Notably, APROH's president was General Gustavo Álvarez Martínez—commander of the armed forces, linked to widespread political assassinations and torture—and its vice-president was businessman Miguel Facussé.

Since the 2009 coup, Honduras has become increasingly militarized. The human rights organization Committee for Relatives of the Detained and Disappeared in Honduras (COFADEH) identifies the current trend as a powerful resurgence of APROH-style authoritarianism: a blend of right-wing extremism, neoliberalism and militarism.[21] US military aid, ramped up in the name of the War on Drugs, has added fuel to the fire. Efforts have targeted the northern coast and the northeast Moskitia region, areas identified as a "strategic drug trafficking corridor." But the north is also a major area of agribusiness, manufacturing, and commercial tourism expansion. US-assisted militarization—combined with the private security forces of large landowners—has been tantamount to an all-out war on peasants, facilitating the expansion of these elite-controlled sectors.

The agroindustrial oligarchy is heavily oriented towards the United States—for trade, investment, and cultural cues for looking and acting like a global business elite[iii]—and supportive of the US political and economic agenda in Central America. Correspondingly, the US has been instrumental in the *making* of these elites through bilateral and multilateral aid (USAID, IDB) and the policy prescriptions of Washington-based financial institutions (World Bank, IMF). A key moment for the consolidation of the neoliberal model promoted by these institutions was also Hurricane Mitch in 1998. Post-Mitch crisis conditions provided cover for fast-tracking the neoliberal development agenda—focused on the maquila, agroindustry, and tourism sectors—newly branded as a plan for "reconstruction."[22]

Global market mechanisms, such as those generated by the new "green capitalism," also play a part. Markets for "green" commodities such as crop-based fuel (agrofuels) and carbon credits not only encourage "new" land grabbing, but also add value to *previously* grabbed lands and a sheen of environmental legitimacy. The carbon credits allotted to Miguel Facussé for the greening of palm oil processing, for example, reinforces his ownership claim on highly contested lands in the Aguán.[iv] Thus, to say that the 2009 coup and expansion of agroindustrial capital are the result of a class process is by no means to dismiss the role of US/Northern imperialism or global capital. Indeed, these forces tend to transform or reinforce local class dynamics in important and historically specific ways.

Grabbing power (back)

The land grabs of the 1990s generated a powerful counter-movement for the recovery of peasant lands in the Aguán Valley. Dozens of peasant organizations emerged, such as the Peasant Movement of Aguán (MCA), formed in 1999, followed by the Unified Movement of Aguán Peasants (MUCA) in 2001. In most cases, the movements began by pursuing legal strategies—filing requests for the nullification of purchase agreements and demanding investigations of fraudulent deals. When politically influential landowners repeatedly obstructed these approaches, the movements began occupying the oil palm plantations claimed by Facussé and other large landowners. What emerged over a decade of organizing in the Aguán is a mass "grab land back" movement.[23]

---

iii Like many Latin American business and governing elites (often educated at US institutions like MIT or Texas A&M), Honduran elites see Miami as their preferred social and cultural hub. This was illustrated by US ambassador to Honduras Charles Ford (2008-2009) in a recent WikiLeaks cable in which he mocks ousted president Manuel Zelaya, saying, "Zelaya's view of a trip to the 'big city' means Tegucigalpa and not Miami or New Orleans." (Reported by anthropologist Adrienne Pine on her blog Quotha.net: "Wikileaks 08TEGUCIGALPA459: Ambassador Charles Ford on Zelaya" December 10, 2010, accessed August 2012, http://quotha.net/node/1432.)

iv It also raises the value of those lands, making their progressive redistribution *with compensation at market value* (as opposed to politically difficult forced expropriation) increasingly unaffordable for peasants and state agencies alike (at least without taking on tremendous debt burdens).

This movement made headway under the Zelaya administration (2006–2009), which found itself in an increasingly tense predicament. On one hand was the powerful agro-oligarchy, jealously protecting its newly acquired power and access to foreign investment. On the other hand were 375,000 landless Honduran families, an increasingly militant peasant movement, and steeply rising food prices.[24] Faced with these conditions, Zelaya chose to make concessions to social movements, raising the monthly minimum wage and enacting agrarian reform legislation. These policies were met with a growing hostility that foreshadowed the 2009 coup.

Pro-peasant legislation passed by Zelaya was overturned after the coup while the militarization of the countryside further reinforced the power of the agro-oligarchy. US military and development aid quickly resumed, and by November 2010, post-coup president Porfirio "Pepe" Lobo Sosa was able to sign agreements with the IMF, IDB, and World Bank for $322.5 million to restore the country's economic stability and promote economic growth.[25] The Aguán suffered immediate and relentless state-sponsored repression. Between September 2009 and August 2012, there have been 53 recorded cases of peasant murders in the context of the Aguán agrarian conflict—with many more injuries, kidnappings, illegal detentions, forced evictions, and cases of torture and sexual assault[26]. Many Aguán peasants and activists now place the death toll at over 60.[27]

Paradoxically, the coup inspired a far-reaching political "awakening," as Hondurans often call it. Students, teachers, trade unions, human rights organizations, indigenous peoples, peasants, feminists, LGBT communities, artists, and faith-based groups were galvanized by the coup and the repression that followed, coming together as the National Front of Resistance Against the Coup (now the National Front of Popular Resistance, or FNRP). In the Aguán Valley, struggles for agrarian reform—a project long tied to the good will of the state—turned into a much more radical struggle to transform state power.

NOTES

1   USAID, "Country Profile: Property Rights and Resource Governance: Honduras," April 2011, accessed July 2012, http://www.usaidlandtenure.net/country-profiles/honduras.

2   *Ibid.*

3   Lorenzo Cotula, "The International Political Economy of the Global Land Rush: A critical appraisal of trends, scale, geography and drivers," *The Journal of Peasant Studies* 39 (2012): 649-680.

4   GRAIN, "Pension Funds: Key payers in the global farmland grab," June 29, 2011, accessed July 2012, http://farmlandgrab.org/post/view/18864.

5   Philip McMichael, "Global development and the corporate food regime," (paper presented at the Symposium on New Directions in the Sociology of Global Development, XI World Congress of Rural Sociology, 2012).

6   Saturnino M. Borras, Jennifer C. Franco, Sergio Gómez, Cristóbal Kay, and Max Spoor, "Land Grabbing in Latin America and the Caribbean," *The Journal of Peasant Studies* 39 (2012): 857.

7   Borras et al., "Land Grabbing in Latin America and the Caribbean," *op. cit.*, 850.

8   GRAIN, "Land Grabbing and the Global Food Crisis" Slideshare presentation, December 2011, accessed July 2012, http://www.grain.org/article/entries/4164-land-grabbing-and-the-global-food-crisis-presentation.

9   Samir Amin, "Food Sovereignty: A Struggle for Convergence in Diversity," in *Food Movements Unite!* ed. Eric Holt-Giménez (Oakland, CA: Food First Books, 2011), xiii.

10   GRAIN, "Land grabs threaten Anuak," April 13, 2010, accessed July 2011, http://www.grain.org/article/entries/4064-land-grabs-threaten-anuak; GRAIN, "GRAIN releases data set with over 400 land grabs," February 23, 2012, accessed July 2012, http://www.grain.org/article/entries/4479-grain-releases-data-set-with-over-400-global-land-grabs.

11   Borras et al., "Land Grabbing in Latin America and the Caribbean," *op. cit.*, 846.

12   Juan-Carlos Arita, "A Life with Dignity: Honduran women raising voices to improve living standards," in *Speaking Out Programme Insights* (Oxford, GB: Oxfam, 2008); DanChurchAid, "Stolen Land Stolen Future: A report on land grabbing in Cambodia and Honduras" (Copenhagen, Denmark, 2011).

13   David Harvey, *A Brief History of Neoliberalism* (Oxford University Press, 2005), 19.

14   Walter LaFeber, *Inevitable Revolutions: The Untied States in Central America* (New York: W.W. Norton, 1984), 62.

15   Mark Ruhl, "Agrarian Structure and Political Stability in Honduras," *Journal of Interamerican Studies and World Affairs* 26 (1984): 37.

16   Darío A. Euraque, *Reinterpreting the Banana Republic: Region & State in Honduras, 1870–1972* (Chapel Hill and London: University of North Carolina Press, 1996).

17   Nancie González. *Dollar, Dove and Eagle: One hundred years of Palestinian migration to Honduras,* (Ann Arbor: University of Michigan Press, 1992); Manzar Foroohar, "Palestinians in Central America: From temporary emigrants to a permanent diaspora," *Journal of Palestine Studies* 11 (2011): 6–22.

18   Foroohar, "Palestinians in Central America: From temporary emigrants to a permanent diaspora."

19   Euraque, *Reinterpreting the Banana Republic: Region & State in Honduras, 1870–1972, op. cit.*, 35.

20   "Honduras: Militarized and Denationalized," *Revista Envio* 35, May 1984, accessed August 2012, www.envio.org.ni/ariculo/3914.

21   James Rodríguez "La Historia se Repite: Comite de Familiares de Detenidos-Desaparecidos de Honduras," MiMundo, February 7, 2010, accessed August 2012, http://www.mimundo-fotorreportajes.org/2010/02/la-historia-se-repite-comite-de.html.

22   Jeff Boyer and Aaron Pell, "Mitch in Honduras: A Disaster Waiting to Happen," NACLA, Vol. XXXIII, No. 2 (September/October), 1999; Paul Jeffrey, "Rhetoric and Reconstruction in Post-Mitch Honduras," *NACLA Report on the Americas*, Vol. XXXIII, No. 2 (September/October), 1999; Naomi Klein, "The Rise of Disaster Capitalism," *The Nation*, April 14, 2005; Susan Stonich, "International Tourism and Disaster Capitalism: The Case of Hurricane Mitch in Honduras," *Capitalizing On Catastrophe: Neoliberal Strategies in Disaster Reconstruction*, eds. Nandini Gunewardena and Mark Schuller (Lanham, MD: Altamira Press, 2008), 47–68.

23   This phrase is borrowed from Ben White, Saturnino M. Borras Jr., Ruth Hall, Ian Scoones, and Wendy Wolford, "The New Enclosures: Critical perspectives on corporate land deals," *The Journal of Peasant Studies* 39 (2012): 635.

24   Vía Campesina et al., "Ley de Transformación Agraria Integral," October 11, 2011, accessed June 2012, http://www.vamosalgrano.org/images/generales/descargas/generales/leyagraria.pdf.

25   Peter J. Meyer, "Honduran-U.S. Relations," CRS Report for Congress, April 25, 2011.

26   FIAN, "International Organisations condemn repression and criminalization of peasant organisations of the Bajo Aguán, Honduras," FIAN International, August 30, 2012, accessed October 2012, http://www.fian.org/news/news/international-organisations-of-the-bajo-augan-honduras; FIDH, "Honduras: Human Rights Violations in Bajo Aguán," Federación Internacional de Derechos Humanos, Report No. 572a. September 2011, accessed April 2012, http://www.fidh.org/IMG/pdf/honduras573ang.pdf; IACHR, "IACHR Condemns Murder of Human Rights Defenders in Honduras," Press Release, September 28, 2012, accessed October 2012, http://oas.org/en/iachr/media_enter/Preleases/2012/12.asp.

27   Annie Bird, "Repression is the 'Negotiation Strategy,'" Rights Action, March 2, 2012, accessed March 2012, http://www.rightsaction.org/action-content/repression-negotiation-strategy-rudy-hernandez-illegally-detained-aguan-human-rights.

FARMLAND MEETS FINANCE: IS LAND THE NEW ECONOMIC BUBBLE?

Madeleine Fairbairn, 2014[i]

At the turn of the 21st century, farmland was still considered an investment backwater by most of the financial sector. Although some insurance companies have had farmland holdings for years, most financial investors found farmland, and agricultural investment in general, unappealing compared to the much higher returns to be made in financial markets. However, this began to shift around 2007 as the prices of agricultural commodities started to climb and land prices followed suit. The recession that began with the bursting of the US housing bubble in 2008 caused investor interest to suffer a momentary dip but also added fuel to the fire, as investors sought alternative, and more secure, places to put their money.

Private investors are flocking to farmland both for the returns it delivers and for the role that farmland can play in an investment portfolio. The sudden enthusiasm for farmland as a portfolio investment is contributing to both the large "land grabs" taking place in developing countries and to roaring land prices in countries with more developed land markets.[1] In the US, skyrocketing land prices have raised concerns about a possible land price bubble.[2]

Farmland is drawing investment from "high net worth individuals" as well as institutional investors such as pension funds, hedge funds, university endowments, private foundations, and sovereign wealth funds. Celebrity investors like George Soros are investing in farmland,[3] and agricultural investment conferences—which provide opportunities for fund managers and farmland operators to network with investors—have exploded in popularity. Asset management companies, which act as investment intermediaries, have responded to this sudden investor interest by creating a lavish buffet of new farmland funds.[4] Despite this rapid growth, the extent of capital markets' interest in farmland is still relatively minor; estimates of total institutional investment in farmland range between $30 and $40 billion globally.[5] However, it is undeniable that since 2007, global farmland real estate has undergone a makeover to become a desirable alternative investment.

The financialization of farmland: "like gold with yield"

"Financialization" is a catchall term for the growing power and prominence of finance since the 1970s. One aspect of this trend is "the tendency for profitmaking in the economy to occur increasingly through financial channels rather than through productive activities."[6] Essentially,

i   Adapted from Madeline Fairbairn, "Farmland Meets Finance: Is Land the New Economic Bubble?" Land & Sovereignty in the Americas Series, No. 5 (Oakland, CA: Food First/Institute for Food and Development Policy and Transnational Institute, 2014).

investors are making more money by lending or investing their capital and waiting for it to grow by itself and less by using that capital to produce and sell commodities. The case of farmland is interesting because the distinction between "productive" and "financial" sources of profit is not always easy to discern.

Land plays two different economic roles: it is an essential means of production, but it also acts as a reserve of value and creates wealth through appreciation. In other words, it is a productive asset that moonlights as a financial asset. Though farmland's financial qualities have always held some appeal to speculators, the financialization of the global economy since the 1970s opened up new possibilities for the incorporation of farmland into financial circuits. The current wave of farmland investment combines a renewed interest in productive, real assets with an underlying logic of financialization.

In the 1970s and 80s, researchers began to notice that investors were increasingly drawn to land for its financial qualities. David Harvey argued that investors were treating land as "ficti-tious capital" that brought in a stream of income just like their other investments in stocks or bonds.[7] Massey and Catalano found that financial investors were buying British farmland and leasing it out to tenant farmers, motivated by the rental income and potential for property value appreciation.[8] They contrasted this behavior with that of farmers, who valued farmland for its productive qualities. They raised concerns that these investors were inflating land prices and outbidding "owner-occupier" farmers. Because they treat land as fictitious capital, their deci-sion to keep or sell it is influenced not just by the agricultural value of the land but also by the wider financial environment, such as inflation and interest rates.

Today, many investors are drawn to farmland because of what it can do for them financially. Farmland's desirability is perhaps best illustrated by the frequent comparisons between farm-land and gold. Like gold, farmland is limited in quantity, appreciates over time, and provides a refuge for anxious investors during economic downturns. Unlike gold, however, farmland is also a means of production, a fact that sometimes gets lost. In media and investment publications, farmland is frequently referred to as "black gold"[9] or "like gold with yield."[10] At one investment conference, a South American agricultural fund manager took this analogy even further, arguing that if Brazilian and Argentine cropland is like gold, then Chilean vineyards are like diamonds, emeralds, and rubies. Such expressions are telling because they imply that farmland's primary appeal is its ability to store and even increase in value, while the fact that it also comes "with yield" from agricultural production is just the icing on the cake.

Due to land's dual nature as a productive and a financial asset, it is possible to use the land productively while simultaneously speculating on financial returns from its appreciation. Con-trary to simplistic portrayals of recent large-scale farmland acquisitions (or land grabs) as *either* productive *or* speculative, this dual nature demonstrates that they can be, and frequently are, both at the same time.

Potential impacts of the financialization of land

Separation of ownership and control

While investors can provide farmers with much needed financing, they also transfer ownership away from the person farming the land. Aside from the obvious impact this has on the social structure of agriculture, it also reduces the farmer's incentive to use sustainable practices by removing his or her stake in future productivity.

Land concentration and reduced access to land

Some of the ways that investors "add value" to farmland before reselling could also reduce access to land for smallholders. Many companies see consolidation of small properties as an integral part of their strategy of land transformation. Their reasoning is that larger plots will be more attractive to agribusinesses and other buyers. In addition, some companies add value by clarifying legal title where it was previously murky. In many parts of the Global South, an ironclad property title will come at the expense of local residents whose legally flimsy claim lies only in years or generations rooted in that place.

Unsustainable, short-term thinking

There is also a danger of importing the short-term thinking of finance into land markets. The idea of entering into land ownership with an "exit strategy" in place—as private equity fund managers often do—would thoroughly confound most of the world's farmers, for whom hanging on to their land is a primary objective. For most financial investors, however, seven or ten years is a long-term commitment. Although many private equity fund managers argue that their short tenure as landowner will involve soil quality or other property improvements as a means to increase profit on resale, it seems equally likely that such a short-term view could lead to careless treatment of soil and water resources.

Rising land prices

Some investors, including many pension funds, do plan to hold on to their farmland properties for many years to come. However, this type of investment could also contribute to changing land market dynamics. Global pension funds alone manage over $30 trillion in assets.[11] If all allocated just 1 percent of their portfolios to farmland investments, there would be $300 billion of pension money competing in global land markets. This amount of capital could raise land prices, putting it out of reach of small farmers.

Conclusion

We may be seeing the emergence of a new type of financialization for an era of growing resource scarcity—one in which farmland's role as a quasi-financial asset will be even more prominent. As McMichael observes, the restructuring of the corporate food regime involves the opening of new investment opportunities for capital with the result that "the so-called rational planning of planetary resources such as land (and water) is driven as much by financial goals as by material considerations."[12] Increasing financial interest in farmland may prove to be a passing phenomenon. The farmland bubble, if indeed one exists, may soon burst or simply deflate. If, however, powerful institutional investors and financial companies continue to embrace farmland as a financial asset, it could have lasting effects on landownership and farming worldwide.

NOTES

1   Knight Frank, "How the land lies: review of the international farmland market," *The Wealth Report*, 2011, accessed May 22, 2012, http://www.knightfrank.com/wealthreport/2011/international-farmland-market.

2   Charles Abbott, "U.S. farmland boom may carry long-term risk: FDIC." *Reuters*, March 10, 2011, accessed March 22, 2012, http://www.reuters.com/article/2011/03/10/us-fdic-farmland idUSTRE72968T2011C310.

3   Brian O'Keefe, "Betting the farm," *Fortune Magazine*, June 16, 2009; Towers Watson, "Global Pension Assets Study 2013." Towers Watson, January 31, 2013, accessed December 31, 2013, http://www.towerswatson.com/en/Insights/IC-Types/Survey-Research-Results/2013/01/Global-Pensions-Asset-Study-2013.

4   Abbi Buxton, Mark Campanale, and Lorenzo Cotula, "Farms and funds: investment funds in the global land rush," IIED Briefing, January 2012, accessed May 15, 2014, http://pubs.iied.org/pdfs/17121IIED.pdf.

5   Bradley Wheaton and William J. Kiernan, "Farmland: an untapped asset class? Quantifying the opportunity to invest in agriculture," *Food for Thought* (Sydney, AU: Macquarie Agricultural Funds Management, December 2012), accessed July 24, 2013, http://www.macquarie.com/dafiles/Internet/mgl/com/agriculture/docs/food-for-thought/food-for-thought-dec2012-anz.pdf.

6   Greta R. Krippner, *Capitalizing on Crisis: The Political Origins of the Rise of Finance* (Cambridge, MA: Harvard University Press, 2011), 4.

7   David Harvey, *The Limits to Capital* (Oxford: Blackwell. 1982).

8   Doreen Massey and Alejandrina Catalano, *Capital and Land: Landownership by Capital in Great Britain* (London: Edward Arnold, 1978).

9   Robert Cole, "The new black gold: U.S. farmland," *The Globe and Mail*, March 22, 2012.

10 Peter Koven, "ETF may stand for exchange-traded farmland," *Financial Post*, January 19, 2012; Massey and Catalano, *Capital and Land: Landownership by Capital in Great Britain, op. cit.*

11 "Global Pensions Asset Study 2013," Towers Watson, January 31, 2013, http://www.towerswatson.com/en/Insights/IC-Types/Survey-Research-Results/2013/01/Global-Pensions-Asset-Study-2013.

12 Philip McMichael, "The land grab and corporate food regime restructuring," *The Journal of Peasant Studies* 39 (2012): 686.

9. CLIMATE JUSTICE VS. CORPORATE PSEUDO-SOLUTIONS

FOOD SOVEREIGNTY AND CLIMATE JUSTICE

Brian Tokar, 2011[i]

In the summer of 2010, nearly 20 million residents of Pakistan's Indus River valley—a fifth of the country's population—were forced to flee their homes and fields as the most severe monsoon rains in nearly a century buried much of the region under water. Now, areas of Nigeria and Cameroon are facing a different kind of deluge—a human wave of climate migrants, forced to flee their homes in the vicinity of Lake Chad, which has lost 90 percent of its area in recent decades due to a relentless long-term drought.[1] Farmers in the once Fertile Crescent of Syria and Iraq—the center of origin for wheat and barley, and perhaps agriculture as we know it—are similarly fighting a losing battle against an ever-encroaching desert.[2]

Most climate scientists will correctly point out that local phenomena and particular weather events cannot be linked unambiguously to the growing destabilization of the earth's climate systems. At the same time, long-term trends have convinced many that climate changes are happening much faster than even the best analytical models once predicted. After less than one degree Celsius of global warming, people around the world are experiencing increasingly chaotic weather patterns, including extreme heat waves and unprecedented cycles of flooding and drought. Barring an extraordinarily rapid change in our energy use and economic systems, the world will undoubtedly see several additional degrees of warming before the end of this century, with catastrophic consequences for many vulnerable people and ecosystems.

It is clear that some people will be far more affected than others, and that indigenous peoples and subsistence farmers in the tropics and subtropics are already experiencing the most serious consequences of an unfolding global climate crisis. This profound inequity in the impacts of climate changes, and the need for a thoroughgoing social transformation in order to alleviate it, are the primary insights of an emerging global movement known as "climate justice." Climate justice advocates believe that the unfolding global climate crisis demands an unprecedented convergence of social movements.

The concept of climate justice reflects somewhat different origins and emphases in various parts of the world. The term was first articulated by Indigenous Environmental Network founder and director Tom Goldtooth in the mid-1990s, was further defined in a 1999 Corpwatch report,[3] and formed the basis for a resolution passed at the second National People of Color Environmental Leadership Summit in the US in 2002. The concept gained international attention following a meeting in Durban, South Africa, in the fall of 2004, that included representatives of social movements and indigenous peoples' organizations based in Brazil, India, Samoa, the US, the UK, and South Africa. That gathering crystallized around the drafting of the first comprehensive international declaration to challenge the emerging global carbon market, which is viewed

i   Adapted from Brian Tokar, "Food Sovereignty and Climate Justice," in *Food Movements Unite! Strategies to Transform Our Food Systems*, ed. Eric Holt-Giménez, (Oakland, CA: Food First Books, 2011), 275–287.

by climate justice activists as a corporate-driven attempt to commodify the atmosphere and perpetuate and rationalize, rather than curtail, the expansion of fossil fuel use.[4] Carbon markets have failed to reduce emissions while offering new indirect subsidies to polluting industries, and thus are increasingly viewed as a false solution to the global climate crisis.[5]

In the United States, the demand for climate justice is voiced most articulately by environmental justice activists, mainly from communities of color that have been resisting daily exposure to chemical toxins and other environmental hazards for the past 30 years or more. At an important 2009 conference organized by West Harlem Environmental Action (WE ACT) in New York City, speakers described the emerging climate justice movement as a continuation of the civil rights legacy, and of the continuing "quest for fairness, equity, and justice," as described by the pioneering environmental justice researcher and author, Robert Bullard.[6]

Food and climate: a "two-way street"

While climate disruptions are already having profound effects on those who grow our food, the practices of industrial agriculture are largely responsible for altering the climate. The International Assessment of Agricultural Knowledge, Science and Technology for Development (IAASTD), a collaborative effort by four UN agencies and the World Bank, affirmed in a 2009 report that "the relationship between climate change and agriculture is a two-way street; agriculture contributes to climate change in several major ways and climate change in general adversely affects agriculture."[7] The IAASTD report acknowledged several well-known consequences of climate changes for agriculture, especially the increasingly disruptive effects on water cycles, and highlighted sustainable agricultural practices as a primary mitigation strategy. The report was widely acclaimed for its acknowledgment that traditional and local agricultural knowledge is central to the attainment of worldwide sustainability and development goals.[8] As several recent studies have noted, peasants and other smallholders contribute far more to the world's agricultural output than is widely acknowledged, and small farms are generally far more productive relative to their size than larger, industrial-scale farms.[9]

Estimates of the current food system's contribution to global emissions of greenhouse gases vary widely, from ten to 20 percent at the low end, up to nearly 60 percent.[10] One anomalous but widely reported study suggests that livestock alone may be responsible for 51 percent of global emissions.[11] This range of estimates is the result of widely varying assumptions about key factors such as animal nutrition and waste handling, land and soil management practices, the impacts of the processing and transportation of food, and agriculture's contribution to global deforestation. These practices vary widely, of course, with the scale and cultivation methods of farms of various sizes. The calculations are also complicated by the fact that greenhouse gases such as methane and nitrous oxide (N_2O) have far greater climate-forcing potential than carbon dioxide in the short term, by factors of 25 and 300, respectively, but do not remain in the atmosphere for nearly as long as CO_2 does.

In the United States, the leading contributors are N_2O—produced when soil bacteria digest chemical-fertilizer residues—and methane released by ruminants, along with the CO_2 directly released from fossil fuel consumption.[12] These three factors represent more than 80 percent of

US agriculture's total emissions, and are highly sensitive to changes in livestock feed, manure management, fertilizer use, and the use of farm machinery.

Researchers who support the widespread adoption of organic agricultural methods—which often mirror traditional peasant practices while bringing current scientific knowledge into their application—suggest that organic methods help reduce agriculture's climate impacts in numerous ways. These include increasing soil's ability to sequester carbon by increasing its organic matter, reducing excess nitrogen from chemical fertilizers, eliminating energy-intensive pesticide production, composting instead of burning crop residues, and feeding ruminants less grain and more grass, among other practices.[13] The need to expand the use of these methods is reinforced by the widespread effects of current and predicted climate changes on growing food.

The comprehensive review of current climate science compiled in 2007 by the Intergovernmental Panel on Climate Change (IPCC) addressed several longer-term trends. In the second volume of their report, the IPCC confirmed that climate-induced disruptions of the global hydrological cycle will bring increased flooding and droughts, most notably in the major river deltas of Asia and Africa. Glacial melting will continue to affect the water supplies of one-sixth of the global population that depends on runoff from glaciers to provide much of its fresh water.[14] The data reviewed by the IPCC points toward a worldwide decrease in crop productivity if global temperatures rise more than three degrees Celsius, although crop yields from rain-fed agriculture could be reduced by half as soon as 2020. In Africa alone, between 75 million and 250 million people will be exposed to "increased water stress."[15]

Overall, the study confirms that those populations with "high exposure, high sensitivity and/or low adaptive capacity" will bear the greatest burdens, and that those that contribute the least to the problem of global warming will continue to face the most severe consequences.[16] These findings affirm the urgency of embedding a justice-centered framework into global efforts to alleviate the impacts of climate change. Politically, this has become an essential counterpoint to the prevailing, rather narrow, climate policy focus on the reliability of climate models and quantitative projections of future CO_2 concentrations.

Converging movements

La Vía Campesina's increasingly potent interventions into the UN's climate policy process help illuminate the central role of activist farmers from the Global South in the development of a worldwide climate justice movement. How can food and farm activists in the Global North also play a more active role in supporting and strengthening this emerging movement?

An impressive variety of local and regional efforts throughout the US and other developed countries promote local food, facilitate direct purchases from farmers, and further the goal of community-based food security. Many of these activities, however, take place in the background of a fashionable localism that is often skewed toward affluent consumers. These middle- and upper-class individuals often embrace local food as part of a high-consumption "green" lifestyle that at best offers only a pale challenge to destructive patterns of conspicuous consumption.

Visionary activists, farmers, and organizers around the world, however, are reaching far beyond the fashions of "green consumerism" and introducing models of solidarity and mutual aid that resonate well with the message of climate justice. For example, neighborhood activists in Hartford, Connecticut, brought an assertive community-organizing model into efforts to alleviate hunger and developed a comprehensive urban food system. They brought community gardens and farmers' markets into inner-city neighborhoods and developed active working relationships between publicly funded nutrition programs and nearby farms.[17] Organizations in many other US cities and towns have developed their own innovative approaches to bringing more fresh and locally grown food to those most in need. New York City now boasts more than 50 farmers' markets, serving neighborhoods at every socioeconomic level, as well as over 30 urban farms and an equal number of public food pantries and soup kitchens that regularly use fresh produce grown in and around the city.[18] In the decaying industrial city of Holyoke, Massachusetts, a large urban farm known as Nuestras Raices ("Our Roots") offers substantial farm plots to aspiring urban farmers and helps recent immigrants identify varieties of culturally important crops that are adaptable to the short New England growing season.[19] Programs in a variety of cities offer subsidized farm-share subscriptions to low-income residents, often combined with environmental education and job training for neighborhood residents.[20] In a more rural setting, a network of nonprofit "food hubs" throughout the state of Vermont is actively linking farmers with local food shelves, hospitals, senior meals programs, and other institutions that once relied exclusively on imported, highly processed foods.

It remains to be seen whether efforts such as these can make a decisive difference in the wider struggles for food sovereignty and climate justice. Recent research suggests that how our food is grown and processed may have far greater climate impacts than how far it travels.[21] Regionalizing produce, reducing meat consumption (particularly from factory farms), and eating more seasonally can have a greater impact than broadly focusing on the geographic origins of our food. Mega-greenhouses in northern climates that aim to keep tomatoes on our plates all winter are clearly not the solution, and curtailing long-distance transportation of staple grains may not be wise either, especially in the short term. However, the development of local food systems that help sustain farmers committed to sustainable agriculture within their regions still ranks among the most immediately practical strategies to enhance both food justice and climate justice. More resilient local and regional food systems contribute to climate mitigation by reducing fossil fuel use, and also help communities cope with future climate instabilities by fending off potential disruptions of long-distance supply chains due to rising energy costs.

Local food systems can also help challenge agribusiness dominance and, ultimately, the climate consequences of agribusiness practices, but only if they move far beyond niche marketing to a selective clientele, toward creating a genuine alternative that serves much larger numbers of people. While more affluent "locavore" activists often shy away from politics, a higher level of political engagement is essential if this movement is to begin realizing its potential. Indeed, many people have come to see local food as part of a broader transition away from dependence on fossil fuels and toward a more fully realized economic self-reliance on both local and regional levels.

In his book, *The Green Collar Economy*, Van Jones[22] recounts an interview with Brahm Ahmadi, executive director of the People's Grocery in Oakland, California, which has also developed community gardens and a two-acre farm. "Food is our medium for achieving broader outcomes in community development and public health and addressing disparities in opportunities and quality of life," Ahmadi explains. He continues:

> We chose food as our tool because it's intimate and universal, regardless of the differences in culture or personal preferences... From there we connect the dots to the structural and systemic issues of the food system: considering the global environmental footprint of food production, how far food travels, and equity issues related to farmworkers and the struggles of small farmers... connecting those to the struggles of low-income consumers.[23]

With the failure of United Nations climate negotiators in Copenhagen and Cancún to reach an international agreement to reduce emissions of carbon dioxide and other greenhouse gases,[24] climate activists are also struggling with the question of what is achievable at the local and regional level. Cities, towns, and entire US states are pioneering important initiatives to reduce energy use and relieve dependence on fossil fuels,[25] even as advocates for climate justice and food sovereignty are arguing for broader systemic changes.

While many food and agriculture activists understand the need to challenge the power of megacorporations in the global food system, systemic change is perhaps even more central to efforts to forestall climate catastrophe. Curtailing the excessive emissions that are threatening to overheat the entire planet requires fundamental changes in almost every area of human activity, including entrenched patterns of energy and land use, the design of our cities and towns, and everyday habits of work and leisure. The survival of threatened ecosystems, and perhaps of complex forms of life on this planet, may now require a pace of technological, political, and economic transformation well beyond anything we have yet experienced.

Ultimately, both food sovereignty and climate justice require greater solidarity and more committed alliance building with people around the world than many in the Global North are accustomed to. Increasingly catastrophic climate disruptions, which now mainly impact people in the tropics and subtropics, are beginning to be felt throughout the world. More than ever, our ability to continue to thrive as humans depends on radically transforming our social and economic systems. The reality is too urgent, and the outlook far too bleak, to settle for anything less. Perhaps more than ever before, we are compelled to realize our vision of a dramatically different kind of world.

NOTES

1   Elias N. Ngalame, "Immigration surging in Cameroon as farmers and fishermen desert shrinking Lake Chad," Thomas Reuters Foundation, October 5, 2010, accessed June 8, 2011, http://www.trust.org/alertnet/news/immigration-surging-n-cameroon-as-farmers-and-fishermen-desert-shrinking-lake-chad.

2   Robert F. Worth, "Searching for Crumbs in Syria's Breadbasket," *New York Times,* October 13, 2010.

3   Kenny Bruno, Joshua Karliner, and China Brotsky, "Greenhouse Gangsters vs. Climate Justice," CorpWatch, November 1, 1999, http://www.corpwatch.org/article.php?id=1048.

4   "Climate Justice Now! A call for people's action against climate change," Durban Group. 2004, unpublished.

5   Brian Tokar, *Toward Climate Justice: Perspectives on the Climate Crisis and Social Change* (Porsgrunn, Norway: Communalism Press, 2010); Larry Lohmann, "Carbon Trading: A Critical Conversation on Climate Change, Privatization and Power," *Development Dialogue* no. 48 (Uppsala: Dag Hammerskjold Center, 2006).

6   Robert Bullard, "Advancing Climate Justice: Transforming the Economy, Public Health and Our Environment" (presentation at The 20th Anniversary National Climate Justice Conference, New York, NY, January 29, 2009).

7   Beverly D. McIntyre, Hans R. Herren, Judi Wakhungu, and Robert T. Watson, *Agriculture at a Crossroads: The International Assessment of Agricultural Knowledge, Science and Technology for Development, Synthesis Report: A Synthesis of the Global and Sub-Global IAASTD Reports, Secretariat* (Washington, DC: Island Press, 2009), 8.

8   McIntyre et al., *Agriculture at a Crossroads, op. cit.,* 11.

9   "Who Will Feed Us? Questions about the food and climate crisis," ETC Group, November 1, 2009, http://www.etcgroup org/content/who-will-feed-us; Peter Rosset, "Fixing Our Global Food System: Food Sovereignty and Redistributive Land Reform," in *Agriculture and Food: Crisis, Resistance and Renewal*, ed. Fred Magdoff and Brian Tokar (New York: Monthly Review Books, 2010).

10   Jennifer Wightman, "Production and Mitigation of Greenhouse Gases in Agriuclture," Cornell University Agriucltural Ecosystems Program Team, 2006, accessed October 25, 2010, heep://www.climate-andfarming.org/pdfs/FactSheets/IV.1GHGs.pdf.; Henry Saragih, "Why We Left Our Farms to Come to Copenhagen," (presented at Klimaforum 09, Copenhagen, Denmark, December 7, 2009).

11   Robert Goodland and Jeff Anhang, "Livestock and Climate Change," *World Watch Magazine,* November/December 2009.

12   Keith Paustian et al., "Agriculture's Role in Greenhouse Gas Mitigation," Pew Center on Global Climate Change, 2006,.

13   Adrian Muller and Joan S. Davis, *Reducing Global Warming: The Potential of Organic Agriculture* (Emmaus, PA: Rodale nstitute, 2009).

14   IPCC (Intergovernmental Panel on Climate Change), 'Contribution of Working Group II to the Fourth Assessment Report of the Intergovernmental Panel on Climate Change: Summary for Policymakers," 2007, accessed October 1, 2007, http://ipcc.ch., 11.

15   IPCC, "Contribution of Working Group II to the Fourth Assessment Report of the Intergovernmental Panel on Climate Change," *op. cit.,* 13.

16   *Ibid.*

17   Mark Winne, *Closing the Food Gap: Resetting the Table in the Land of Plenty* (Boston: Beacon Press, 2008).

18   Grow NYC, "Our Markets," 2010, accessed November 1, 2010, http://www.grownyc.org/ourmarkets.; Just Food, 2010, accessed November 1, 2010, http://justfood.org/about-us.

19   Robert Gottlieb and Anupama Joshi, *Food Justice* (Cambridge: MIT Press, 2010), 123–126.

20   Elizabeth Henderson and R. Van Eyn, *Sharing the Harvest: A Guide to Community Supported Agriculture* (White River Junction, VT: Chelsea Green, 1999), 204–205.

21   Christopher L. Weber and H.S. Matthews, "Food-Miles and the Relative Climate Impacts of Food Choices in the United States," *Environmental Science and Technology* 42 (2008): 3508–3513.

22   Van Jones, *The Green Collar Economy: How One Solution Can Fix Our Two Biggest Problems* (New York: HarperCollins, 2008).

23   Van Jones, *The Green Collar Economy, op. cit.*, 130–31.

24   Brian Tokar, *Toward Climate Justice, op. cit.;* Martin Khor, "Complex Implications of the Cancun Climate Conferences," *Economic & Political Weekly* 45 (2010): 10–15.

25   Tommy Linstroth and Ryan Bell, *Local Action: The New Paradigm in Climate Change Policy* (Burlington, VT: University of Vermont Press, 2007).

FIVE MYTHS OF THE AGROFUELS TRANSITION

Eric Holt-Giménez, 2007[i]

Biofuels invoke an image of renewable abundance that allows industry, politicians, the World Bank, the UN, and even the Intergovernmental Panel on Climate Change to present fuel from corn, sugarcane, soy, anc other crops as a smooth transition from peak oil to a renewable fuel economy. Myths of abundance divert attention away from powerful economic interests that benefit from this biofuels transition, avoiding discussion of the growing price that citizens of the Global South are beginning to pay to maintain the consumptive oil-based lifestyle of the North. Biofuels mania obscures the profound consequences of the industrial transformation of our food and fuel systems—the agrofuels transition.

The agrofuels boom

Industrialized countries have unleashed an "agrofuels boom" by mandating ambitious renewable fuel targets. Renewable fuels are to provide 5.75 percent of Europe's transport fuel by 2010, and 10 percent by 2020. The US goal is 35 billion gallons a year. These targets far exceed the agricultural capacities of the industrial North. Europe would need to plant 70 percent of its farmland to fuel. The US's entire corn and soy harvest would need to be processed as ethanol and biodiesel. Northern countries expect the Global South to meet their fuel needs, and Southern governments appear eager to oblige. In Brazil—where fuel crops already occupy an area the size of Netherlands, Belgium, Luxembourg, and Great Britain combined—the government is planning a five-fold increase in sugarcane acreage with a goal of replacing 10 percent of the world's gasoline by 2025.

Agrofuel champions assure us that because fuel crops are renewable, they are environmentally friendly, can reduce global warming, and will foster rural development. But the tremendous market power of agrofuel corporations, coupled with weak political will of governments to regulate their activities, is a recipe for environmental disaster and increasing hunger in the Global South. It's time to examine the myths fueling this agrofuel boom—before it's too late.

Myth no. 1: agrofuels are clean and green

Because photosynthesis from fuel crops removes greenhouse gases from the atmosphere and can reduce fossil fuel consumption, we are told fuel crops are green. But when the full "life cycle" of agrofuels is considered—from land clearing to automotive consumption—the moderate emission savings are undone by far greater emissions from deforestation, burning, peat

---

i   Adapted from Eric Holt-Giménez, "Biofuels: Myths of the Agrofuels Transition," Food First Backgrounder, Vol. 13, No. 2, Summer 2007.

drainage, cultivation, and soil carbon losses. Every ton of palm oil produced results in 33 tons of carbon dioxide emissions—ten times more than petroleum.[1] Tropical forests cleared for sugarcane ethanol emit 50 percent more greenhouse gasses than the production and use of the same amount of gasoline.[2]

Industrial agrofuels also require large applications of petroleum-based fertilizers, whose global use—now at 45 million tons/year—has more than doubled the biologically available nitrogen in the world, contributing heavily to the emission of nitrous oxide, a greenhouse gas 300 times more potent than CO_2. In the tropics—where most of the world's agrofuels will soon be grown—chemical fertilizer has ten to 100 times the impact on global warming compared to temperate soil applications. Producing a liter of ethanol requires three to five liters of irrigation water and produces up to 13 liters of wastewater. It takes the energy equivalent of 113 liters of natural gas to treat this waste, increasing the likelihood that it will simply be released into the environment to pollute streams, rivers, and groundwater. Intensive cultivation of fuel crops also leads to high rates of erosion, particularly in soy production—from 6.5 tons/hectare in the US to up to 12 tons/hectare in Brazil and Argentina.

Myth no. 2: agrofuels will not result in deforestation

Proponents of agrofuels argue that fuel crops planted on ecologically degraded lands will improve, rather than destroy, the environment. Perhaps the government of Brazil had this in mind when it reclassified some 200 million hectares of dry tropical forests, grassland, and marshes as "degraded" and apt for cultivation.[3] In reality, these are the biodiverse ecosystems of the Mata

Palm oil plantation (Photo by Tanya Kerssen)

Atlantica, the Cerrado, and the Pantanal, occupied by indigenous people, subsistence farmers, and extensive cattle ranches. The introduction of agrofuel plantations will simply push these communities to the "agricultural frontier" of the Amazon where deforestation will intensify.

Myth no. 3: agrofuels will bring rural development

In the tropics, 100 hectares dedicated to family farming generate 35 jobs. Oil palm and sugarcane provide ten jobs, eucalyptus two, and soybeans just one half job per 100 hectares, all poorly paid. Until this boom, agrofuels primarily supplied local markets, and even in the US, most ethanol plants were small and farmer-owned. Big Oil, Big Grain, and Big Genetic engineering are rapidly consolidating control over the entire agrofuel value chain. The market power of these corporations is staggering: Cargill and ADM control 65 percent of the global grain trade, Monsanto and Syngenta a quarter of the $60 billion gene-tech industry. This market power allows these companies to extract profits from the most lucrative and low-risk segments of the value chain—selling inputs, processing, and distributing. Agrofuels growers will be increasingly dependent on this global oligopoly of companies. Farmers are not likely to receive many benefits.[4] Smallholders will likely be forced off the land. Hundreds of thousands have already been displaced by the soybean plantations in an area over 50 million hectares, covering southern Brazil, northern Argentina, Paraguay, and eastern Bolivia.[5]

Myth no. 4: agrofuels will not cause hunger

The world's poorest people already spend 50–80 percent of their total household income on food. They suffer when high fuel prices push up food prices. Now, because food and fuel crops are competing for land and resources, high food prices may actually push up fuel prices. Both increase the price of land and water. This perverse, inflationary spiral puts food and productive resources out of reach for the poor. The International Food Policy Research Institute has estimated that the price of basic food staples will increase 20–33 percent by the year 2010 and 26–135 percent by the year 2020. Caloric consumption typically declines as price rises by a ratio of 1:2. With every one percent rise in the cost of food, 16 million people are made food insecure. If current trends continue, some 1.2 billion people could be chronically hungry by 2025—600 million more than previously predicted.[6] World food aid will not likely come to the rescue because surpluses will go into our gas tanks. What is urgently needed are massive transfers of food-producing resources to the rural poor—not converting land to fuel production.

Myth no. 5: better "second generation" agrofuels are just around the corner

Proponents of agrofuels argue that present-day agrofuels made from food crops will soon be replaced with environmentally friendly crops like fast-growing trees and grasses. This myth, wryly referred to as the "bait and switchgrass" shel game, makes food-based fuels socially acceptable. The agrofuel transition transforms land use on a massive scale, pitting food production against fuel production for land, water, and resources. The issue of which crops are converted to fuel is irrelevant. Wild plants cultivated as fuel crops won't have a smaller "environmental footprint." They will rapidly migrate from hedgerows and woodlots onto arable lands to be intensively cultivated like any other industrial crop, with all the associated environmental externalities.

Cellulosic ethanol, a product that has yet to demonstrate any carbon savings, is unlikely to replace agrofuel within the next five to eight years—in time to avoid the worst impacts of global warming. Major breakthroughs in plant physiology that permit the economically efficient breakdown of cellulose, hemi-cellulose, and lignin are required. Industry is either betting on miracles or counting on taxpayer bailouts. Faith in science is not science. Selective faith in unproven and possibly unattainable second-generation biofuel—rather than working to improve existing solar, wind, or conservation technologies—is a bias in favor of agrofuel corporations.

Building food and fuel sovereignty

Food sovereignty movements are already squaring off with the agrofuels boom. When US president George Bush arrived in Brazil to establish an ethanol partnership with President Lula, 700 women from La Vía Campesina protested by occupying Cargill's sugar mill in São Paulo. But derailing the agrofuels juggernaut entails changing the agrofuels transition from an agrarian transition that favors industry to one that favors rural communities—a transition that does not drain wealth from the countryside, but that puts resources in the hands of rural peoples. This is a far-reaching project. A good next step would be a global moratorium on the expansion of agrofuels. Time and public debate is needed to assess the potential impacts of agro-fuels, and to develop the regulatory structures, programs, and incentives for conservation and food and fuel development alternatives. We need the time to forge a better transition—an agrarian transition for both food and fuel sovereignty.

NOTES

1   Delft Hydraulics, as cited in George Monbiot, "If we want to save the planet, we need a five-year freeze on biofuels," *The Guardian*, March 27, 2007.

2   David Tilman and Jason Hill, "Corn Can't Solve Our Problem," *Washington Post*, March 25, 2007.

3   Plano Nacional de Agroenergia 2006-2011, in Camila Moreno, "Agroenergia X Soberania Alimentar: a Questão Agrária do século XXI," 2006.

4   Annie Dufey, "International trade in biofuels: Good for development? And good for environment?" International Institute for Environment and Development, 2006.

5   Elizabeth Bravo, "Biocombustibles, cutlivos energeticos y soberania alimentaria: encendiendo el debate sobre biocommustibles." *Acción Ecológica*, 2006.

6   C. Ford Runge and Benjamin Senauer, "How Biofuels Could Starve the Poor," *Foreign Affairs*, May/June 2007.

AGROFUELS: A TROJAN HORSE FOR BIOTECHNOLOGY

Annie Shattuck, 2009[i]

Biotechnology is poised to strike at our agricultural system on a scale never before imagined. Consumers, farmers' organizations, social movements, and environmental advocates all fiercely oppose biotechnology in agriculture, while the industry has continued to expand its presence in the developing world, often through undemocratic means. But resistance, and effectively all public debate on biotech, may well be put to rest for good by the world's growing dependence on agrofuels. The sunny glow of alternative fuels helps lend biotech the public credibility it has lacked since its market debut. While new traits for agrofuels are already helping corporations amass unprecedented market power, a pipeline of new fuel crops stands waiting in the wings. Agrofuels are the perfect Trojan horse, promising not only whole new markets for biotech products, but also the irreversible entrenchment of genetically modified crops throughout the world.

The birth of an oligopoly

How did we get here? A brief look at the history of consolidation in the biotech industry paints a disturbing picture of what is to come. Riding the waves of the Green Revolution in the 1960s and '70s, large agricultural chemical corporations that formerly specialized in chemical weapons began buying up small seed companies to complement their nascent agricultural chemicals businesses. In the 1980s, when agricultural biotechnology was being developed, these companies were the first to jump on board. Over the last decade, the hybrid seed-chemical-biotechnology industry (from here on biotech) became consolidated. In 1998, the top ten seed companies controlled 30 percent of the global market. Now, only two companies control that same market share.[1] This latest round of consolidation was fueled by biotechnology. Genetic modification (GM) has been used to vertically integrate market power, allowing the same companies that sell seed to also sell the herbicides and other inputs these GM crops require.

The pattern of technological development in GM is to develop traits that increase dependence of farmers on the biotech industry. The first and most widely planted products are the "Roundup Ready" or herbicide-tolerant products—crop species like corn, soy, and cotton that are resistant to the herbicide glyphosate. Monsanto, Syngenta, and DuPont all sell glyphosate-resistant seeds as well as the herbicide itself, often in a package. This technology has not only dramatically boosted the sales of glyphosate, but it has become so widespread as to undercut farmers' use of nonchemical alternatives and integrated weed management systems, fostering farmers' dependence on both the patented seed and the herbicide.[2] The much-discussed "terminator

i   Adapted from Annie Shattuck, "The Agrofuels Trojan Horse: Biotechnology and the Corporate Domination of Agriculture," in *Agrofuels in the Americas*, ed. Richard Jonasse (Oakland, CA: Food First Books, 2009), 139–154.

gene," another early biotech trait, would have served to ensure farmers' dependence on licensed products by physically preventing farmers from saving seed, had the technology gained regulatory approval (the industry is still pushing for this). Even Bt corn, a variety that produces a natural pesticide in the stem of corn plants, increases the share of the seed market subject to strong-arm patent laws and licensing fees, while eroding the effectiveness of Bt as part of a more holistic integrated pest management system.[3] The economic function of these foreign genetic traits is not to decrease chemical use, but to increase market dominance and control over the agro-input industry by the corporations holding the patents.

Integrating agrochemical sales with patented seed has worked extremely well for big biotech. In 2006, Monsanto alone controlled 20 percent of the global seed market, worth nearly $4.5 billion annually. The top three seed companies now control nearly 40 percent of the global market.[4] All of this investment and market dominance have fueled the quest for even more control. In the past ten years, the pace of mergers and acquisitions between former chemical companies, smaller biotechnology firms, and the big seed sellers has outstripped all expectations. In a span of eight weeks in 1998, Monsanto absorbed four major agricultural biotechnology firms, including two of the top ten seed sellers in the world at the time.[5] This pattern of swallowing up smaller biotechnology and seed companies continues apace.

Consumer rejection

Even in the US—where 50 percent of corn, 90 percent of soy, and 80 percent of cotton are genetically modified—consumers are still resistant to GM foods. A 2004 survey done by the Food Policy Institute at Rutgers University indicated that 41 percent of Americans disapproved of the technology.[6] The level of awareness of GM foods however is low. The Rutgers study indicates that only 31 percent of American consumers believe they have ever consumed a GM product (nearly all processed foods sold in the US contain GM ingredients), and 89 percent said they think GM products should be labeled. After labels were required on all food products that contain GM ingredients in Europe, GM food virtually disappeared from European shelves.[7] Rejection of GM technology is strongest in the European Union, where, according to a recent World Trade Organization (WTO) ruling, the reticence of EU regulators to approve new GM varieties constitutes an illegal trade barrier.[8] From small nations like Sri Lanka, whose government only withdrew plans for a popular GM ban when threatened with WTO lawsuits,[9] to powerful social movements like Brazil's Landless Worker's Movement,[10] the global tide of public opinion is turning against transgenic food.

The biotech industry is constantly faced with the threat of market contraction and consumer rejection. This leaves the industry two options: either quickly recycle their capital, as they did in the 1970's when chemical companies switched from producing warfare-related chemicals like Agent Orange to producing agricultural inputs, or somehow turn global public opinion in their favor. With the onset of the agrofuels boom, the biotech industry hopes to do both.

Corn ethanol: harbinger of the new agricultural economy

With the signing of the 2007 Energy Bill, President Bush committed the nation to a Renewable Fuels Standard (RFS) that will, according to Republican Senator Pete Domenici, "use ethanol and a new generation of advanced biofuels to disp ace oil."[11] The standard pushes an already growing market for liquid biofuels, to 36 billion gallons a year by 2022. While 36 billion gallons represents only a fraction of the US's total fuel consumption, it opens a bonanza of investment and even further consolidation in the agricultural industry, what many have dubbed the "agrofuels boom." The RFSs in Europe and the US mandate the use of more corn ethanol than is physically possible for either region to produce, driving the transformation of corn for food to GM "dedicated energy crops." While language in both RFSs suggests an eventual move to alternate feedstocks, the biotech industry's foray into fuel corn gives us a picture of what future markets for agrofuel feedstocks might look like.

Both Monsanto and Syngenta have recently come cut with genetically modified varieties specifically for processing into ethanol. According to the industry, increased processing efficiency and a higher yield of ethanol per bushel for these varieties will benefit both the ethanol refiners and farmers. However, farmers' marketing options are much more limited with these newly patented energy crops. In an indication of what is to come, Monsanto and agribusiness giant Cargill have recently launched a joint venture called Renessen, a whole new corporation with an initial investment of $450 million dollars. Renessen is the sole provider of the first commercially available GM dedicated energy crop, Mavera High-Value Corn. Mavera corn is stacked with foreign genetic material coding for increased o I content and production of the amino acid lysine, along with Monsanto's standard Bt pesticide and its Roundup Ready gene. The genius of this operation, and the danger to farmers, is that farmers must sell their crop of Mavera corn to a Renessen-owned processing plant to recoup the "higher value" of the crop (for which they paid a premium on the seed).

Cargill's agricultural processing division has created a plant that only processes this brand of corn. Further, due to the genetically engineered presence of lysine, an amino acid lacking in the standard feedlot diet, they can sell the waste stream as a high priced cattle feed. Renessen has achieved for Monsanto and Cargill nearly perfect vertical integration. Renessen sets the price of seed, Monsanto sells the chemical inputs, Renessen sets the price at which to buy back the finished crop, Renessen sells the fuel, and farmers are left to absorb the risk. This system robs small farmers of choices and market power, while ensuring maximum monopoly profits for Renessen/Monsanto/Cargill.

Resistance to corn ethanol, however, is strong among farmers' movements and environmental groups. Even in official policy circles, corn ethanol is seen as a temporary step towards "second generation" fuel crops. US federal subsidies to corn ethanol are politically unsustainable, and numerous studies have questioned its energy efficiency, claiming ethanol yields less energy than it eats up in production.[12] Civil society groups have also accused ethanol of robbing food from the mouths of the poor. This food vs. fuel debate has been the most damaging for the image of agrofuels. Agrofuels were blamed as one of the reasons the price of tortillas in Mexico shot up 400 percent, leading to widespread protests and an eventual government cap on prices.[13] For many people, burning food in a world with 824 million hungry people is clearly immoral.

While sales of GM corn and soy for agrofuels climb steadily, these crops do little to solve the biotech industry's PR problem. Advanced energy crops, like cellulosic ethanol, promise to open new markets for biotech products and put to bed the issue of consumer rejection once and for all.

Second generation energy crops: power and profit painted green

The biotech industry promises to develop a "second generation" of new cellulose-based energy crops that can grow on land unusable for modern agriculture, eliminating the food vs. fuel debate currently plaguing the agrofuels industry. They promise to use environmentally friendly native plants like switchgrass to produce carbon-neutral fuels, and to reduce chemical inputs on these new green energy plantations by engineering plants to grow in resource-poor areas. Greater efficiency, opportunities for small farmers, and nothing less than the complete revitalization of rural economies are all supposed to come down the magic biotechnology pipeline in the form of cellulosic energy crops. Cellulosics are inedible but little understood, making all the mythology surrounding them easier for the public to swallow. Perhaps best of all for the biotech industry, second-generation ethanol, like cellulosic, promises to open brand new proprietary markets for the biotechnology products being rejected by consumers worldwide.

Cellulosic energy crops can conceivably be produced from any plant material: corn stalks, trees, sugar cane biomass, or grasses. One might ask, with so many possibilities for feedstock, why biotechnology stands to play such a large role. Biotechnology addresses two key factors: processing efficiency and yield. For example, Energycane, a new product in the pipeline at Ceres, Inc., in which Monsanto is a key equity shareholder, is merely sugarcane with genetic coding for increased biomass and decreased sugar content, i.e., a higher yield of cellulose. Other biotech traits aim at faster growth, shorter time until maturity, increased oil content, and frost or drought tolerance, all traits that attempt to conform nature to an industrial model.

Like first generation biotech traits, many of the energy traits being developed are designed for opening and dominating markets. In fact, many of these traits will create markets from scratch, augment the already lucrative markets for chemical inputs, and deliver the full control of these markets to the tightly packed corporations of the biotech industry. What do these new traits look like?

- **Range expansion, drought/freeze tolerance, growth on marginal land:** Some of the most highly advertised traits being developed allow a plant to escape its own physiological limitations—to grow on poor soils, in water-scarce regions, and in below-freezing temperatures. In other words, these traits aim to make industrial monocrops grow where they otherwise could not. Expanding the range of energy crops will expand the acreage under industrial agriculture worldwide, resulting in a dramatic expansion in the market for seed, fertilizers, pesticides, and other inputs, conveniently sold by the same group developing this technology.

- **Increased biomass and faster growth:** The biotech industry is working on code for faster-growing plants that put more energy into producing biomass, or overall material, than specific products like sugars, nuts, oils, and tubers. What fast growing really means, though, is high nitrogen consuming. Nitrogen, in the form of nitrates and ammonium, is the primary limiting factor in plant growth. Plants that are good at using nitrogen, and can use a lot of it quickly, will grow faster and produce more biomass. This is all well, except that in industrial agriculture the pressure of high-density, high-nitrogen-using plants rapidly depletes soil nutrients, making the system more dependent on chemical fertilizers.

- **Reduced lignin content in trees:** Lignin is the woody compound in the cell wall that gives trees both their structural integrity and their resistance to pests. Lignin is also what makes it difficult to pulp trees into paper and unlock cellulose in wood to produce ethanol. ArborGen, a biotechnology firm with heavy investments from the industrial forestry industry, is developing trees with 20 percent reduced lignin content. This development could necessitate the use of pesticides in plantation forests, because some of the natural pest resistance will have been engineered out of the trees.

- **Proprietary GM enzymes, bacteria and catalysts:** Processing cellulose into sugars is the largest hurdle in making cellulosic ethanol practical. At its current stage, processing is vastly inefficient. Much disagreement exists as to when and if cellulosic processing will be efficient. Some reports say it will arrive within the next two years, others claim it will never come. Regardless of doubts about the technology, the engineering of new enzymes and bacteria that can break down cellulose is a multi-million-dollar race. Large agriculture and biotech corporations and oil companies are partnering with smaller startup biotech firms to control the keys to unlocking the potential of cellulosic ethanol. Whoever controls the most efficient catalysts will have a virtual monopoly on processing fuel, meaning that feedstock prices paid at the farm gate will be set by the processor, robbing farmers of market power yet again.

If the horse enters the gates...

Once in the field, there is no way to prevent GM fuel crops from contaminating their food-crop cousins. Cases of genetic contamination are commonplace. In the past two years alone, there were at least 73 publicly documented cases of genetic contamination.[14] Proving contamination can be difficult, making the actual amount of genetic pollution hard to judge, but it is likely much higher than reported. GM corn traits were even found in native corn varieties in the mountains of Oaxaca, Mexico, where GM corn was never legally grown.[15] In fact, every commercial fuel crop so far is under consideration or has been approved for human consumption in the US without long-term independent testing. This includes Syngenta's fuel corn with traits from deep-sea bacteria that have never come in contact with humans, much less entered our food chain.[16] The danger of an agronomically flat, genetically modified world is that it leaves our food systems vulnerable to climate change events and pest and disease outbreaks.

Agrofuels based on genetically modified organisms (GMOs) and controlled by a handful of corporate giants do not lessen our vulnerability; they worsen it. Once GM agrofuels have entered the agricultural gates, they will soon escape into the wild, contaminating food crops across the globe. Nothing short of a sustained, coordinated (and expensive) international eradication campaign will rein them in.

Conclusion

The fact that agrofuels have exacerbated the vulnerabilities in our food systems, leading to rampant food-price inflation and food rebellions across the globe, reveals an evil irony. In a sleight of hand that draws our attention away from the fact that they created the crisis in the first place, big grain, seed and chemical companies now claim that in order to solve the crisis we need more GMOs. Their message is clear: "Don't worry about the displacement of food crops by agrofuels, or the contamination of our genetic diversity; just buy more crop-based fuel and more GM seeds, and we will consume our way out of the food and fuel crises."

We don't need agrofuel plantations to solve our energy problems. Neither do we need GMOs to overcome food-price inflation or to combat hunger. The vision for a new food system is well reflected in the growing movement for food sovereignty, "the right of all people to healthy and culturally appropriate food produced through ecologically sound and sustainable methods, and their right to define their own food and agriculture systems." This means dismantling the control companies like ADM, Cargill, Bunge, Monsanto, Syngenta, and DuPont exercise over our food systems—control that is held in place both by regulations like the RFSs that force us to consume their products, and the GM technologies that limit our options to one: theirs. We need to support movements for food sovereignty that promote policies and technologies for local rather than international markets; for keeping people on the land, rather than driving them off; and for bringing genetic diversity back into agriculture, rather than reducing it to the GMO patents held by a few corporate oligopolies.

Rolling back the industrial onslaught of GMOs is key to establishing food systems that serve the needs of the majority. Stopping the agrofuels boom, with its attendant corporate-owned GMOs, is an essential step in this challenge.

NOTES

1   ETC Group, "The World's Top Ten Seed Companies 2006," October 2007,
     http://www.etcgroup.org/en/materials/publications.html?pub_id=615; RAFI (Rural Advancement
     Foundation International), "Seed Industry Consolidation: Who Owns Whom?" *Communiqué*, July/
     August 1998.

2   Charles Benbrook, "Principles Governing the Long-Run Risks, Benefits, and Costs of Agricultural
     Biotechnology" (paper presented at Conference on Biodiversity, Biotechnology and the Protection of
     Traditional Knowledge, April 3, 2003), http://www.biotech-info.net/biod_biotech.pdf.

3   *Ibid.*

4   ETC Group, "The World's Top Ten Seed Companies 2006," *op. cit.*

5   RAFI, "Seed Industry Consolidation: Who Owns Whom?" *op. cit.*

6   William K. Hallman, W. Carl Hebden, Cara L. Cuite, Helen L. Aquino, and John T. Lang, "Americans and GM Food: Knowledge, Opinion and Interest in 2004," Food Policy Institute Report No. RR-1104-007, 2004, http://foodpolicy.rutgers.edu/docs/pubs/2004_Americans%20and%20GM%20Food_Knowledge%20Opinion%20&%20Interest%20in%202004.pdf.

7   Martina Holbach and Lindsay Keenan, "EU Markets: No Market for GM Labeled Food in Europe," Greenpeace International, January 2005, http://www.greenpeace.org/eu-unit/press-centre/reports/no-market-for-gm-labelled-food.

8   James Kanter, "WTO gives EU more time on genetically modified foods," *International Herald Tribune*, November 22, 2007.

9   Juan Lopez, Ann Doherty, Niccolo Sarno and Larry Bohlen, "Genetically Modified Food: A decade of failure (1994-2004)," Friends of the Earth International, February 2005, http://www.foei.org/en/publications/pdfs/gm_decade.pdf.

10   MST, "Small Scale Sustainable Farmers are Cooling Down the Earth," MST Informa, Movimento dos Trabalhadores Rurais Sem Terra N. 145, November 30 2007, http://www.mstbrazil.org/?q=node/552.

11   Matthew Letourneau, "President Bush Signs Energy Bill Into Law," Press Release, United States Senate Committee on Energy and Natural Resources, December 19, 2007.

12   David Pimentel, "Weighing in on Renewable Energy," *Geotimes* 50 (2005); Paul J. Crutzen et al., "Nitrous oxide release from agro-biofuel production negates global warming reduction by replacing fossil fuels," *Atmospheric Chemistry and Physics*, 2007; Timothy Searchinger et al., "Use of U.S. Croplands for Biofuels Increases Greenhouse Gases Through Emissions from Land Use Change," *Science* 319 (2008).

13   "Mexicans Stage Tortilla Protest," *BBC News*, February 1, 2007, http://news.bbc.co.uk/2/hi/americas/6319093.stm.

14   "GM Contamination Register," GeneWatch UK and Greenpeace International, accessed April 8, 2008, www.gmcontaminationregister.org.

15   David Quist and Ignacio H. Chapela, "Trasgenic DNA introgressed into traditional maize landraces in Oaxaca, Mexico," *Nature* 414 (2001).

16   Richard E. Bonnette, "Biotechnology Consultation Note to the File BNF No. 000095," Center for Food Safety and Applied Nutrition, Office of Food Additive Safety, US Food and Drug Administration, August 7, 2007, http://www.cfsan.fda.gov/~rdb/bnfm095.html; African Centre for Biosafety, "Comments on Syngenta's Application for Commodity Clearance of Genetically Modified Maize, Event 3272," May 29, 2006, http://www.biosafetyafrica.net/.

10. BUILDING A TRANSFORMATIVE FOOD MOVEMENT

FOOD SECURITY, FOOD JUSTICE, OR FOOD SOVEREIGNTY?

Eric Holt-Giménez, 2010[i]

The New Year saw renewed food riots in India and Africa—and record levels of hunger here in the US. This year also saw transformation in the food movement, with new power and national recognition. The food movement has successfully shone the spotlight on hunger and food access in the US, created a drive for more local food, and achieved better policy from the federal to the local level. The question now is: how do we turn these initial reforms into lasting food system transformation?

How do we know the food movement is a force for transformative change, rather than a passing fad, a collection of weak reforms, or a smattering of isolated local efforts? To know this, we need a moment of reflection on how the food system is structured historically, politically, and economically. We need to build alliances to take on the root of our failing food system.

Corporate food regimes

One way to imagine the food system is as a "regime." A food regime is a "rule-governed structure of production and consumption of food on a world scale." The first global food regime spanned the late 1800s through the Great Depression and linked food imports from Southern and American colonies to European industrial expansion. The second food regime reversed the flow of food from the Northern to the Southern Hemisphere to fuel Cold War industrialization in the Third World.

Today's corporate food regime is characterized by the monopoly market power and mega-profits of agrifood corporations, globalized meat production, and growing links between food and fuel. Virtually all the world's food systems are tied into today's corporate food regime. This regime is controlled by a far-flung agrifood industrial complex, made up of huge monopolies like Monsanto, ADM, Cargill, and Walmart. Together, these corporations are powerful enough to dominate the governments and the multilateral organizations that make and enforce the regime's rules for trade, labor, property, and technology. This political-economic partnership is supported by both public and private institutions like the World Bank and International Monetary Fund, the World Food Program, USAID, the USDA, and Big Philanthropy.

---

i   Adapted from Eric Holt-Giménez, "Food Security, Food Justice or Food Sovereignty?" Food First Backgrounder, Vol. 16, No. 4, Winter 2010.

Liberalization and reform

Like the larger economic system of which they are a part, global food regimes alternate between periods of liberal zation—characterized by unregulated markets, corporate privatization, and massive concentrations of wealth—followed by devastating financial busts. When these busts provoke widespread social unrest—threatening profits and governability—governments usher in reformist periods in which markets, supply, and consumption are re-regulated to rein in the crisis and restore stability to the regime. Infin tely unregulated markets would eventually destroy both society and the natural resources that the regime depends on for profits. Therefore, while the "mission" of reform is to mitigate the social and environmental externalities of the corporate food regime, its "job" is identical to that of the liberal trend: the reproduction of the corporate food regime. Though liberalization and reform may appear politically distinct, they are actually two sides of the same system.

Reformists dominated the global food regime from the Great Depression of the 1930s until Ronald Reagan and Margaret Thatcher ushered in our current era of neoliberal "globalization" in the 1980s, characterized by deregulation, privatization, and the growth and consolidation of corporate monopoly power in food systems around the globe.

With the global food and financial crises of 2007–2010, desperate calls for reform have sprung up worldwide. However, few substantive reforms have been forthcoming, and most government and multilateral solutions simply call for more of the same policies that brought about the crisis to begin with: extending liberal ("free") markets, privatizing common resources (like forests and the atmosphere), and protecting monopoly concentration while mediating the regime's collateral damage to community food systems and the environment. Unless there is strong pressure from society, reformists will not likely affect (much less reverse) the present neoliberal direction of the corporate food regime.

Food enterprise, food security, food justice, food sovereignty

Combating the steady increase in global hunger and environmental degradation has prompted governments, industry, and civil society to pursue a wide array of initiatives, including food enterprise, food security, food justice, and food sovereignty. Some seek to ameliorate hunger and poverty through charity. Others see it as a business opportunity and call for public-private partnerships. Human rights activists insist that government and industry should be held accountable when they undermine the right to food. Those who can afford good food promote individual consumer choices (vote with your forks). Food justice activists from underserved communities struggle against structural racism in the food system. Some efforts are highly institutionalized, others are community-based, while still others build broad-based movements aimed at transforming our global food system.

Photo by USDA

Understanding which strategies work to stabilize the corporate food regime and which seek to actually change it is essential if we are to move toward more equitable and sustainable food systems.

Some actors within the growing global food movement have a radical critique of the corporate food regime, calling for food sovereignty and structural, redistributive reforms regarding land, water, and markets. Others advance a progressive, food justice agenda calling for access to healthy food by marginalized groups defined by race, gender, and economic status. Family farm and sustainable agriculture advocates, as well as those seeking quality and authenticity in the food system, also fall in this progressive camp. While progressives focus more on localizing production and improving access to good, healthy food, radicals direct their energy at changing regime structures and creating politically enabling conditions for more equitable and sustainable food systems. Both overlap significantly in their approaches. Together, folks in this global food movement seek to open up food systems to serve people of color, smallholders, and low-income communities while striving for sustainable and healthy environments. Radicals and progressives are the arms and legs of the same food movement.

The Food Regime-Food Movement Matrix helps describe the dominant trend in the food system according to the politics, production models, tendencies, issues, and approaches to the food crisis:

Figure 3: Food movement matrix

	Corporate Food Regime		Food Movements	
Politics	Neoliberal	Reformist	Progressive	Radical
Discourse	Food Enterprise	Food Security	Food Justice	Food Sovereignty
Main Institutions	International Finance Corporation (World Bank); IMF, WTO; USDA (Vilsak); Global Food Security Bill; Green Revolution; Millennium Challenge; Heritage Foundation; Chicago Global Council; Bill and Melinda Gates Foundation; Feed the Future (USAID)	International Bank for Reconstruction and Development (World Bank); FAO; UN Commission on Sustainable Development; USDA (Merrigan); mainstream fair trade; some Slow Food Chapters; some Food Policy Councils; most food banks & food aid program	Alternative fair trade and many Slow Food chapters; many organizations in the Community Food Security Movement; many CSAs; many Food Policy Councils and youth food and justice movements; many farmworker and labor organizations	Via Campesina, International Planning Committee on Food Sovereignty; Global March for Women; many food justice and rightsbased movements
Orientation	Corporate	Development	Empowerment	Entitlement
Model	Overproduction; corporate concentration; unregulated markets and monopolies; monocultures (including organic); GMOs; agrofuels; mass global consumption of industrial food; phasing out of peasant and family agriculture and local retail	Mainstreaming/ certification of niche markets (e.g. organic, fair, local, sustainable); maintaining northern agricultural subsidies; "sustainable" roundtables for agrofuels, soy, forest products, etc.; market-led land reform	Agroecologically produced local food; investment in underserved communities; new business models and community benefit packages for production, processing, and retail; better wages for agriculture workers; solidarity economies; land & food access	Dismantle corporate agrifoods monopoly power; parity; redistributive land reform; community rights to water and seed; regionally based food systems; democratization of food systems; sustainable livelihoods; protection from dumping/ overproduction; revival of agroecologically managed peasant agriculture to distribute wealth and cool the planet; regulated markets and supply
Approach to the food crisis	Increased industrial production; unregulated corporate monopolies; land grabs; expansion of GMOs; public-private partnerships; liberal markets; international sourced food aid	Same as neoliberal but with increased medium farmer production and some locally sourced food aid; more agricultural aid but tied to GMOs and "bio-fortified/ climateresistant" crops	Right to food; better safety nets; sustainably produced, locallysourced food; agroecologically based agricultural development	Human right to food sovereignty; locally sourced, sustainably produced, culturally appropriate, democratically controlled focus on UN/FAO negotiations
Guiding Document	World Bank 2009 Development Report; "Realizing a New Vision for Agriculture (World Economic Forum)"	World Bank 2009 Development Report; "Realizing a New Vision for Agriculture (World Economic Forum)"	International Assessment on Agriculture Science Technology and Development	Peoples' Comprehensive Framework for Action to Eradicate Hunger

Time for transformation

The current food crisis reflects the environmental vulnerability, social inequity, and economic volatility of the corporate food regime. Absent profound changes, we will continue to experience cycles of free market liberalization and mild regime reform, plunging the world's food systems into ever more serious crises. While food system reforms—such as localizing food assistance, increasing aid to agriculture in the Global South, increasing food stamps, and funding research in organic agriculture—are certainly needed and long overdue, they don't alter the balance of power within the food system, and in some cases, may even reinforce existing inequities.

Progressive projects are tremendously energetic, creative, and diverse, but they can also be locally focused and issue—rather than system—driven. For example, the movement to improve access to food in low-income urban communities has received high-level support from the White House and the USDA. But the causes of nutritional deficiency among underserved communities go beyond the location of grocery stores. The abysmal wages, unemployment, skewed patterns of ownership and inner-city blight, and the economic devastation that has been historically visited on these communities are the result of structural racism and class struggles lost. No amount of fresh produce will fix urban America's food and health gap unless it is accompanied by changes in the structures of ownership and a reversal of the diminished political and economic power of low-income people of color. To end hunger at home and abroad, practices, rules, and institutions (structures) determining the world's food systems must be transformed.

Food movements unite!

The challenge for food movements is to address the immediate problems of hunger, malnutrition, food insecurity, and environmental degradation, while working steadily towards the structural changes needed to turn sustainable, equitable, and democratic food systems into the norm rather than a collection of projects. This means that both reform and transformation are needed. Historically, substantive reforms have been introduced to our political and economic systems, not by the good intentions of reformists per se, but through massive social pressure on legislators—who then introduce reforms. The social pressure for system change comes from social movements.

The food crisis of 2007–2010 has opened up new opportunities for reform and transformation, but has also led to a retrenchment of liberalization. This suggests that substantive changes to the corporate food regime will originate outside the regime's institutions—from the food movement. Whether or not the food movement can bring about change depends on whether or not progressive and radical trends unite.

The inequities and injustices of the corporate food regime are the default condition between food movement organizations. These social, economic, and political divides of race and class can't be ignored or willed away. An honest and committed effort to the original food justice principles of anti-racism and equity within the food movement is just as important as working for justice in the food system. Rural-urban and North-South divides must also be addressed in practice and in policy for the food movement to unite in a significant way.

In this regard, the progressive trend is pivotal: if progressive organizations build their primary alliances with reformist institutions from the corporate food regime, the regime will be strengthened, and the food movement will be weakened. In this scenario, we are unlikely to see substantive changes to the status quo. However, if progressive and radical trends find ways to build strategic alliances, the food movement will be strengthened. Social pressure from a united food movement has a much higher likelihood of bringing about reforms and of moving our food systems towards transformation.

RACISM AND CAPITALISM: DUAL CHALLENGES FOR THE FOOD MOVEMENT

Eric Holt-Giménez, 2015[i]

Our modern food system has co-evolved with 30 years of neoliberal globalization that privatized public goods and deregulated all forms of corporate capital worldwide. This has led to the highest levels of global inequality in history. The staggering social and environmental costs of this transition have hit people of color the hardest, reflected in the record levels of hunger and massive migrations of impoverished farmers in the Global South, and the appalling levels of food insecurity, diet-related diseases, unemployment, incarceration, and violence in under-served communities of color in the Global North.

The US food movement has emerged in response to the failings of the global food system. Everywhere, people and organizations are working to counteract the externalities inherent to the "corporate food regime." Understandably, they focus on one or two specific components—such as healthy food access, market niches, urban agriculture, organic farming, community supported agriculture, local food (farm to table), food and farm workers' rights, animal welfare, pesticide contamination, seed sovereignty, genetically modified organism (GMO) labeling, etc.—rather than the system as a whole. But the structures that determine the context of these hopeful alternatives remain solidly under control of the rules and institutions of the corporate food regime, e.g. the farm bill, free trade agreements, the USDA, the World Bank and International Monetary Fund, USAID, global supermarket oligopolies, meat, fisheries, grain, seed, and input oligopolies, and big philanthropy.

Neoliberal globalization has also crippled our capacity to respond to problems in the food system by destroying much of our public sphere. Not only have the health, education, and welfare functions of governments been gutted; the social networks within our communities have been weakened, exacerbating violence, intensifying racial tensions, and deepening cultural divides. People are challenged to confront the problems of hunger, violence, poverty, and climate change in an environment in which social and political institutions have been restructured to serve global markets rather than local communities.

Notably, the food justice movement has stepped up—with support from the nonprofit sector—to provide services and enhance community agency in our food systems. Consciously or not, in many ways the community food movement, with its hands-on, participatory projects for a fair, sustainable, healthy food system, is rebuilding our public sphere from the ground up. This is simply because it is impossible to do one without the other.

---

i   Adapted from Eric Holt-Giménez, "Racism and Capitalism: Dual Challenges for the Food Movement," *Journal of Agriculture, Food Systems, and Community Development* (March 2015): 23-25.

But as many organizations have discovered, we can't rebuild the public sphere without addressing the issues that divide us. For many communities, this means addressing racism in the food system. The food movement itself is not immune to the structural injustices that it seeks to overcome. Because of the pervasiveness of white privilege and internalized oppression in our society, racism in the food system can and does resurface within the food movement itself, even when the actors have the best of intentions. It does no good to push the issue aside because this undermines the trust we need in order to work together. Understanding why, where, and how racism manifests itself in the food system, recognizing it within our movement and our organizations and within ourselves, is not extra work for transforming our food system; it *is* the work.

Understanding how capitalism functions is also the work, because changing the underlying structures of a capitalist food system is inconceivable without knowing how the system functions in the first place. And yet many people trying to change the food system have scant knowledge of its capitalist foundations.

This is because in capitalist countries the foundational political-economic structures are assumed to be immutable and are rarely systematically (or systemically) questioned. Doing so immediately uncovers the structural causes of the profound economic and political disparities between social classes, thus contradicting the notion of a classless society. Tragically, critical knowledge of capitalism—vital to the struggles of social movements throughout the 19th and 20th centuries—has largely disappeared from the lexicon of social change, precisely at a time when neoliberal capitalism is penetrating every aspect of nature and society on the planet and is exacerbating the intersectional oppressions of race, class, ethnicity, and gender.

Luckily, this is changing as activists in the food movement dig deeper to fully understand the system behind the problems they confront. Many people in the Global South, especially peasants, fishers, and pastoralists, can't afford not to understand the socio-economic forces destroying their livelihoods. The rise of today's international food sovereignty movement, for instance, is part of a long history of resistance to violent, capitalist dispossession and exploitation of land, water, markets, income, labor, and seeds. Underserved communities of color in the Global North—as the result of recent and historical waves of colonization, dispossession, and exploitation—form the backbone of the food justice movement. Understanding why people of color are twice as likely to suffer from food insecurity, obesity, hypertension, diabetes, and other diet-related diseases even though they live in affluent northern democracies requires an understanding of the intersection of capitalism and racism.

Activists across the food movement are beginning to realize that the food system cannot be changed in isolation from the larger economic system. Sure, we can tinker around the edges of the issue and do useful work in the process. However, to fully appreciate the magnitude of the challenges we face and what will be needed to bring about a new food system in harmony with people's needs and the environment, we need to understand and confront the social, economic, and political foundations that created—and maintain—the food system we seek to change.

TRANSFORMING OUR FOOD SYSTEM BY TRANSFORMING OUR MOVEMENT

A conversation with Rosalinda Guillen, Community to Community Development, 2011[i]

If we can't respect ourselves enough to feed ourselves food that is not damaged and, most of all, is not hurting something else in the production of that food, then what are we? Are we really human, then? We know in our current food system we are doing something wrong; how do we get millions of people to understand that?

I firmly believe that the whole idea of how we build movements in the United States has gone terribly awry; we think that we are doing the right thing, but I am certain we are not: I know this by the suffering of the farmworkers in this country; I know this by the suffering of the poor, and the lack of food in many areas. I know this by the fact that through being fed, we're becoming ill.

Our culture is being destroyed by the food we are being given to eat, when Mexican farmworkers are stopped from feeding themselves the way they want to be fed, which often requires that we grow our own food because we can't find what we need to eat—that the food we need for self-sustenance is not permitted in many areas.

Working with the US Food Sovereignty Alliance, I've been thinking through what food sovereignty is—and that food security and food justice really are just not good enough for us in this country. I've been thinking that we really do need a movement toward food sovereignty. But again, the question keeps coming up: "What does a movement toward food sovereignty really mean?"

To me, food justice is about how we as humans are going to take responsibility for feeding ourselves in a way that doesn't hurt people, the land, and the resources that we need so badly just to survive. The need to make a change quickly is accelerating because we've ignored so much for so long. It's not because we didn't know about it. Cesar Chavez was telling us about it in the 1950s and '60s—millions of people stopped eating grapes for almost a whole generation because people understood when he said that there's something wrong with the way these grapes are being grown, and the best way for you to help us correct that is to stop eating the grapes. Food justice has so much to do with ourselves as human beings, period. I think this is taking longer than anybody ever hoped, what Cesar hoped, what Martin Luther King hoped. But how are we going to take responsibility? *Everything we put into our mouth makes a difference.*

It seems we don't have the sense or willingness to sacrifice to make the difference. It's difficult to pull people out of their comfort zones. We used to pull people out of their physical comfort

---

i   Adapted from Rosalinda Guillen, "Transforming Our Food System by Transforming Our Movement," in *Food Movements Unite! Strategies to Transform Our Food Systems*, ed. Eric Holt-Giménez (Oakland, CA: Food First Books, 2011), 307–314.

zones by showing them how farmworkers were living in the labor camps like organizers did in the '60s, but now it's the emotional comfort zone. Today we hear demands such as, "Don't call me racist, don't call me privileged, don't call me insensitive, because then you're moving into my comfort zone of who I believe I am as a good person." Even that is becoming a problem; to really tell people the truth we have to speak truth to power. The power of the corporation to influence the emotional being of people is becoming a barrier to us as food justice activists.

At Community to Community, we are trying to learn from the social forum model, based on creating space and dialogue and intersecting movements, and to see if we in the United States can develop a women-led organization that replicates that model in a smaller way in local communities. In our case, we are trying to do it by intersecting regionally and then linking nationally. Even our own internal structure and organizing dynamics are an experiment, as is everything else that we are trying to do to move farmworker justice forward. Women's leadership is our first goal; farmworker justice is next; and then immigrant rights and environmental justice. We are looking at it through the ecofeminist lens.

One of the things we talk about in terms of ecofeminism is building power—and I don't even know if power is the right word. A lot of organizations and a lot of organizers talk about power, how we're going to "get the power." They talk about shifting power. But we don't want to take somebody's power; we don't want to be in that place of power. We want to transform what power is. We need to claim that and act on it, regardless of who is claiming it in any other way.

A transformation of what power is should be the ultimate goal of community organizing today. Simply shifting power from here to there doesn't change the structures, it doesn't change the

Photo by Detroit Unspun

systems. It just places our people in losing situations. We've done that over and over again. We support one person, they become elected, and then we say they sold out. But they haven't sold out. We have just placed them in a box for them to bang their head against. They're never going to get to us because we moved them out of here, and put them in there, and now we are alone. This is just so clear to me.

I talk to other organizations and other leaders and try to talk about our model of organizing, and they say, "Well, you know that's a wonderful dream, but we've got to change this regulation, we've got to change this law," and I'm thinking, you are trapped inside that box.

We have to find a way to use our current system to move ourselves out of that structure and to create a new one, or to just forget about it completely. These are the decisions we need to make as organizers and leaders. This is what I'm trying to teach young people: don't fall into that trap! I'm challenging them, I'm speaking to students as much as possible and saying: if out of 300 of you I can get one to move out of this box and go over here and start thinking differently, then today is a successful day.

Community organizers need to be effective at modeling, and at being public in modeling what we believe another world should be. This means a lot of very public presentations and public demonstrations of how we should behave as humans. It's been done in the past. All experienced organizers will tell you that you just need a really strong core moving things quickly, with a lot of people around you. Remember, every single movement that you see that has brought change and transformation—more than just legislative change but transformation of relationships between humans in a community—has included music, food, orators, a lot of dialogue, a lot of activity.

But how do we convince all the people around us to think about what they're putting in their mouths? Despite the power of the internet to connect people, our first major sacrifice is figuring out how we can have face-to-face contact to really feel the full strength of each other's thoughts and commitments and feelings and goals. The only way it is going to work is for us to be able to understand each other. And it's going to take a long time. By a long time, I mean concerted effort over years—if we can make that effort. But we have to be honest with each other. I think that's a first step: if we can really say what we think in a way that is respected.

Food sovereignty is the best way to describe our struggle because it speaks more to the dignity of the human person. While food justice is a great term, it speaks more to a struggle based on legislation, on policy regulation. It's become a way of struggle that needs to be fought within the existing structures that we recognize. We are relying on the same government and corporate food system to insure justice, the same institutions that are depriving us of our human right to healthy food that does not harm people or the environment.

Political struggle in this country today is controlled. It's almost like there is a monopoly on it. We bang our heads on walls that just don't give way. I envision this soft metal box that we're in. We think that reform is putting a dent in the structure we're being held in, that we can bang our heads against its walls and claim, "Victory, victory!" There is a way out of that box that we don't see because we believe in the box. It's going to be hard to break through a consciousness that has been created through several generations in this country. So, new laws and the enforcement of existing laws are important, but it is not enough if we want to transform our food systems.

Food sovereignty demands that we move out of that box and think as human beings of our own personal dignity, and the dignity of our communities, in a deeper, transformative way. What is it that I need to do to ensure my community's liberation, not just from the effects of oppression—like bad treatment of workers and food insecurity—but also from the structures of oppression? Some of the older activists in this country, like Grace Lee Boggs, understand this. We need to get people to listen to her to grasp what this struggle means before it's too late.

The damage that's done to the earth is getting worse, but we're not stopping it. We are putting poison in our mouths that the corporations are giving us, and we're not saying anything. We're just eating more of it, because it's cheaper or convenient. If we can think of every piece of food that we put in our mouths, that we can honored it by the fact that we know nothing's been hurt or damaged by it, it will be good for us and good for the earth.

People say, "That's impossible! What kind of campaign is that?" But the truth is, it is not a campaign; it's more than that. We need to say, "Stop! You're back in your box! We're working within the box that has been given to us by the corporations. They already have that system down; it's theirs. We have to do something else!"

There are rules and restrictions to this process. Not just legislative rules, but social and cultural conformity about how we're supposed to be. In the social justice movement, we have organizing models and organizing protocols, but by breaking out of these we really take the ultimate action that's going to move us out of the box.

We need to rethink all of our relationships when it comes to the food movement. Some folks from Brazil have an interesting thought about coalitions, networks, movements, about relationships and how we relate to each other to create that political will to make change. In addition, writer Manuel De Landa has introduced a useful distinction between two general network types: hierarchies and flexible, nonhierarchical, decentralized, and self-organizing "meshworks."[1] This is an articulation of something that for many years we, and the farmworker community, starting with the farmworker movement that Cesar Chavez started in the Central Valley of California, did. We self-organized through chaotic networks, chaotic verbal communications, and face-to-face meetings of farmworkers where emotions come into action from the bottom up and create masses of people coming together. We saw it again in the immigrant rights movement a short time ago, with the marches that happened. This meshing of people coming together in this country gets swallowed up and created into hierarchical "networks." And then whatever it was we started from the beginning dissolves into something totally different that all of a sudden needs to be "funded," needs to be "organized," and needs to be "directed."

Today, grassroots movements are coming from the bottom up—made up of folks who with their hearts and their spirits seek to change something wrong in American society—and are swallowed up by these other structures. We immediately get put into a box. We must think through what that means, and how we might be able to get out of these "containments" of organized movements to really free ourselves up to allow for some sort of thinking of how we create meshworks. Even better, we must recognize when this grassroots meshwork is coming up and, for God's sake, leave it alone! Let it grow! Adopt a position of solidarity that in this country has created so many successful social change movements.

If anything requires great sacrifice from all of us, it is the food movement, because every day each one of us puts into our mouths something that has hurt somebody, has poisoned the earth, and that continues to create that kind of damage to Mother Earth. And we are eating it. At some point we are going to have to say, "No more!" We have to stop eating food that is hurting another person or is hurting the earth."

That, to me, is going to be the greatest sacrifice that we all can make. When will we get to that point? I don't know, but hopefully it won't be too late.

NOTES

1   Manuel De Landa. *Real Virtuality Meshworks and Hierarchies in the Digital Domain* (Netherlands: Netherlands Architecture Institute, 2006).

SURVIVAL PENDING REVOLUTION: WHAT THE BLACK PANTHERS CAN TEACH THE US FOOD MOVEMENT

Raj Patel, 2012[i]

Over the past decade, the US food movement has grown to become a potent force for social change. Precisely because of its success, the movement now is being called to shore up the status quo. Revisiting some radical roots suggests ways that the food movement can end hunger in America, rather than becoming just another Band-Aid alleviating poverty.

It's no accident that the food movement grew widely after the terrorist attacks of September 11, 2001. With the criminalization of dissent, it became increasingly difficult to confront corporate capitalism through other politics. As Michael Pollan has noted,

> Food is the place in daily life where corporatization can be most vividly felt... By the same token, food offers us one of the shortest, most appealing paths out of the corporate labyrinth.`

Under the Bush regime, environmentalists, social justice campaigners, anti-capitalists, and organic foodies found a government, media, and general public far less responsive than a decade before. Membership of umbrella groups like the Community Food Security Coalition swelled, with a proliferation of food organizations, consultants, academics, and activist groups throughout the US.

Part of the success of the movement has been its largely nonsectarian, big-tent approach, committed to the idea that food should be available to all, and that, above all, food is a domain in which something can and ought swiftly to be done.[ii] Indeed, it's the very success of community farms, gardens, feeding programs, kitchens, and food banks that has helped recruit a new generation of activists into a movement that seems to offer transcendence from the "old politics."

Yet it's the movement's practical success that puts it in a precarious position today. At the time of this writing (fall 2011), hunger is at its highest level in a generation[2]—50.2 million Americans and one-third of female-headed households are food insecure. Food prices are rising, unemployment remains stubbornly high, and a Republican-led Congress has ambitions to amputate social

---

i   Adapted from Raj Patel, "Survival Pending Revolution: What the Black Panthers Can Teach the US Food Movement," Food First Backgrounder, Vol. 18, No. 2, Summer 2012.

ii   In part, this vision has roots that can be traced to the outsized anarcho-Marxist organizing that produced Slow Food. See G. Andrews, *The Slow Food Story: Politics and Pleasure* (Montreal: McGill-Queen's University Press, 2008), and Pew Research Center, *The Millennials: A Portrait of Generation Next. Confident. Connected. Open to Change* (Washington DC: Pew Research Center, 2010).

programs from the body of government in the name of fighting inflation.[3] In the resulting vacuum, community organizations have been pressed, with government's approval, into providing service to the poor. As Suzi Leather remarked of a similar period in the UK government's history:

> It is easy to see the appeal of this community development approach for the present administration: it smacks of the self-help ethos, involves vanishingly small resources, and can be encouraged without at the same time having to admit the existence of poverty.[4]

To inoculate ourselves against the dangers of being co-opted into the very food system we have spent a decade criticizing, we need food politics. I don't just mean policies mediating the interactions between the government and the private sector of the corporate food regime. I'm referring to politics as an ideology, as a positive system of beliefs, analytical principles, and values that informs practice.

The Black Panthers feed the world

Since World War II, African American income has consistently stayed at around 60 percent of white household income.[5] The government's persistent refusal to address poverty in African American communities was compounded in the 1960s by an ongoing criminalization of poor, urban African Americans by local and state police, with attendant and systematic police violence against black men. It was the encounter with this "police logic" that spurred two students at Merritt College in Oakland, Huey Newton and Bobby Seale, to launch the Black Panther Party for Self Defense in 1966—later shortened to the Blank Panther Party (BPP).[6]

The party soon expanded its ambit beyond police surveillance, dropping "for Self Defense" from its name and, through dialogue with community members, setting up a range of community service programs. By 1968, the most successful of these was the Breakfast for School Children Program. David Hilliard, the Panthers' chief of staff, recalls the first donation of food that kicked off the program, given by Emmett Grogan of the San Francisco "Diggers":

> Emmett left off some bags of food his group distributes to the runaways, draft resisters and freaks who have flocked to Berkeley… We told him to put the stuff outside the office: in a few minutes people were flocking by, stocking up on onions and potatoes. Now Emmett donates the food regularly. Like the newspaper, the food serves a double purpose, providing sustenance but also functioning as an organizing tool: people enter the office when they come by, take some leaflets, sit in on an elementary PE [political education] class, talk to cadre, and exchange ideas.[7]

What distinguished the Black Panther Party's food distribution was its part in a far wider vision for social change. Parts of the mechanisms of the Black Panther Party's self-defense were programs for survival, ranging from the provision of free shoes and education to land banking and the school breakfast program.[8] In the provision of these services, Newton understood the ambiguities and contradictions within the programs:

> All these programs satisfy the deep needs of the community but they are not solutions to our problems. That is why we call them survival programs, meaning survival

pending revolution. We say that the survival program of the Black Panther Party is like the survival kit of a sailor stranded on a raft. It helps him to sustain himself until he can get completely out of that situation. So the survival programs are not answers or solutions, but they will help us to organize the community around a true analysis and understanding of their situation.[9]

The Panthers' breakfast program eventually served 45 branches nationwide. New York's chapters fed numbers in the hundreds, California's in the thousands. Nonetheless, the universal aspiration was for a balanced diet of fresh fruit twice a week, and always a starch of toast or grits; protein of sausage, bacon, or eggs; and a beverage of milk, juice, or hot chocolate.[10] Done without a penny from the government or organized philanthropy, the meals were the only source of nutrition in many a child's day.

The breakfast program was part of a suite of survival programs with explicit goals of transforming relations around private property—the vision of a land bank, for instance, called for the creation of trusts that would suspend the profit motive from land tenure, making other arrangements possible.[11] Land reform was, in turn, part of a broader political strategy, enshrined in the Panthers' Ten Point Plan, which featured "power to determine the destiny of our black and oppressed communities," "full employment," "an end to... robbery by the capitalists," "decent housing," "decent education," "completely free health care," and an end to war, militarism, police brutality, and, in the final point, "land, bread, housing, education, clothing, justice, peace and people's community control of modern technology." It was the political vision, the possibility of a different tomorrow after surviving today, that transformed the Panthers' feeding into radical social work.[12]

Effect and aftermath

Jesse Jackson called the breakfast program "creative and revolutionary."[13] People across the country copied it. Nationally, because the breakfast program actually fed children, it stoked grassroots pressure that eventually led to increased funding for kids' food. In a Senate hearing, George McGovern asked the school lunch program administrator, Rodney Leonard, if the Panthers fed more poor children than did the state of California... Leonard admitted that it was "probably true."[14]

The Panthers' success in providing food also intensified the government's efforts to crush them. Through its COINTELPRO program, the FBI was trying to destroy the Panthers, but found it much harder to summon popular support for its work when the Panthers were engaged in radical social work. As Ward Churchill observed, "[FBI director J. Edgar] Hoover was quite aware that it would be impossible to cast the party as merely 'a group of thugs' so long as it was meeting the daily nutritional requirements of an estimated 50,000 grade-schoolers in forty-five inner cities across the country. Rather than arguing that the government itself should deliver such a program, however, he targeted the Panthers' efforts for destruction."[15]

Though the FBI eventually did succeed in bringing down the Panthers—and the breakfast program—the program has an important legacy. Not only was it responsible for creating what today might be called a "temporary autonomous zone"[16] for instigating real "school meal revolutions" (as opposed to the kind shown on today's TV), and for embarrassing the federal government into taking child nutrition seriously, but—at least in some cases—it involved a transformation within the domain in which the Panthers have consistently been considered remiss: gender.

One female activist recalled the lengths to which the Panthers earnestly, but inconsequentially, paid lip service to questions of gender equality and then said:

> You could have a thousand dialogues on gender issues and you would have never gotten that result faster than you did by saying look, if you love these children, if you love your people, you better get your ass up and start working in that breakfast program.[17]

It was the active participation in the program that transformed gender relations, not merely the talking about it.

This vision of gender transformation isn't, however, widely shared. When I asked one activist these ideas, she was unimpressed. She wasn't alone—many of the women who were part of the Panthers engaged not because of the enlightened gender praxis, but despite it.[18] Indeed, the only way in which many women were taken seriously within the movement was not because of equality over the cooking range, but because they were armed. For some women within the Black Panther Party, power grew out of the barrel of a gun. But it's not inconceivable that, among the dozens of Panther chapters, even if women have reported the persistence of patriarchy, this sexist bubble might also have been punctured by moving men into kitchens and onto serving lines for children.

Conclusion

The food movement today might benefit from the Black Panthers' vision for radical change. The Panthers understood that while the needs of the hungry deserved immediate attention, those needs could only be banished permanently by a far more radical transformation than the government was ready to provide. The Panthers knew political education was vital to understanding the reasons behind their hunger. So they read Mao, Frantz Fanon, and Marx. They also knew that the combination of political education and effective action made them dangerous, turning them into enemies of a status quo that produced hunger. Hence the massive government-sponsored attempts to murder their example, and parade its body as a warning to those whose hearts might harbor similar hopes.

Yet the Panthers' example remains important for today's food movement. Clearly, it is difficult to balance the desire to recruit a broad movement under a single banner, and the need to broach the potentially divisive subject of capitalism. You can find this tension within the notion of "food sovereignty" that guides the international peasant movement, La Vía Campesina. Their definition of "food sovereignty" has changed over time,[19] though it is at heart a call for political equality at every level of the food system, so that decisions about the food system might be made democratically. With an organizational structure as diverse as La Vía Campesina's, vagueness is politically expedient. In a movement peopled with landed peasants and landless workers, any talk about "the means of production" is fractious—some folk in La Vía Campesina have land

and are reluctant to talk about giving it up—even if talking about all of this might provide more political focus. Food sovereignty is, from the outset, an idea built on postponing certain difficult political discussions to another day—just as long as everyone gets a say in what a new food system might look like.

Precisely because equality in political participation has to come first, the one conversation that can't be avoided or postponed is the one about gender. Although questions about unequal ownership may be punted to tomorrow, the consequences of gender inequality need to be addressed today. Hence a recently launched campaign confronting violence against women, which itself is the product of hard conversations, and concerted organizing by women within La Vía Campesina.[20] The campaign stretches not only to domestic violence, but the structural violence of poverty, i.e. to those inequities magnified by capitalism.

For La Vía Campesina, some of the most powerfully transformative and practical parts of a theory about global change in the food system come from actual gendered fights for the future of food. The Black Panthers' struggles for survival may not yet have brought the revolution, but at least they saw the scale of change needed so that hunger might finally be banished in our communities. And in the US today, the group most likely to be food insecure is households headed by women. It's possible to explain why this is so why women are paid less than men, why hunger flourishes among the poor, and why capitalism will not willingly provide food to those unable to afford it.

In providing these explanations, and organizing effective actions to address inequity, we will make the food movement more threatening to the powerful. That sounds frightening, but every movement that has ever accomplished social change—whether the civil rights movement, the Indian independence movement, or indeed the global justice movement—has put the demands of justice ahead of the need to accommodate oppressive thinking. Instead, such movements have been armed with radical ideas for a better future, in which all people are possessed of dignity, and able to govern themselves. The Black Panther Party's vision of a world where all children are fed, where food, healthcare, education, access to land, and housing and clothes are rights and not privileges is a vision that can and should spark the food movement today. Inspired by their example, and learning the lessons from their experience, we can dream beyond the limitations imposed by capitalism, of a world in which hunger is, for the first time, a specter of the past.

NOTES

1   Michael Pollan, "Food Movement Rising," *New York Review of Books*, June 10, 2010.

2   Mark Nord et al., "Household Food Security in the United States, 2009," USDA Economic Research Service, 2010, http://www.ers.usda.gov/Publications/ERR108/ERR108.pdf.

3   Raj Patel, "That witch, inflation, hurts us more without protection," *The Guardian*, January 19, 2011.

4   Suzi Leather, *The Making of Modern Malnutrition: An Overview of Food Poverty in the UK* (London: Caroline Walker Trust, 1996), 47–48.

5   Carmen DeNavas-Walt, Bernadette D. Proctor, and Jessica C. Smith, "Income, Poverty, and Health Insurance Coverage in the United States: 2008," US Census Bureau, 2009, http://www.census.gov/prod/2009pubs/p60-236.pdf.

6   Katheryn Cleaver and G. Katsiaficas, eds., *Liberation, Imagination and the Black Panther Party: A New Look at the Panthers and Their Legacy* (New York/London: Routledge, 2001); David Hilliard and Lewis Cole, *This Side of Glory: The Autobiography of David Hilliard and the Story of the Black Panther Party* (Boston: Little, Brown, 1993); Jacques Rancière, *Disagreement: Politics and Philosophy*, (Minneapolis: University of Minnesota Press, 1998); Bobby Seale, *Seize the Time: the Story of the Black Panther Party and Huey P. Newton* (London: Hutchinson, 1970).

7   David Hilliard and Lewis Cole, *This Side of Glory, op. cit.*, 158.

8   Huey P. Newton Foundation and David Hilliard, eds., *The Black Panther Party Service to the People Programs* (Albuquerque: University of New Mexico Press, 2008).

9   Huey P. Newton Foundation and David Hilliard, eds., *The Black Panther Party Service to the People Programs, op. cit.*, 4.

10   Huey P. Newton Foundation and Hilliard, *The Black Panther Party Service to the People Programs, op. cit.*, 31.

11   John E. Davis, "Origins and Evolution of the Community Land Trust in the United States" in *The Community Land Trust Reader*, ed. John E. Davis (Cambridge, MA: Lincoln Institute of Land Policy, 2010), 3–47.

12   Roy V. Bailey and M. Brake, *Radical Social Work* (London: Edward Arnold, 1976).

13   Susan Levine, *School Lunch Politics: The Surprising History of America's Favorite Welfare Program* (Princeton/Woodstock, UK: Princeton University Press, 2008), 139.

14   *Ibid.*

15   Ward Churchill, "To Disrupt, Discredit and Destroy: The FBI's Secret War against the Black Panther Party," in *Liberation, Imagination and the Black Panther Party: A New Look at the Panthers and Their Legacy*, ed. Katheryn Cleaver and G. Katsiaficas (New York/London: Routledge, 2001), 78–117.

16   Hakim Bey, *T.A.Z.: The Temporary Autonomous Zone, Ontological Anarchy, Poetic Terrorism*, 2nd ed. (Brooklyn, NY: Autonomedia, 2003).

17   Nik Heynen, 2009, "Bending the Bars of Empire from Every Ghetto for Survival: The Black Panther Party's Radical Antihunger Politics of Social Reproduction and Scale," *Annals of the Association of American Geographers* 99 (2): 406–422.

18   Angela D. LeBlanc-Ernest, "The Most Qualified Person to Handle the Job: Black Panther Party Women, 1966–1982," in *The Black Panther Party [Reconsidered]*, ed. Charles E. Jones (Baltimore: Black Classic Press, 1998), 305–36; and Tracye A. Matthews, 1998. "No One Ever Asks, What a Man's Role in the Revolution is: Gender and the Politics of the Black Panther Party, 1966–1971," in *The Black Panther Party [Reconsidered]*, ed. Charles E. Jones (Baltimore: Black Classic Press, 1998), 267–304.

19   Raj Patel, "Food Sovereignty: An Introduction," *The Journal of Peasant Studies* 37.3 (2010): 663-672.

20   La Vía Campesina, "Message from Dakar: Peasants Confront Land Grabs, Violence against Women, and AGRA," February 2, 2011, http://rajpatel.org/2011/02/07/message-fromdakar-peasants-against-land-grabs-violence-against-womenand-agra/.

EPILOGUE: FOOD FIRST LOOKING AHEAD

Eric Holt-Giménez, Executive Director

"The arc of the moral universe is long, but it bends towards justice."

— Rev. Martin Luther King, 1964

To envision a world without hunger is to bend our political will towards justice. When we look ahead to a food system in which everyone has fresh, healthy food and a dignified livelihood, we are imagining a just, sustainable, vibrant food system under community control. We are envisioning food sovereignty.

The violent persistence of hunger, malnutrition, and diet related disease in the midst of abundance has placed our food systems at the center of our social and environmental future. The corporate capture of land, water, air, and the genetic foundations of life itself has pushed not just our food systems, but our economies, the environment, and our societies to the brink of disaster. Technological development, global markets, and endless economic growth—once unquestioned solutions to hunger and poverty—are now widely recognized as the problem. Indeed, after four years of extensive research on the global food crisis the International Agricultural Assessment on Science Technology and Knowledge for Development concluded: "The way the world grows its food will have to change radically to better serve the poor and hungry if the world is to cope with growing population and climate change while avoiding social breakdown and environmental collapse." Food First is committed to this radical change.

Successful social movements are formed by integrating activism with livelihoods. These integrated movements create the sustained social pressure that produces political will—the key to changing structures, institutions, and rules.

To end hunger we need to transform our food system. Human civilizations emerged with our ability to collectively manage our food systems to overcome scarcity. Eight thousand years of complex food system development brought us a wide diversity of seeds, cultivars, cropping, and fishing methods, as well as knowledge, norms, and social organization. How we produce, process, distribute, and consume our food will again largely determine the future of human civilization. However, this time the challenge is not scarcity, but sustainability and equity.

The future of food is a political question. A new food politics—one that prioritizes needs and rights over market demand, that builds rather than undermines popular democracy, and that measures success in terms of well-being and empowerment rather than Gross National Product—is as necessary as it is radical. Transforming our food systems also depends on transforming our politics and, as Rosalinda Guillen points out, depends on "transforming power itself."

Food justice and food sovereignty are impossible without strong systems of justice, democracy, and equity in the societies that produce our food. Beneath the call for good, clean, and fair food is a demand—and an urgent need—for a new society. Apart from the biophysical and economic linkages with our energy, health, and political systems, our food system is inextricably linked to climate justice, labor justice, racial justice, indigenous rights, and all other movements for liberation.

The deep power of our food movements lies as much in the irrepressible desire for dignity and liberation as it does in the basic need for healthy food. Food First is privileged to work with the growing social movements for food justice, food sovereignty, indigenous rights and immigrant and workers' rights, #BlackLivesMatter, and others for whom giving up hope is not an option.

Successful social movements are formed by integrating activism with livelihoods. These integrated movements create the sustained social pressure that produces political will—the key to changing structures, institutions, and rules. Our movements are also the key to changing how we think, believe, and act—they are not just a path towards our utopias; they are a reflection of who we want to be.

We are humbled and proud to be part of a movement that is ending the injustices that cause hunger.

FOOD FIRST TIMELINE: BOOKS, ACHIEVEMENTS & WORLD EVENTS

1971

Food First co-founder Frances ("Frankie") Moore Lappé publishes **Diet for a Small Planet**, which has now sold over three million copies.

1975

Joseph Collins and Frances Moore Lappé attend the first **World Food Conference in Rome** and found the Institute for Food and Development Policy, aka Food First.

1977

Food First publishes the groundbreaking book **Food First: Beyond the myth of scarcity** by Frances Moore Lappé and Joseph Collins and **Needless Hunger: Voices from a Bangladeshi village** by James Boyce and Betsy Hartmann.

1979

The **Sandinistas overthrow the Somoza dictatorship in Nicaragua** and establish a revolutionary government, which lasts until 1990 in spite of a US-funded and trained militia known as the Contras.

1981

Food First publishes the book ***Circle of Poison*** by David Weir and Mark Schapiro, which leads to the formation of Pesticide Action Network, an international coalition of groups concerned with pesticide poisoning.

1982

Food First publishes the book ***Nicaragua: What difference could a revolution make?***

1984

Food First publishes an integrated social studies curriculum designed to help sixth grade students understand their food's journey from the farm to the dinner table, and the causes of hunger at home and abroad. Food First founds the **Television Organizing Project**, which splits off in 1986 as Neighbor-to- Neighbor, to put political pressure on Congress to stop US military aid to right-wing forces in Central America.

1986

Food First co-founders publish ***World Hunger: Twelve Myths***, which examines the policies that have kept hungry people from feeding themselves around the world. *World Hunger* is now in its third and revised edition (forthcoming 2015).

Food First publishes ***Alternatives to the Peace Corps***. Now in its 12th edition, it was the first guide to offer options for volunteer service focused on social change.

1987

Frances Moore Lappé accepts the **Right Livelihood Award** (Alternative Nobel Prize) on behalf of Food First "for revealing the political and economic causes of world hunger and how citizens can help to remedy them." Food First publishes *Don't Be Afraid Gringo* by Elvia Alvarado, translated and edited by Medea Benjamin which tells the story of peasant land struggles and US interventionism in Honduras. The book wins the Bay Area Book Publishers best biography of the year award.

Medea Benjamin accepts the Bay Area Book Award for Don't Be Afraid Gringo, 1987. Photo by Elliott Smith

1988

Food First publishes **A Fate Worse than Debt** by Susan George, which analyzes the World Bank and IMF's structural adjustment programs in the Third World. Food First staffers Kevin Danaher and Medea Benjamin start the human rights organization Global Exchange.

1989

The Soviet Union falls. Cuba loses access to petroleum inputs, eventually leading to its widespread adoption of sustainable agriculture. Food First publishes **Kerala: Radical reform as development in an Indian state** by Richard Franke and Barbara Chasin.

1990

Frances Moore Lappé founds the Center for Living Democracy. Among its publications is the 1997 report **Bridging the Racial Divide** describing how citizens across the country are sponsoring interracial dialogues.

1992

Food First publishes **Dragons in Distress** by Food First Executive Director Walden Bello and Stephanie Rosenfeld, which challenges prevailing wisdom on Asia's "miracle economies."

Walden Bello, TV interview with Edward Klamm, 1990

1993

The international peasant movement La Vía Campesina is founded in Mons, Belgium, which now includes over 150 member organizations in 70 countries representing 300 million farmers.

1994

The North American Free Trade Agreement (NAFTA) goes into effect. On the morning of January 1, 1994, the Zapatista movement is born in the southern Mexican state of Chiapas, inspiring anti-globalization activists around the world. The Community Food Security Coalition—which reaches a membership of 500 organizations—is founded to provide leadership to the rapidly expanding food movement in North America.

1994

Food First publishes *Chile's Free-Market Miracle: A second look*, which examines the gap between free market rhetoric and socioeconomic realities in Pinochet's Chile.

1995

The World Trade Organization (WTO) comes into existence with the goal of extending free trade and investment across the globe. Former Food First Executive Director Walden Bello founds the Bangkok-based think tank Focus on the Global South aimed at counteracting neoliberalism and militarization. Food First publishes *Breakfast of Biodiversity* by John Vandermeer and Yvette Perfecto, which describes the global economic forces responsible for rainforest destruction. Executive Director Peter Rosset leads Food First's first delegation to Cuba.

1996

La Vía Campesina launches the concept of "food sovereignty" at the World Food Summit: "the right of all peoples to healthy and culturally appropriate food produced through sustainable methods and their right to define their own food and agriculture systems."

1997

Food First publishes *Benedita da Silva: An Afro-Brazilian woman's story of politics and love*, which tells the story of the first Black woman from a favela to become a congress-woman and senator in Brazil. Starting in Thailand, a devastating financial crisis strikes East Asia.

1999

Executive Director Peter Rosset and board vice president Miguel Altieri are invited to the Vatican to provide a consultation on hunger in the 21st century. Food First publishes three books: *America Needs Human Rights*, which argues that human rights are routinely violated in the US; *A Siamese Tragedy: Development and degradation in modern Thailand*, which looks at the role of foreign investment in causing that country's economic collapse; and *Basta! Land and the Zapatista rebellion in Chiapas*, now in its third and revised edition. In November, **Food First participates in massive protests at the WTO Ministerial in Seattle, WA**, which catalyzed the US anti-globalization movement. The Congressional Progressive Caucus launches its "Economic Human Rights" bus tour of economic injustices in the US, co-sponsored by Food First and the Institute for Policy Studies. The tour kicks off in Georgia joined by Danny Glover and Harry Belafonte.

2001

Food First publishes ***The Future in the Balance: Essays on globalization and resistance*** by Walden Bello. Food First founder Frances Moore Lappé and her daughter Anna Lappé establish the Small Planet Institute and Small Planet Fund, channeling resources to social movements worldwide.

2002

Food First publishes ***Sustainable Agriculture and Resistance: Transforming food production in Cuba*** by Fernando Funes, Peter Rosset, Luis García, Nilda Pérez, and Martin Bourque, which tells the story of Cuba's remarkable recovery from a food crisis brought on by the collapse of the Soviet Union and turn toward organic farming. Former Food First staffer Medea Benjamin founds Code Pink: Women for Peace, a grassroots organization working to end US-funded wars and occupations.

2003

Activists shut down the WTO in Cancún. Food First works with indigenous and peasant activist groups protesting the inclusion of agriculture within WTO trade rules and, as a UN NGO on the inside, influences India to withdraw. Talks collapse.

2004

Food First publishes ***Genetic Engineering in Agriculture: The myths, environmental risks, and alternatives*** by Miguel Altieri.

2006

Food First publishes *Campesino a Campesino: Voices from Latin America's farmer to farmer movement for sustainable agriculture* by Eric Holt-Giménez and *Promised Land: Competing visions of agrarian reform* edited by Peter Rosset, Raj Patel, and Michael Courville, produced in partnership with organizations in Thailand, Brazil, and South Africa. The Bill and Melinda Gates Foundation and Rockefeller Foundation come together to form the Alliance for a New Green Revolution in Africa (AGRA).

2007

Food First participates in the Forum for Food Sovereignty in Nyéléni, Mali, which includes more than 500 people representing organizations from over 80 countries. Food First warns delegates of the colonial intent behind the new Green Revolution for Africa. At Nyéléni, Food First co-organizes an international conference with 150 participants from 35 African and northern countries to discuss African Alternatives to the Green Revolution. Planning for the African-led "We Are the Solution" campaign begins. The Nyéléni Declaration asserts that: Food sovereignty implies new social relations free of oppression and inequality between men and women, peoples, racial groups, social and economic classes and generations."

In 2007 and 2008, world food prices increase dramatically, creating a global crisis and causing political and economic instability in both poor and developed nations. The number of hungry people in the world tops one billion.

2008

Food First is selected to incubate the newly-created Oakland Food Policy Council, now a thriving a 21-seat council that makes recommendations to the City of Oakland on ways to make the system more equitable and sustainable.

2009

Food First publishes three books: *Agrofuels in the Americas*, edited by Rick Jonasse; *Beyond the Fence: A journey to the roots of the migration crisis* by Dori Stone; and *Food Rebellions: Crisis and the hunger for justice* by Eric Holt-Giménez, Raj Patel, and Annie Shattuck, which analyzes of the events that led to the global food crisis of 2007-2008 and documents the grassroots initiatives working to create food sovereignty. Food First also publishes the report "Food Policy Councils: Lessons Learned," an in-depth study of 48 North American Food Policy Councils.

On June 28, 2009, democratically elected Honduran president Manuel Zelaya is overthrown in a military coup.

2010

Food First launches its educational travel program Food Sovereignty Tours geared toward helping farmers, scholars, activists, and consumers connect with the global movement for food sovereignty. Food First co-publishes the book *Food Sovereignty: Reconnecting food, nature and community*, edited by Annette Desmarais, Nettie Wiebe, and Hannah Wittman, which has since become a definitive text on food sovereignty. Food First is a founding member of the US Food Sovereignty Alliance, launched on World Food Day (Oct. 16), which evolved out of the US Working Group on the Food Crisis convened in 2008 with the goal of promoting the principles of food sovereignty in the US.

2011

The campaign "We Are the Solution: Celebrating African family farming" is launched at the World Social Forum in Dakar, Senegal, led by rural women from six West African countries. Food First supports the campaign with resources, analysis, and agroecological training materials. Food First publishes the book *Food Movements Unite! Strategies to transform our food systems* edited by Eric Holt-Giménez, which highlights the voices of farmers, workers, and activists from rural and urban communities around the globe.

On November 2, **Occupy Oakland calls for a General Strike**. Food First co-organizes a Food Justice Teach In & Eat In with other Bay Area organizations in a joint call to "Occupy the Food System."

Food First co-hosts the 13th Annual Community Food Security Coalition conference in Oakland, CA, with a record 1,100 attendees. Food Sovereignty Tours organizes ten Food Justice Tours allowing 400 conference participants to visit Bay Area food justice organizations.

2012

Food First convenes a group of researchers and activists in Oakland, CA, to discuss land grabbing and resistance in the Americas—North and South, urban and rural—in an initiative that becomes the Land & Sovereignty in the Americas Collective. Food First publishes *Unfinished Puzzle: Cuban agriculture, the challenges, lessons and opportunities.*

2013

Food First publishes **Grabbing Power: The new struggles for land, food and democracy in northern Honduras** about the history of agribusiness and peasant struggles in Honduras, and the repression of rural movements following the 2009 coup. Food First co-organizes the first major academic conference focused on food sovereignty at Yale University: "Food Sovereignty: A Critical Dialogue." La Vía Campesina celebrates its 20th anniversary and moves its secretariat from Indonesia to Zimbabwe.

Food First launches the East Bay Urban Farmer Field Schools (EBUFFS) project using farmer-to-farmer education to build sustainable urban agriculture. Food Sovereignty Tours hosts 13 farmers from the Basque Farmers' Union for a Food Justice Tour of the Bay Area and takes its first delegation to South Korea co-organized by the Korean Women's Peasant Association.

Executive Director Eric Holt-Giménez leads a workshop of the EBUFFS project in San Leandro, CA, 2013. Photo by Leonor Hurtado

2014

Food First publishes a landmark action-research study on the "Food Insecurity of Restaurant Workers" in partnership with Restaurant Opportunities Center (ROC) and Food Chains Workers Alliance. Food First also publishes three important briefs in its Land & Sovereignty series on the financialization of farmland; land grabbing and peasant resistance in Paraguay; and land grabbing in the United States.

The police killing of Black teenager Michael Brown in Ferguson, MO, and public outcry put racial injustice in the spotlight. Food First identifies "dismantling racism in the food system" as an institutional priority. The Obama administration lifts restrictions on travel and trade with Cuba.

2015 Food First celebrates its 40th anniversary with a national speaking tour

featuring Executive Director Eric Holt-Giménez; special events in the Bay Area including a Food Day gala and auction; and a 40th anniversary book. Join us in celebrating four decades of Food First!

ABOUT THE EDITORS

Tanya M. Kerssen writes and teaches on the political economy of food, agriculture, and rural development with a focus on Latin America and Africa. She holds an MA in Latin American Studies from the University of California Berkeley and is the author of the Food First book *Grabbing Power: The new struggles for land, food, and democracy in Northern Honduras*.

Teresa K. Miller holds an MFA from Mills College and is the author of *sped* (Sidebrow) and *Forever No Lo* (Tarpaulin Sky Press). Her essays and other writings have appeared in more than two dozen publications, including *Common Dreams*, *AlterNet*, and FoodFirst.org.

ABOUT FOOD FIRST

The Institute for Food and Development Policy, better known as Food First, is a nonprofit research and education-for-action center dedicated to investigating and exposing the root causes of hunger in a world of plenty. Our 40 years of research have shown that hunger is caused by poverty and injustice—not scarcity. Resources and decision-making are in the hands of a privileged few, depriving the majority of land, markets, dignified work, and healthy food.

Founded in 1975 by author of the bestselling *Diet for a Small Planet* Frances Moore Lappé and food policy analyst Dr. Joseph Collins, Food First has published over 60 books. Hailed by *The New York Times* as "one of the most established food think tanks in the country," Food First's groundbreaking work continues to shape local, national, and international policies and debates about hunger and development. Learn more at www.foodfirst.org

BECOME A MEMBER!

We count on our broad network of members for support so that we can maintain our independent and critical voice. We invite you to join Food First. As a member you will receive a 20 percent discount on all Food First books. You will also receive our quarterly newsletter and backgrounders, providing information for action on current food and land struggles in the United States and around the world. All contributions are tax-deductible. Please visit our website for details at www.foodfirst.org or contact us at foodfirst@foodfirst.org or (510) 654-4400, ext. 221.

MORE TITLES FROM FOOD FIRST BOOKS

Available from www.foodfirst.org

World Hunger: 10 Myths

By Frances Moore Lappé and Joseph Collins

Full of new insight and astonishing facts, *World Hunger: 10 Myths* is the definitive text on hunger from the internationally recognized Institute for Food and Development Policy/Food First.

ISBN: 9780802123466

September 2015, $18.00

Grabbing Power: The New Struggles for Land, Food and Democracy in Northern Honduras

By Tanya M. Kerssen

Foreword by Eric Holt-Giménez

In 2009, Honduran elites financed a coup to grab land and power. The peasants of the Aguán Valley are fighting to grab it back—for their families, local economies, and the future of democracy.

ISBN 978-0-935028-43-0

February 2013, $14.99

Food Movements Unite! Strategies to Transform Our Food System

Edited by Eric Holt-Giménez, Preface by Samir Amin

This book brings together the insights of farmers, workers and activists from rural and urban communities around the globe, covering topics such as the global fight for climate justice; the Black Panther Party's food justice legacy; women's autonomy; and food sovereignty in Africa. Contributors to this volume address the critical question: "How can we unite to transform the global food system?"

ISBN: 978–0–935028–38–6

November 2011, $24.99, also available in Italian

Food Sovereignty: Reconnecting Food, Nature and Community

Edited by Annette Desmarais, Nettie Wiebe, and Hannah Wittman

This book argues that food sovereignty is the means to achieving a system that will provide for the food needs of all people while respecting the principles of environmental sustainability, local empowerment, and agrarian citizenship. Contributors include: Miguel Altieri, Walden Bello, Rachel Bezner Kerr, Jack Kloppenburg, Paul Nicholson and Raj Patel.

ISBN: 978-0-935028-37-9

November 2010, $24.95

Beyond the Fence: A Journey to the Roots of the Migration Crisis

By Dori Stone

Beyond the Fence examines how US/Mexico policy affects families, farmers, and businesses on both sides of the border, exposing irretrievable losses, but also hopeful advances.

ISBN: 978-0-935028-33-1

March 2009, $16.95

Alternatives to the Peace Corps: A Guide to Global Volunteer Opportunities (Twelfth Edition)

Edited by Caitlin Hachmyer

This easy-to-use guidebook is the original resource for finding community-based, grassroots volunteer work—the kind of work that changes the world, one person at a time.

ISBN: 978-0-935028-31-7

April 2008, $11.95

Campesino a Campesino: Voices from Latin America's Farmer to Farmer Movement for Sustainable Agriculture

By Eric Holt-Giménez

The voices and stories of dozens of farmers are captured in this history of the farmer-to-farmer movement in Central America, which describes the social, political, economic, and environmental circumstances that shaped this important movement.

ISBN: 978-0-935028-27-0

April 2006, $19.95

Basta! Land and the Zapatista Rebellion in Chiapas (Third Edition)

By George A. Collier with Elizabeth Lowery-Quaratiello

Foreword by Peter Rosset

Now in its third and revised edition, this book paints a vivid picture of the Zapatista rebellion that shot into the international spotlight on January 1, 1994, in the impoverished state of Chiapas in southern Mexico.

ISBN: 0-935028-97-8

June 2005, $16.95

To Inherit the Earth: The Landless Movement and the Struggle for a New Brazil

By Angus Wright and Wendy Wolford

To Inherit the Earth tells the dramatic story of Brazil's Landless Workers' Movement, or MST, the millions of poor, landless, jobless men and women who, through their own nonviolent efforts, have secured rights to over 20 million acres of farmland.

ISBN: 978-0-935028-90-4

May 2003, $15.95

Food First books are available online at www.foodfirst.org/store or from your local independent bookseller. To find an independent bookseller in your area, visit www.booksense.com. You can also order most Food First books directly from our distributor, Perseus Distribution, by calling (800) 343-4499.

CPSIA information can be obtained
at www.ICGtesting.com
Printed in the USA
FSOW04n1834071015
11936FS